Adam Smith, Radical and Egalitarian

In memoriam John Anderson McLean (1915–2001)

Adam Smith, Radical and Egalitarian

An Interpretation for the Twenty-First Century

Iain McLean

Edinburgh University Press

Edinburgh University Press Ltd
22 George Square, Edinburgh

Typeset in 10.5/13 Sabon
by Servis Filmsetting Ltd, Manchester, and
printed and bound in Great Britain by
The Cromwell Press, Trowbridge, Wilts

A CIP record for this book is available from the British Library

ISBN-10 0 7486 2352 3 (hardback)
ISBN-13 978 0 7486 2352 5 (hardback)

Contents

Adam Smith, 1759

He is a bold surgeon, they say, whose hand does not tremble when he performs an operation upon his own person; and he is often equally bold who does not hesitate to pull off the mysterious veil of self-delusion, which covers from his view the deformities of his own conduct . . . This self-deceit, this fatal weakness of mankind, is the source of half the disorders of human life. If we saw ourselves in the light in which others see us, or in which they would see us if they knew all, a reformation would generally be unavoidable. We could not otherwise endure the sight.

The Theory of Moral Sentiments 1759; fifth edn (probably the one used by Burns in 1786) 1781; sixth edn 1790, III, iv, 4 and 6.

Robert Burns, 1786

To a Louse: on Seeing One on a Lady's Bonnet at Church

Ha! whaur ye gaun, ye crowlin ferlie?
Your impudence protects you sairly;
I canna say but ye strunt rarely,
Owre gauze and lace;
Tho', faith! I fear ye dine but sparely
On sic a place.

Ye ugly, creepin, blastit wonner,
Detested, shunn'd by saunt an' sinner,
How daur ye set your fit upon her –
Sae fine a lady?
Gae somewhere else and seek your dinner
On some poor body.

Swith! in some beggar's haffet squattle;
There ye may creep, and sprawl, and sprattle,
Wi' ither kindred, jumping cattle,
In shoals and nations;
Whaur horn nor bane ne'er daur unsettle
Your thick plantations.

Now haud you there, ye're out o' sight,
Below the fatt'rels, snug and tight;
Na, faith ye yet! ye'll no be right,
Till ye've got on it –
The verra tapmost, tow'rin height
O' Miss' bonnet.

My sooth! right bauld ye set your nose out,
As plump an' grey as ony groset:
O for some rank, mercurial rozet,
Or fell, red smeddum,
I'd gie you sic a hearty dose o't,
Wad dress your droddum.

I wad na been surpris'd to spy
You on an auld wife's flainen toy;
Or aiblins some bit dubbie boy,
On's wyliecoat;
But Miss' fine Lunardi! fye!
How daur ye do't?

O Jenny, dinna toss your head,
An' set your beauties a' abread!
Ye little ken what cursed speed
The blastie's makin:
Thae winks an' finger-ends, I dread,
Are notice takin.

O wad some Power the giftie gie us
To see oursels as ithers see us!
It wad frae mony a blunder free us,
An' foolish notion:
What airs in dress an' gait wad lea'e us,
An' ev'n devotion!

Foreword by Rt Hon. Gordon Brown

In 2002 I had the privilege to chair public lectures in the 'Enlightenment Series' at Edinburgh University, on the theme 'Can Both the Left and Right Claim Adam Smith?'. I asked whether Adam Smith would feel more at home in the right-of-centre Adam Smith Institute or in the left-of-centre (John) Smith Institute, named after my good friend John Smith, the leader of the Labour Party, who died suddenly in 1994. I am delighted that Iain McLean has responded to my challenge. In this book he sets out why Adam Smith deserves to be seen in a new light.

Adam Smith had a good start in the world – he was born in Kirkcaldy. He went to study, and later teach, at Glasgow University. He spent time in Edinburgh, in London and in France. But for his deepest thoughts, he returned to Kirkcaldy. It was in Kirkcaldy that he worked tirelessly on what became the *Wealth of Nations*, taking long solitary walks on the foreshore as he thought through his great plan. He observed the jarring effects of the union of 1707 both on Kirkcaldy (which did badly out of it in his time) and on Glasgow (which did very well out of it).

For most of the time since his death in 1790, Smith has had the reputation of an apologist for 'laissez-faire' at its most heartless. In one of the lectures I introduced in 2002, Emma Rothschild showed that this reputation was born in the shadow of the French Revolution, where it was not safe to admit that Smith's work could be interpreted in any other way. In this book, Iain McLean brings the story forward to the present day. He argues that Smith was not opposed to all government, but merely government by vested interests. In book five of the *Wealth of Nations*, Smith – according to McLean – sets out the proper roles of the state and the market in a way that sounds almost contemporary. In the same book, Smith also sets out some famous canons of taxation which – as I told the audience in Edinburgh that day in 2002 – I kept beside me while preparing my budgets.

Adam Smith also published *The Theory of Moral Sentiments* in 1759. Many people have argued that Smith's two books contradict one another: the *Moral Sentiments* advocating altruism and the *Wealth of Nations* assuming that everybody is selfish. Like many, I challenge this interpretation.

'All for ourselves and nothing for other people' is 'a vile maxim', wrote Adam Smith. Coming from Kirkcaldy as Adam Smith did, I have come to understand that his *Wealth of Nations* was underpinned by his *Theory of Moral Sentiments*, his invisible hand dependent upon the existence of a helping hand. Indeed he wrote a new chapter in 1790 for the new edition of *Theory of Moral Sentiments* entitled 'On the Corruption of our Moral Sentiments' which, according to Smith, is occasioned by 'the disposition to admire the rich and great and to despise or neglect persons of poor and mean condition'.

Of course Smith wanted people freed from the shackles of obedience to kings and vested interests, hence the *Wealth of Nations*, but while he wanted people freed from the old constraints he certainly did not envisage people free of civic bonds and civic duties. Hence his theory of moral sentiments. 'Whenever we feel the fate of others is our personal responsibility we are less likely to stand idly by,' he wrote. For Smith the moral system encompassed the economic system, generating the responsible virtues of industry, honesty and reliability – and the stable associations in which we accept our responsibilities each to one another, habits of cooperation and trust, the moral sense upon which the market depended.

So Adam Smith always believed that the town centre was far more than a marketplace. And when he stood under the banner of freedom, he did not argue for a freedom that gave men immunity from a responsibility to serve their society. Liberty was always more than self-interested individualism. Ideas of active citizenship, 'neighbourliness', civic pride and the public realm would have appealed to him.

Iain McLean has lived in Fife and he has studied history and social and political change for a long time. Like Adam Smith – who helped draw up the budget of 1767 – he has also been an academic adviser to the government. In this book, he shows that Smith's two books arose out of the lectures he gave at 7.30 every weekday morning for thirteen years in Glasgow, and he suggests there is not a contradiction between them.

And Iain McLean locates Adam Smith in his roots in the Scottish Enlightenment, the period that produced thinkers like Francis Hutcheson and David Hume, but also practical men such as James Watt, who was developing the steam engine in the same building as Professor Smith was lecturing. Quoting two poems by Smith's admirer Robert Burns, Iain McLean argues that Smith's thought has reverberated round the globe. Adam Smith may be the hero of the Scottish Enlightenment, but his work makes him also a citizen of the world.

A Note on Citations

Like all other modern academics writing on Smith, I cite the standard Glasgow edition of his works (for bibliographic details see References). I follow the convention of labelling the individual volumes as follows.

TMS:	The Theory of Moral Sentiments. Glasgow edn Vol. I.
WN:	Inquiry into . . . the Wealth of Nations. Glasgow edn Vol. II in two parts.
EPS:	Essays on Philosophical Subjects. Glasgow edn Vol. III.
LRBL:	Lectures on Rhetoric and Belles-lettres. Glasgow edn Vol. IV.
LJ(A):	Lectures on Jurisprudence, report of 1762–3. Glasgow edn Vol V.
LJ(B):	Lectures on Jurisprudence, report dated 1766. Glasgow edn Vol V.
Corr.	Correspondence of Adam Smith. Glasgow edn Vol VI.

In *TMS* and *WN*, I cite passages using Smith's own part and chapter divisions, as codified by the editors of the Glasgow edition. Since parts and chapters are of very different lengths, the number of symbols in a citation varies between three and four. An example of a full four-symbol citation is *WN* V.i.f.16. The first element (roman capital numeral) is the Book. The second element (roman lower-case numeral) is the Chapter. The third element (lower-case letter in *WN*, arabic numeral in *TMS*), where there is one, is a subdivision of Smith's into a 'Part' or an 'Article', or simply a subheading of Smith's. The fourth element (arabic numeral) is a paragraph within the next higher subdivision.

This system has become an industry standard, like the QWERTY typewriter and the VHS video recorder. Therefore no individual user has an incentive to break away. However, it does have some drawbacks, the main one being that the symbol i may either be a lower-case roman numeral or a letter. There is a *WN* V.i.i. That is not the introduction to Book V, Chapter 1 – it is the ninth element of that chapter, which is in fact the Conclusion.

LRBL, *LJ(A)*, and *LJ(B)* are all printed from manuscript notebooks discovered in 1895 (*LJ(B)*) and 1958 (the others). I cite the Glasgow subdivisions, which give the original manuscript volume numbers in lower-case roman (for *LRBL*, which was in two volumes, and *LJ(A)*, which was in six), followed by paragraph number in arabic.

The most important parts of *EPS* are:

- the 'History of Astronomy', cited as *Astronomy* with Section (roman caps) and paragraph (arabic numeral); and
- Dugald Stewart's *Account of the Life and Writings of Adam Smith, Ll.D*, cited as Stewart, with Section (roman caps) and paragraph (arabic numeral).

In *Corr.*, I cite the letters by their number (using the # symbol) or letter. The lettered correspondence comprises items discovered late in the preparation of the volume and printed at the end.

Citations from manuscripts and rare books relating to Smith in Glasgow University Library or Glasgow University Archives & Business Record Centre are accompanied by the archive's own reference number. Other citations follow the Harvard author–date system. Citations to websites were all checked during summer or autumn 2005 and found to be live. Any reader discovering a non-functioning link is asked to kindly let me or the publishers know.

Preface: A Scotsman Looks at the World

In the academic year 2001–2, Edinburgh University held an 'Enlightenment Lecture Series' to honour the leading figures of the Scottish Enlightenment, who had all had connections with Edinburgh and its university. The final lecture in the series was on Adam Smith (1723–90). Smith was born and brought up in the (then) small port of Kirkcaldy. He never studied at Edinburgh, his relatives having rather surprisingly sent him to Glasgow University in 1737. But after completing his degree there and six years of solitary study in Oxford, Smith first went back to Kirkcaldy for rest and recuperation, and then came to Edinburgh in 1748 to give private lectures on 'rhetoric and belles-lettres', also on government and on the history of science, under the patronage of Edinburgh literati. He moved back to Glasgow as a professor in 1751 and remained there until 1764, when the opportunity to accompany a young aristocrat, the Duke of Buccleuch, on his travels to France made Smith financially independent for the rest of his life. He stayed with the Duke in France until 1766, and spent the rest of his life in either Kirkcaldy or Edinburgh, with four visits to London of a few months each. The Buccleuch family continued to pay Smith a pension. In 1778 Smith was appointed as a Commissioner of Customs for Scotland, in which post he served diligently for the rest of his life.

The 2002 Edinburgh lecture on Smith actually took the form of a mini-symposium, introduced by the UK Chancellor of the Exchequer, Gordon Brown. Like Smith, Brown is a native of Kirkcaldy, and, since 2005, MP for the constituency that includes Kirkcaldy. He took his degrees at Edinburgh University. He is clearly fascinated by both the writings and the personality of his eminent fellow-townsman. The symposium was entitled 'Can Both the Left and Right Claim Adam Smith?'[1] The economic historian Emma Rothschild was to speak for the left; the economist and journalist Irwin Stelzer for the right. Introducing their papers, Chancellor Brown said:

> Is Smith, the author of the invisible hand, also the Smith of the helping hand?

> Would the Adam Smith who has been the inspiration behind the right-of-centre Adam Smith Institute be more likely to feel at home with the left-of-centre John Smith Institute?
>
> Or is the Smith of 'The Theory of Moral Sentiments' the Jekyll to 'The Wealth of Nations'' Hyde?
>
> Is it possible two centuries and more on from his famous work 'The Wealth of Nations' to find a way of reconciling his apparently contrasting views: that social behaviour is influenced by sympathy and that economic behaviour is motivated by self-interest?[2]

The question continues to fascinate Gordon Brown. He has aired it at least twice more since then: once implicitly, while answering it (Brown 2003), and once more explicitly, in a series of events surrounding the visit to Scotland of Alan Greenspan, Chairman of the US Federal Reserve, in February 2005. Greenspan was awarded an honorary degree at Edinburgh University and gave the Adam Smith Memorial Lecture in Kirkcaldy, the latter in the church of which Gordon Brown's father had been the parish minister.[3] Brown and Greenspan both paid more than ordinary tribute to Smith, Brown wondering how Smith's upbringing in Kirkcaldy would have exposed him to the disruption of Scotland's international trade after the Union with England in 1707.

This book is my response to Gordon Brown's challenge. As this is not a detective story, I am not ashamed to say now that my answers to his four questions are *Yes*; *Yes*; *No*; and *Yes* in that order. I am not the only person to take this view; for other relevant recent scholarship see Rothschild 2001 and Kennedy 2005. If Rothschild, Kennedy, Brown and myself are right, then the still conventional view that Smith is the founder and apologist for capitalism at its most naked must be wrong. That view bubbled up in Kirkcaldy in October 2005. The further education colleges there and in neighbouring Glenrothes have recently been merged under the name 'Adam Smith College', of which Chancellor of the Exchequer Gordon Brown became the first Chancellor. However, the Students' Union at the College reportedly took a unanimous decision to name itself not the 'Adam Smith' but the 'Jennie Lee' Students' Association. Their reported grounds were that:

> 'We didn't feel that Adam Smith represented the values a student association should stand for,' said student leader Paul Muirhead. 'He is associated with socio-economic policies that work against the people, that were synonymous with Thatcherite and Reaganite governments. Jennie Lee[4] would be an excellent role model for the students because of the courage and conviction she showed in achieving the aims she believed passionately in. This isn't an attack upon Adam Smith as a person, but upon what his name has

> come to represent. Adam Smith's name is linked to exploitation and greed'. (Brown 2005)

Even though Mr Muirhead distinguishes between Adam Smith's name and Adam Smith's persona, I think that he is wrong. The aim of this book is to explain how and why. But first, like Gordon Brown, I believe that the importance of Smith's Scottishness has been understated, and needs to be brought centre stage.

Let us first stand in Edinburgh and look north to Fife. In August 1769 Smith's best friend David Hume wrote to him from his flat in James Court in Edinburgh's Old Town. Hume, like Smith's other friends, was sometimes infuriated by Smith's failure to answer letters or to meet his friends. But, being the most even-tempered philosopher in history, he made a joke of it:

> Dear Smith
>
> I am glad to have come within sight of you, and to have a View of Kirkaldy from my Windows: But as I wish also to be within speaking terms of you, I wish we coud concert measures for that purpose. I am mortally sick at Sea, and regard with horror, and a kind of hydrophobia the great Gulph that lies between us . . . I therefore propose to you to come hither, and pass some days with me in this Solitude . . . There is no Habitation on the Island of Inchkeith; otherwise I shoud challenge you to meet me on that Spot, and neither [of] us ever to leave the Place, till we were fully agreed on all points of Controversy. (*Corr.* # 121)

You can stand in Hume's flat now and get the same view. (It is currently part of a set of luxury residential suites available for short-term lettings.) You will be breathing the air, much purer now than in 1769, of the Scottish Enlightenment – not only of Smith and Hume, but also of James Boswell, to whom Hume let the flat before moving to St Andrew Square in the newly built New Town for the last few years of his life. There is still no habitation on the island of Inchkeith. You can turn left out of Hume's flat and down the Royal Mile (past the Deacon Brodie pub) for one block, when you will see on your left the grand eighteenth-century building that is now the Edinburgh City Chambers (for its construction see Youngson 1966, pp. 53–9). In 1778 part of it was the office of the Commissioners of Customs for Scotland, where Adam Smith put in four solid days' work a week. The Edinburgh caricaturist John Kay drew him in 1787 on his daily walk up from his home, Panmure House, which still stands at the bottom of the Royal Mile, near the Scottish Parliament building. The cover of this book incorporates Kay's sketch, showing Smith's sprightly military bearing. He approved of military service, though he was cooler than his friends on the idea of a citizen militia. As you walk down to Panmure House, you pass Canongate church and its churchyard on your left. The grave of Adam Smith is on the left as you go in. From there, you can look up the hill in front of you to see the great Greek pile that housed the (Royal) High School of Edinburgh from 1829 to 1968 – the school attended by many of Smith's friends including his publisher William Strahan. The school is flanked by two monuments. To its right is a monument to Scotland's greatest poet, Robert Burns – an admirer of Smith, whose copies of Smith's two great books are among the prized relics in Glasgow University Library. Smith and Burns never met – Burns sought him out in 1787, but narrowly missed him. However, Burns's friend Mrs Dunlop told him that Commissioner of Customs Smith would try to get a job for Burns as a Salt Officer in order to provide him with a better income (Mrs Dunlop to R. Burns, 29.03.1787, in Wallace 1898, pp. 13–16; Ross 1995, p. 374). Burns did not then join the Excise service, but did later. Higher up Calton Hill to the left stands a monument to Dugald Stewart, friend and first biographer of Smith, who continued the Scottish Enlightenment into the next generation but was rather intimidated by the anti-French backlash in Scotland of the 1790s.

If you retrace your steps up the Royal Mile, you may turn left at the crossroads above the City Chambers on to George IV Bridge. This high-level street, completed in 1834, flies over the southern chasms of the Old Town to open up new suburbs of the later New Town and the modern city beyond. It was named in honour of the visit of George IV to Scotland, stage-managed by Sir Walter Scott in 1822 to signal Scotland's attachment to the parliamentary Union of 1707. George IV was the first monarch to visit Scotland since 1707. Smith and Hume lived in a weakly and distantly governed Scotland.

George IV Bridge did not exist in Smith's day, and so the Edinburgh wits called the house of Adam Ferguson, Smith's contemporary and rival, 'Kamschatka' as a mark of its impossible remoteness at Sciennes,[5] a mile south of the city. It was at Kamschatka that Robert Burns met the young Walter Scott in 1786. Dugald Stewart was there too.[6]

For another mental experiment, we could stand in Fife and look back at Edinburgh. The tough knobbly heights of North Queensferry, northern landing of the Forth Bridges, make a good vantage point. Ten miles away to our left is Smith's home in Kirkcaldy that he was so reluctant to leave, even to meet David Hume, while working hard on the *Wealth of Nations*. Immediately in front is the estuary of the Forth, dotted with islands including Inchkeith. Before 1707 the little ports on the Fife side – from Crail at the seaward end, through Anstruther, Pittenweem, Elie,

Leven, Kirkcaldy, Kinghorn and up to Culross where Fife ends – were the richest places in a poor country. As Smith recalled in an early draft of *WN*, King James VI had described Fife as 'like a coarse woollen coat edged with gold lace'.[7] In Smith's boyhood and young adulthood, the rest of Scotland was growing rich from the Union, but Kirkcaldy and its neighbours were actually suffering from the disruption of their pre-1707 trade ties with Holland, which had brought the Dutch red pantile roofs to the better-off houses along the Fife coast. Smith lived through the 'creative destruction' – as a later economist, Joseph Schumpeter, was to call it – of the Scottish economy after the Union. In front of us stands one of the greatest monuments of Scottish engineering, the Forth Railway Bridge; away out to sea on the left we can just see another, the lighthouse on the Isle of May built in 1816 by Robert Stevenson (1772–1850), the grandfather of Robert Louis Stevenson. Stevenson's lighthouse replaced a crude coal-burning affair that Smith would have seen on his daily walks along the Kirkcaldy foreshore. Stevenson was also consulting engineer for one of the boldest strokes in the New Town, Waterloo Bridge. The three generations of 'Lighthouse Stevensons' and one poet (see Bathurst 1999) were amongst the most eminent products of the Scottish parish school system that Smith extols in *WN*, giving it as one of the grounds for contemporary Scotland's superiority to England.

To our south-east lies Edinburgh in dramatic profile (as it is from most directions). It was 'Auld Reekie' (Old Smoky) in Smith's day, as it still was in my childhood in the 1950s and early 1960s, before the Clean Air Acts took hold. (See a wonderfully atmospheric picture in Youngson 1966, Plate 8.) The medieval city runs down the Royal Mile, from the Castle on its impregnable rock eastwards to the palace of the Scottish kings at Holyrood (now adjacent to the Scottish Parliament). Surrounding the medieval city is Britain's greatest classical creation, the New Town, planned and built in stages from the 1760s to the 1830s as Edinburgh leapt at unprecedented speed from filth and poverty to gentility and elegance (Youngson 1966). Smith and Hume saw the start of that process.

Between our viewpoint and Edinburgh stands a piece of green belt, which is the Dalmeny Estate, ancestral home of the Earls of Rosebery. Robert Louis Stevenson sets the opening scenes of *Kidnapped* in a location which is unmistakably Dalmeny. More relevantly to our theme, it was in Dalmeny House, on a sheet of Lord Rosebery's notepaper, that William E. Gladstone first sketched out a scheme for Irish Home Rule in November 1885, without telling his host. In *WN*, Smith anticipated that uniting Ireland with Great Britain would produce even greater benefits than those from the Union of 1707, because the people of Ireland

> would gain an equally compleat deliverance from a much more oppressive aristocracy . . . founded . . . in the most odious of all distinctions, those of religious and political prejudices. (*WN* V.iii.89)

Alas, when Irish union came in 1800, the two largest religious groups (Catholics and Presbyterians) were not delivered from the oppressive Ascendancy (Church of Ireland) aristocracy. As a result, most of them never regarded the Union as legitimate. It could have been dismantled without bloodshed if most British politicians had shared Smith's or Gladstone's far-sightedness. They did not; and it was not.

Such a mental experiment is a bit harder to conduct in Adam Smith's Glasgow. Because it rose so fast in his day and continued to rise for a century after his death, before going into an equally rapid decline, there are far fewer physical relics of the Glasgow Smith knew than of the Edinburgh or Fife. Glasgow University, the 'College' where Smith studied and later taught, moved out to the suburbs in 1870 when its city-centre site was hemmed in by working-class slums. The old college was demolished to make way for a railway yard, now also gone. Only a few landmarks of the Glasgow that Smith knew survive. They include the Cathedral, the Trongate and – relevantly for our story – the satellite port of Port Glasgow, created by the city downstream and on the opposite side of the Clyde. Port Glasgow was to give Glasgow the competitive edge that enabled it to rise far and fast in Smith's lifetime. Another survivor is the model Newcomen steam engine used in chemistry and physics teaching in Smith's day. The laboratory technician James Watt, who worked in the same building as Professor Smith, was asked to repair it. Watt discovered that the problems lay not with the model but with Newcomen's design. Smith's colleague and close friend Joseph Black provided the theoretical background for Watt's design modification, in the theory of latent heat. Watt made his first great advance in designing the separate condenser, which creates a vacuum on one side of the piston at the same time as the steam creates pressure on the other side. Therefore a Watt engine has something like double the efficiency of a Newcomen engine. From that, in some simple accounts at least, arose the Industrial Revolution. It is nice to think that it happened in the next room to Smith's lectures on the nature and causes of the wealth of nations. The model engine that Watt was asked to repair is on display at the Hunterian Museum on the Glasgow University campus.

The point of these imaginary tours is to plant Adam Smith firmly in the Scotland of his time, a Scotland whose physical remains are all around us. Getting into Smith's mental universe may be a little harder.

Intuition is an unreliable guide but it may be a start. It would be extremely arrogant to claim that only a Scot can see into Adam Smith's mental world. But at least Scots share a common cultural background that may make it easier for them than for others to pick up cues about what mattered to Smith. So here are my credentials, for what they are worth. I was born, brought up and educated in classical Edinburgh. I attended the Royal High School, when it was on Calton Hill with the Burns monument to one side, the Stewart monument on the other and overlooked Adam Smith's home in Panmure House. So this book feels like a homecoming. Like Adam Smith, I was well coached in Latin and Greek at school. Like Adam Smith, I have quite appalling handwriting.[8] In my father's last years, my parents lived in North Queensferry, and his daily walk took him past the viewpoint just described. My father was an Edinburgh accountant: quiet, upright, meticulous. I like to think that he and Adam Smith would have got on extremely well. This book is dedicated to his memory.

Like Smith, I went from Scotland to Oxford, and found it a distinct culture shock, although unlike Smith I recovered from it. Like Smith, I have wandered between the worlds of academe and public policy; unlike him, however, I have never been the personal tutor of a duke nor the Budget adviser of a Chancellor of the Exchequer.

My interest in Smith in his own time derives from two areas of my recent research, namely

- the French and American Enlightenments, where Smith has a fascinating but elusive relationship with the Marquis de Condorcet, Thomas Jefferson and James Madison (cf. McLean and Hewitt 1994; McLean 2003, 2004);
- work on the Union (of the United Kingdom) and Unionism, recently funded by the Leverhulme Trust (McLean 2005a; McLean and McMillan 2005). A Smithian sideline is the proper relationship (if any) between the state and the established church (McLean and Linsley 2004). A fascinating section of *WN*, discussed later, compares Smith's preference for hundreds of little competing sects with Hume's preference for an established church.

My interest in Smith in our time derives from my current work in political economy, tax policy, the spatial distribution of public expenditure and related subjects (cf., for example, McLean and McMillan 2003; McLean 2005b, c; McLean and Jennings 2006). Time and time again I find myself drawn back to Adam Smith. In the pages that follow, I will try to show that he has a lot to teach us on tax policy, the role and limits of the state, and the frontier between the state and the market. Smith was a backroom adviser to UK Government ministers at least twice and probably three times in his career, as discussed later.

The purpose of this book is to explain the Scottish Smith of the eighteenth century to the citizens of the twenty-first. As my title indicates, I believe that Smith was both a radical – for his own time and ours – and an egalitarian. I shall try to explain why and how his radical egalitarianism is rooted in the Scotland he grew up in. More broadly, I see the book as part of a campaign by many people to show the continued relevance of the Scottish Enlightenment, cropping up in unexpected places. For instance, readers of Alexander McCall Smith may (or may not) come to share my view that the moral philosophy of Isobel Dalhousie – who edits the *Review of Applied Ethics* – and of Domenica Macdonald derives more from Adam Smith's *Theory of Moral Sentiments* than from any other single source (McCall Smith 2004, 2005).

As recorded above, this book was prompted by Gordon Brown's questions. I am very grateful to him for his interest in this project, and for contributing a Foreword. Financial help for Alistair McMillan's and my *Attitudes to the Union* project came from the Leverhulme Trust. The project was part of a Programme administered for the Leverhulme Trust by the Constitution Unit, School of Public Policy, University College, London. Thanks to these institutions, to Alistair for his long-standing collaboration and to project partners in the Leverhulme and parallel ESRC research programmes on devolution for acting as sounding boards for some of the themes of this book. Elizabeth Martin and her colleagues at Nuffield College Library (and beyond), and the librarians and archivists of the University of Glasgow and of Balliol College, Oxford, helped me locate and read scarce material relating to Smith. Fonna Forman-Barzilai, Andrew Glyn, Dirk Haubrich, David Hendry, Will Hopper, Alistair McMillan, David Miller, Dennis Rasmussen (whom I thank for allowing me to cite an unpublished presentation to the 2005 meeting of the American Political Science Association), John Robertson, David Vines (formerly Adam Smith Professor of Economics, Glasgow University) and Stewart Wood all commented helpfully on drafts or outlines. My discussions on a related project, on the nature of establishment in the Church of Scotland, with Marjory Maclean and Scot Peterson have helped to form my views on Smith and the Kirk in his day. Wolfgang Müller invited me to give a lecture at the Mannheim Institute for Social Research in June 2005, an opportunity which enabled me to try out the themes of the book. I am grateful for the feedback I received then. Edinburgh University Press have been supportive and efficient. For the third or fourth time, David Penny has proved how quickly and accurately he can prepare copy to publishers' specifications.

Interest in Adam Smith and the Scottish Enlightenment has never been higher. I hope that these pages make a modest contribution to explaining him and it.

Oxford
October 2005

NOTES

1. Details are still available at www.ed.ac.uk/events/lectures/enlightenment/adamsmith.html, consulted 21.06.05.
2. Source: Edinburgh audio and video transcript. For the Adam Smith Institute, see www.adamsmith.org/. For the (John) Smith Institute, which co-sponsored the lecture series, see www.smith-institute.org.uk/default.htm. The reference to Jekyll and Hyde is to the Edinburgh novelist Robert Louis Stevenson's *Strange Case of Dr Jekyll and Mr Hyde*, itself based on the true story of the respectable but larcenous Deacon Brodie of Edinburgh Town Council (1746–88).
3. Greenspan's lecture is at www.federalreserve.gov/boarddocs/speeches/2005/20050206/default.htm.
4. Jennie Lee (1904–88) MP (ILP) North Lanark 1929–31; (Labour) Cannock 1945–70. Wife of Aneurin Bevan, and regarded as being well to his left. Inaugurated the Open University as Minister for the Arts between 1964 and 1970. Created Baroness Lee of Asheridge 1970.
5. Pronounced 'Sheens'. The name is a corruption of *Siena*. Part of Ferguson's house was demolished in the nineteenth century; the rest is incorporated into a tenement block.
6. Source: Letter from Scott to Burns's biographer Lockhart, 10.04.1827, quoted at www.robertburns.org/encyclopedia/ScottSirWalter1770–1832.778.shtml.
7. 'Second Fragment on the division of Labour' in *LJ* p. 585. The phrase is usually given as 'a beggar's mantle fringed with gold', and it has been attributed to more than one Scottish king.
8. Scott (1937, p. 178n) quotes an unnamed French friend as describing Smith's handwriting as 'griffoné comme un chat' ('scribbled like a cat'). Surviving documents confirm this. Surviving drafts of *TMS* and *WN* are in a secretary's hand, with Smith's cat-like corrections scrawled on them.

1

The Life of an Absent-minded Professor

EARLY YEARS

Adam Smith led a quiet, uneventful life. As a child, he was initially sickly and protected by his widowed mother. As an adult, he was notoriously absent-minded. In 1767 a society hostess recorded in her diary:

> I said many things in his [AS's] praise, but added that he was the most Absent Man that ever was . . . Mr Damer . . . made him a visit the other morning as he was going to breakfast, and, falling into discourse, Mr Smith took a piece of bread and butter, which, after he had rolled round and round, he put into the teapot and pour'd the water upon it; some time after he poured it into a cup, and when he had tasted it, he said it was the worst tea he had ever met with. (Lady Mary Coke, aunt of AS's tutee the Duke of Buccleuch. Cited by Ross 1995, p. 226)

Part of this may have been a front. As a professor, political adviser and administrator, Smith was anything but absent-minded. Another part probably reflected his hyperactive mental life, not always connected with the physical universe around him. But this absent-minded professor has profoundly shaped the world from his day to ours. The events of his quiet life give us vital clues as to how and why he shaped the world.

Adam Smith was born in Kirkcaldy, Fife, in 1723. His exact date of birth is unproven, but he was baptised into the Church of Scotland on 5 June, the date which his tombstone also gives as his birthday. His father, also Adam Smith, was a collector of customs in Kirkcaldy, and died before his son Adam was born. His mother, Margaret Douglas (1694–1784), was the second wife of Adam Smith senior. She came from a line of smallish Fife landowners; their estate was at Strathenry, just west of Kirkcaldy. The bond between her and her son was exceptionally close, and the already elderly Adam Smith seems to have been devastated in 1784 by her death at the age of 90. He never married, and when in Scotland lived with his mother and with a cousin, Janet Douglas, who died in about 1787.

A colourful story, relished by the older biographers but prissily neglected by modern ones, has it that at three years old Adam was snatched by a band of gipsies and later recaptured by his relatives at Leslie Wood, not far from Strathenry. Smith's nineteenth-century biographer John Rae comments that Smith 'would have made, I fear, a poor gipsy' (Rae [1895] 1965, p. 5).

Smith attended the burgh school of Kirkcaldy. The curriculum survives, in the form of a report from the head teacher to Kirkcaldy Burgh Council. In his final year, Smith and his schoolmates would have been set Latin translation homework every night 'to Exercise their Judgements to teach them by degrees to spell rightly to wryte good wryte Good Sense and Good Languadge' (memo by D. Miller, quoted by Ross 1995, p. 19). Alas, Smith never developed 'good wryte', that is, handwriting, but wisely employed secretaries to draft all his academic work.

In 1737, aged fourteen – not an unusually early age for Scots students of the period – Smith was sent to Glasgow University. This was a surprising choice as Scottish students have always been culturally drawn to their local university,[1] and both St Andrews (small and sleepy in Smith's day) and Edinburgh were closer to Kirkcaldy than was Glasgow. Whatever the reason (we simply do not know), the choice of Glasgow was very happy for intellectual and environmental reasons.

The Acts of Union of 1707 had united Scotland and England under a single monarch and parliament and had profound effects on Scotland. They integrated both the Scottish market and the Scottish executive with their much larger counterparts in England. They freed Scotland from the restraints on its trade imposed previously by the mercantilist governments of England. The Union was, in short, a classic jurisdictional integration which produced the benefits classically to be expected from such integration.

But this was not to happen immediately. As with the fall of Communism in central and eastern Europe beginning in 1989, things in Scotland got worse before they got better. The Union was initially unpopular, its unpopularity symbolised by several riots (especially the lynching of the crew of the *Worcester* in 1705 – McLean and McMillan 2005, Chapter 2 – and of Captain Porteous in 1736); and two full-scale rebellions, the Jacobite Risings of 1715 and 1745–6. However, by the time of Bonnie Prince Charlie's final defeat at Culloden in April 1746, the benefits of the Union were already becoming clear. Smith and his friends – from what it is perhaps anachronistic but useful to call the Scottish middle class – were among the first to benefit. Before the Union, the city of Glasgow had set up a satellite port, imaginatively called Port

Glasgow, on the south bank of the tidal Clyde about fifteen miles downstream. The river was not yet dredged up to Glasgow itself, and Daniel Defoe walked across it without getting his feet wet on one of his visits (Defoe 1724–7, III.2.82). Before the Union, Port Glasgow had only coastal trade, as the English Navigation Acts banned Scottish ships from international trade. The Union removed this restriction. Article 4 creates the unified economic jurisdiction of Great Britain:

> All the Subjects of the United Kingdom of Great Britain shall from and after the Union have full Freedom and Intercourse of Trade and Navigation. (Quoted by McLean and McMillan 2005, p. 36)

Accordingly, after the Union, Glasgow-cum-Port Glasgow rapidly became one of the four most important ports on the British west coast (the others being Bristol, Liverpool and Whitehaven). West-coast trade expanded dramatically with the British settlements in America. Defoe, who had been an English spy during the 1707 negotiations, visited Glasgow during his *Tour Thro' the Whole Island of Great Britain*, originally published in three volumes between 1724 and 1727. Defoe had a vested interest in talking up the benefits of the Union, but his story of the comparative advantage of Glasgow in American trade rings true. From the Clyde a Glasgow ship could head out direct into the Atlantic, whereas a London one had to sail east down the Thames before rounding the English Channel:

> take the Weather to happen in its usual Manner, there must always be allow'd one Time with another, at least fourteen or twenty Days Difference in the Voyage, either Out or Home. (Defoe 1724–7, III.2.91)

This average of five weeks' advantage on a return trip meant that a (Port) Glasgow vessel could make two return trips to America in the sailing season, whereas a ship from London could only make one.

Port Glasgow became primarily an entrepot, where American goods, especially sugar and tobacco, were landed before being repackaged and re-exported for final sale elsewhere. It had relatively little part in the most notorious American trade, namely slaves. The city of Glasgow grew rapidly on the surplus generated by its satellite port. Defoe called it 'the cleanest and beautifullest and best built' British city outside London (quoted in Hook and Sher 1995, p. 3). While still little more than a medieval village, it had acquired both a cathedral and a university – the latter chartered by the pope in 1451. By 1707, Scotland had four universities (Edinburgh, Glasgow, St Andrews and Aberdeen) to England's two. But they were all tiny; three in the shadow of the established church and the fourth, Edinburgh, in the shadow of the town council. The explosive intellectual growth of Edinburgh, Glasgow and Aberdeen in the eighteenth century depended on money, students, intellectual freedom and the rapid growth of a Scots literary elite. Adam Smith experienced all four.

In 1727, Glasgow University had been substantially reformed. It abandoned the old system of 'regents', who taught everything, in favour of professors, who taught just their specialist subject. The first Professor of Moral Philosophy was Gershom Carmichael (1672–1729), who was succeeded by Francis Hutcheson (1694–1746). Both were eminent scholars. Carmichael published a commentary on the German jurist Samuel Pufendorf, who held a social-contractarian view of man and the citizen. Carmichael shared this view, believing (after John Locke) that men had natural rights, including the right not to be enslaved. He saw the Act of Union and the parliamentary choice of the Hanoverian monarchy in 1715 as contracts that guaranteed the liberties of the Scots.

Hutcheson, Smith's teacher, was to become even more eminent. He held similar political views but differed from Carmichael in his philosophy, moving away from Carmichael's natural theology as Smith was later to move further still. Hutcheson's philosophy and Smith's reaction to it are discussed in later chapters of this book.

The University had been founded by papal bull in 1451. At the Reformation, it slipped out of the grip of the Catholic Church but not firmly into the grip of any other. As discussed below, a battle between Episcopalians (Anglicans) and Presbyterians[2] for the Scottish church lasted for over a century, from the time of John Knox until 1690. The Presbyterians secured control in 1690, and embedded their control in the 1707 Acts of Union.

In principle, the Presbyterian Church of Scotland was a wide-ranging instrument of social control. The population was liable before the church courts for moral and theological discipline. Fornicators and heretics might equally find themselves arraigned by the local presbytery, and punished if found guilty. Glasgow in Smith's day was a stronghold of popular Calvinism; Edinburgh was not. Calvinists were naturally suspicious of liberal philosophers like Hutcheson, but the Presbytery of Glasgow was unable to discipline him. Hutcheson and Smith worked under a weak church, as well as a weak state, two facts which are central to the argument of this book.

Smith admired Hutcheson, later describing him as 'the never to be forgotten Dr Hutcheson' (*Corr.* # 274, 1787). For his part, Hutcheson was probably one of those behind the nomination of Adam Smith as one of two Snell Exhibitioners to go to Balliol College, Oxford, where Smith arrived in June 1740. Like his contemporary Edward Gibbon, he later expressed vivid contempt for the intellectual torpor of the Oxford they both attended. But Smith's contempt for Oxford may derive from personal as well as educational disaffection. Because Smith's time as a Snell Exhibitioner was unhappy, and either created or confirmed his prejudices against English institutions, it deserves closer inspection: an inspection which I hope, will, help to dispel some misconceptions about Smith, religion and, indeed, Balliol.

BALLIOL AND THE LESS THAN PERFECT UNION

There was (and still is) a widely held belief that Balliol College is a 'Scots foundation'. The misconception is based on confusing John Balliol (c. 1208–68), founder of the college, who was a landowner in rough and lawless Co. Durham, with his son John (c. 1248–1314), briefly and ingloriously (or prudently) king of even rougher and more lawless Scotland while it was under attack by Edward I of England. John Balliol senior did set up a lodging house in Oxford for a handful of students, but it was his widow Devorguilla, a pious and practical landowner in Galloway, who endowed the college and gave it its first statutes in 1282. The Scottish connection, such as it is, comes from Devorguilla, not from either John (Jones 1988, pp. 2–10).

By the seventeenth century this was lost in the mists of time. The religious and political wars of that century threatened the tenuous Union of the Crowns of 1603, when James VI of Scotland became James I of England. By the time he moved to London, James had had enough of Presbyterian clerics such as Andrew Melvill, who recurs in this story (see Chapter 2 *passim*). One of his first acts was to commission the 'King James bible' – the 'Authorised Version', designed to unite the warring strands of Protestantism in his tenuously united kingdom. He disliked the Scottish Presbyterians but, unlike his son Charles I or his grandsons Charles II and James VII and II, made no serious attempts to oust them from the church. Some of his contemporaries were more militant. One such was John Warner (1581–1666), a fellow of Magdalen College, Oxford from 1604 to 1610, and later Bishop of Rochester. When a Scots army invaded northern England in 1639 in protest at Charles I's attempts to promote episcopacy in Scotland, Warner 'gave £1500 to swell the royal coffers in the campaign against the Scots' (Green 2004). In his will, Warner bequeathed money to Balliol – his own college, Magdalen, having rejected the offer – to endow scholarships for four Scots a year, so that they could be ordained in the Church of England and return to Scotland after their ordination. The most recent historian of the college believes that Warner's motive was not love of the Scots but rather 'creating a means of indoctrinating young Scots with the ways of the Church of England' (Jones 1988, p. 124). Warner's choice of then-obscure Balliol may well have reflected the mistaken belief that it was founded by a king of Scotland – a king, incidentally, who struck a bargain with Edward I of England that was repudiated by William Wallace in the first Scottish war of independence.

John Snell (c. 1628–79) was an Ayrshire man who did well in England. Educated at Glasgow University, he moved to Oxford, marrying the sister of the registrar of Oxford University. He became secretary to a prominent lawyer who was one of the executors of Warner's will, and modelled his own will of 1677 on that, presumably for the same ideological purpose of binding Scots elites to the Episcopalian Church of England. Each scholar should be nominated by Glasgow University from among its students. He should be liable to pay a penalty of £500 if he failed to enter holy orders, and also if having entered them he accepted a promotion in England or Wales, 'it being my will and desire that every such scholar soe to be admitted shall returne into Scotland' (Jones 1988, 1999, 2004; Addison 1901, quoted on p. 199).

But the best laid schemes of mice and men gang aft agley. In 1690 the Presbyterian faction in the Scottish Parliament found itself unopposed, because the Episcopalian faction had walked out under Bonnie Dundee to regain the crown for King James (see Chapter 2). They quickly established the Presbyterian church as *the* Church of Scotland. That establishment was further secured by the Acts of Union of 1707. This posthumously frustrated Warner's and Snell's plans. Indeed, Snell's daughter went to court in 1692 to say that, as the scholarship plan was now frustrated, she should get all her father's money herself. She lost. The court made a *cy pres*[3] order passing control of the endowment to Balliol, and allowing Balliol to keep any surplus after providing for the Snell Exhibitioners. Glasgow University later claimed that it knew nothing about this decision, and went to court in 1738 to object to Balliol pocketing the surplus. This case stayed in the (English) courts for no less than twenty-one years – covering the whole of Smith's time at Balliol – and absorbed huge amounts of energy and money on all sides. One of Smith's later colleagues at Glasgow, William Ruat, worked full-time on the Snell litigation for four years (Glasgow University Archives: call number GUA 26640 f. 50). Finally, in 1759, the court rejected the schemes of all the parties and made a scheme of its own, which dropped the requirement for holy orders. The costs came out of the Snell trust, which must have lost most of its value in the process; instead of Snell's four scholars a year, the trust, which still exists, has ever since been able to make only one nomination a year. It had to fight off another long-drawn-out raid, by the Scottish Episcopal Church, which spent four years from 1844 to 1848 unsuccessfully trying to show that its ordinands should get the proceeds of the trust (Addison 1901, pp. 18–28).

Some writers on Smith, aware of Snell's intentions but not of the above sorry history, have assumed either that Smith intended in 1740 to become an Episcopalian priest and later changed his mind (cf. Kennedy 2005, pp. 6–9), or that he accepted the Snell Exhibition in bad faith, never intending to become an Episcopalian priest (cf. Ross 1995, p. 59). These hypotheses fall at the first fence. No party ever tried to enforce Snell's intentions. Glasgow University, which nominated Smith, had two years earlier stated that it was unaware of the conditions relating to holy orders, even though the form letter from Balliol inviting nominations stated that the nominees should be 'such whose Education and principles shall lead them to ye promoting of ye Doctrine and Discipline established in the Church of England' (Addison 1901, p. 203). The Presbyterian nominators of Glasgow seem to have paid no attention to this requirement. It is hard to imagine the Ulster Presbyterian Hutcheson doing so. The correct morals to draw are two: that the Union of 1707 was seriously incomplete in Smith's time, especially in religious and legal matters; and that the atmosphere at Balliol was always likely to be sulphurous.

The English and Scottish court systems were very poorly integrated (and remained so until the late nineteenth century). Litigants had a vested interest in shopping for a jurisdiction. The Snell litigation was heard in England, to the detriment of the Glasgow litigants; and the judgments up to and including that of 1848 showed no understanding of Scots law. The English and Scottish religious systems have remained unintegrated up to the present day. The Queen is bound by her coronation oath and by the Act of Union to protect Protestant truth in both England and Scotland. There can, however, be at most one set of true religious doctrines and therefore at least one of her promises must be unfulfillable. Ordinary citizens including Adam Smith have faced similar dilemmas. As a member of Balliol College he had to swear loyalty to the thirty-nine Articles of the Church of England. As a new professor at Glasgow University, he had to appear before the Presbytery of Glasgow in January 1751 and swear loyalty to the Westminster Confession of the Church of Scotland (GUA 26640 f. 51). The thirty-nine Articles and the Westminster Confession contradict one another in many places; most obviously, the first requires the swearer to uphold bishops, and the second to deny that the church has any role for bishops. The state (albeit indirectly) imposed two conflicting obligations on any citizen of the United Kingdom who moved between England and Scotland. This alone should have sufficed to persuade Smith that an established state church was a bad idea.

The Scots were very unpopular at Balliol, and the resentment was mutual. The Scots resented Balliol's appropriations from the Snell trust, to which Balliol believed it had a perfect right. Adam Smith's earliest surviving letter, to his cousin and guardian, sets the tone, complaining about his first year's

> extraordinary and most extravagant fees we are obligd to pay the College and University on our admittance; it will be his own fault if anyone should endanger his health at Oxford by excessive Study, our only business here being to go to prayers twice a day, and to lecture twice a week. (AS to William Smith, 24.08.1740, *Corr.* # 1)

Eighteenth-century Oxford was notoriously Tory, and sentimentally Jacobite. Smith's political views may not yet have been formed in 1740; but his training under the sceptical, liberal, Ulster Protestant Hutcheson would have given him no reason to sympathise with Oxford Toryism, let alone Jacobitism. The Master of Balliol in Smith's time, Dr Theophilus Leigh, was a fervent Jacobite who 'is said to have fomented prejudice against the Snell Exhibitioners because they were Scotsmen', and certainly joined a Tory drinking club which annually drank the health of the Old Pretender, the Jacobite claimant to the throne of Great Britain, and father of Bonnie Prince Charlie (Ross 1995, pp. 68–9).

Smith therefore learnt nothing from any tutors at Balliol, but spent his six lonely years there in a self-directed programme of extensive reading in classical and contemporary literature and social science. He was notably interested in classical ethical writings, above all those of the Stoic philosophers; and in (mostly French) writings about anthropology and sociology – about societies, such as Native Americans, whom Europeans were meeting for the first time. This was to become source material for Smith's four stages of history, which play a prominent role in *LJ* and *WN*, but not in *TMS*.

KIRKCALDY, EDINBURGH, GLASGOW AGAIN, FRANCE AND LONDON

After Oxford, Smith returned for two years to live with his mother in Kirkcaldy. He seems to have regarded his native town as a place for rest and recreation. While on his later visit of 1767–73, drafting the *Wealth of Nations*, he wrote to David Hume:

> My Business here is Study in which I have been very deeply engaged for about a Month past. My Amusements are long, solitary walks by the Sea side. You may judge how I spend my time. I feel myself, however, extremely happy, comfortable and contented. I never was, perhaps, more so in all my life. (AS to Hume, 07.06.1767, *Corr.* # 103)

But although Kirkcaldy gave Smith peace and quiet it cannot have given him intellectual networks, nor much in the way of libraries. In 1748 he moved to Edinburgh and set up as a private lecturer on a wide range of subjects, including both literature and the philosophy of science. He continued to refine these Edinburgh lectures when he moved to Glasgow, and they give rise to the sets of student lecture notes that we now know as *LRBL*. Smith's few published works other than *TMS* and *WN* also mostly date back ultimately to his Edinburgh years, and are collected in *EPS*. If Balliol was the wrong place to be at the wrong time – and, although we have no direct evidence, it is safe to assume that Smith's relations with the fellows of Balliol became even worse during the Jacobite rebellion of 1745–6 – then Kirkcaldy, and even more Edinburgh, were the right places for Smith to go to recover.

Where Oxford was sentimentally Jacobite, literary and commercial Edinburgh was hard-headedly Hanoverian – or at least anti-Jacobite. Several of Smith's Edinburgh literary friends, but not Smith himself who was in Oxford, had turned out in 1745 for the Edinburgh militia to help repel Bonnie Prince Charlie's troops, but failed to prevent his occupation of Edinburgh and were themselves defeated at the Battle of Prestonpans (21 September 1745).

It was between 1748 and 1752 that Smith became a close friend of David Hume[4] and other members of the Edinburgh literary establishment that was just beginning a remarkable flowering. Just as Smith was preparing to leave Edinburgh for his chair of Moral Philosophy in Glasgow, his friend Gilbert Elliot of Minto wrote, or co-authored, a prospectus for the development of a new town that captured the revolutionary developments that were overtaking both Edinburgh and Glasgow:

> Proposals for carrying on certain public works in the city of EDINBURGH
>
> Among the several causes to which the prosperity of a nation may be ascribed, the situation, conveniency, and beauty of its capital, are surely not the least considerable. A capital where these circumstances happen fortunately to concur, should naturally become the centre of trade and commerce, of learning and the arts, of politeness, and of refinement of every kind.

The authors go on to say that the dirt and overcrowding of the cramped high-rising Old Town, with few public buildings, drive away the upper and middle classes:

> EDINBURGH, which ought to have set the first example of industry and improvement, is the last of our trading cities that has shook off the unaccountable supineness which has so long and so fatally depressed the spirit of this nation[5] . . . To enlarge and improve this city, to adorn it with public buildings, which may be a national benefit, and thereby to remove, at least in some degree, the inconveniencies to which it has hitherto been liable, is the sole object of these proposals . . . The [1707] union of the two kingdoms, an event equally beneficial to both nations, is the great aera from which we may justly date the revival of that spirit and activity which the union of the crowns [in 1603] had well nigh suppressed . . . ; yet in EDINBURGH and the neighbourhood of it, there was still a total stagnation. But since the year 1746, when the rebellion was suppressed, a most surprising revolution has happened in the affairs of this country. (Quoted by Youngson 1966, pp. 4–8)

The prospectus goes on to propose the building of an exchange (to become Smith's Custom House) and other public buildings in the Old Town, to drain a swamp to the north of it, 'removing the markets and shambles',[6] to bridge the gap and form a grid-plan new town on the ridge to the north of that.

The prospectus marks a remarkable recovery of nerve by the Edinburgh bourgeoisie, only seven years after Bonnie Prince Charlie. Everything it proposed was done, resulting in the New Town. David Hume was one of the first people to move there – in a Humean touch, the plot he bought was in St David Street.[7] The public buildings were all constructed, presaging the arguments for the state as promoter of public works that Smith was to celebrate in Book V of *WN*.

By the time of Minto's 1752 *Proposals*, Adam Smith had returned to Glasgow University, although he frequently visited Edinburgh to hold court with his literary and intellectual friends there (Rae [1895] 1965, chapter VIII *passim*). In 1751 he was appointed to the chair of Logic, but did not break his Edinburgh connections until he moved over in 1752 to the chair of Moral Philosophy. He held that chair until 1764, when he left to travel in France with the Duke of Buccleuch.

Glasgow in Smith's time was rising fast because of its western trade. The first reliable estimate, made in 1755, put its population at about 30,000, half that of Edinburgh, which it was first to surpass in the 1801 Census. We have a good description of Glasgow University in Smith's time as professor from a young English visitor, Henry Wyndham:

> [T]he chief ornament of the town is the College. It consists of 3 neat Courts & has a pretty front towards the street. The members of the College are 16 Professors & about 300 students. Here is no Chapell or common Hall as at Oxford for the Students to attend, but ev'ry member dines and lodges where he pleases, & is only expected to be present at the proper Lectures. Over the entrance of this College in a long Room is an extraordinary good collection of all the best old Painter's pictures. Painting is very much encourag'd here, for there is a school on purpose for it, another for Sculpture & another for Engraving. (H. Wyndham to his father, 25.07.1758, quoted in Hook and Sher 1995, p. 10)

Wyndham caught a difference in style between Oxbridge and the Scottish universities that persists to this day. Adam Smith was later to make clear, in *WN* V.i.f–g, his strong preference for the Scottish model. Glasgow University in his time featured an extraordinary galaxy of talents, given its tiny size by modern standards. As well as Smith, there was his friend Joseph Black, chemist and medical researcher, who discovered the principle of latent heat; the laboratory technician James Watt; and the printers Robert and Andrew Foulis, sponsors of the painting school and printers of what are generally reckoned to be the finest books produced in Scotland. Belying his reputation for absent-mindedness, Smith was an active and successful administrator, dealing with the hard issues of personnel and finance (and therefore having an uneasy relationship with both Watt and the Foulises, who occupied quite a lot of space).

The pattern of Smith's lectures is known from a report by his star student John Millar (1735–1801), as well as from the notes that now comprise *LJ* and *LRBL*. As Professor of Moral Philosophy, Smith gave a lecture at 7.30 a.m. every weekday from October to June. His lecture series fell into four parts. The first, 'Natural theology', was presumably required by the nature of his post. He seems to have got through it very quickly. In Millar's report,

> he considered the proofs of the being and attributes of God, and those principles of the human mind upon which religion is founded. The second comprehended Ethics, strictly so called, and consisted chiefly of the doctrines which he afterwards published in his Theory of Moral Sentiments. In the third part, he treated at more length of that branch of morality which relates to *justice*, and which, being susceptible of precise and accurate rules, is for that reason capable of a full and particular explanation . . . In the last part of his lectures, he examined those political regulations which are founded, not upon the principle of *justice*, but that of *expediency*, and which are calculated to increase the riches, the power, and the prosperity of a State . . . [This]

> contained the substance of the work he afterwards published under the title of An Inquiry into the Nature and Causes of the Wealth of Nations. (John Millar to Dugald Stewart, 1790, in *EPS* pp. 274–5)

It has often been said that we know 'nothing' about Smith's lectures on Natural Theology. Actually, Millar's one-sentence report tells us a lot. It tells us specifically that Smith's attitude to religion is the same as that of his Edinburgh contemporary and rival Adam Ferguson (and Ludwig Feuerbach, and Karl Marx, who studied Ferguson and Smith): that is, that religion is an artefact of the human imagination. As Millar goes on to indicate, two of the four parts of this lecture series were published in Smith's lifetime. *The Theory of Moral Sentiments* came out in 1759 to a chorus of acclaim. David Hume's letter of acclamation is long and witty. Hume was in London at the time, and Smith in Glasgow, so Hume sets out to tell Smith how his book has been received in London. I have no room to reproduce it all but cannot resist some of it:

> Nothing indeed can be a stronger Presumption of Falsehood than the Approbation of the Multitude . . . I proceed to tell you the melancholy News, that your Book has been very unfortunate: For the Public seem disposd to applaud it extremely. It was lookd for by the foolish People with some Impatience; and the Mob of Literati are beginning already to be very loud in its Praises. Three Bishops calld yesterday at Millar's Shop in order to buy Copies, and to ask Questions about the Author: The Bishop of Peterborough said he had passed the evening in a Company, where he heard it extolld above all Books in the World. You may conclude what Opinion true Philosophers will entertain of it, when these Retainers to Superstition praise it so highly. (Hume to AS, 12.04.1759, *Corr.* # 31)

Smith continued to work on revisions of *TMS*, including some to meet criticisms from Hume, and in the last decade of his life the revisions for the sixth edition, published in 1790, occupied most of Smith's spare time. The *Wealth of Nations* came out in 1776 to wide but slightly cooler praise, as some of Smith's friends thought that the dryness and complexity of the subject would make it less of a smash hit than *TMS*. Nevertheless, it too sold well in Smith's lifetime.

The rest of the lecture course remained unpublished. A few days before his death, Smith asked two friends, Joseph Black and James Hutton, to destroy all his manuscripts except what they later published as *EPS*. For a hundred years, therefore, the contents of the third section of his Glasgow lectures remained unknown beyond Millar's report. However, in 1895, a set of student notes taken in the session of 1763–4 was found. In 1958 a second set, taken in the session of 1762–3, surfaced, as did a set of Smith's 'private' lectures on rhetoric and belles-lettres, which he delivered later in the day to a more select group of students. These in turn derived from the Edinburgh lectures on the same subjects that we know Smith gave between 1748 and 1751. These three sets of notes are now available as *LJ(B)*, *LJ(A)* and *LRBL* respectively. Of these, *LRBL* for sure, and probably some parts of the rest, derive from the Edinburgh private lectures. I return to these discoveries later.

On Millar's account, Smith was a good lecturer, although other witnesses say that he was too dry to be as successful as his detractors.

> In delivering his lectures, he trusted almost entirely to extemporary elocution.[8] His manner, though not graceful, was plain and unaffected; and, as he seemed to be always interested in the subject, he never failed to interest his hearers. Each discourse consisted commonly of several distinct propositions, which he successively endeavoured to prove and illustrate. (Millar, *ibid.*)

In *LRBL*, Smith strongly recommends a plain and unaffected style for scholarly writing. Millar's description captures the style of *TMS* and *WN* but misses two main things about both books: the rise of Smith's style to epigrammatic anger when he is protesting against some abuse; and the hiding of deeply subversive opinions behind the plain style. I quote several examples in this book.

One of Smith's administrative talents was to work the patronage system on which eighteenth-century public life depended. Scotland, and in a microcosm of Scotland Glasgow University, depended on its political patrons. The political patron of Scotland in Smith's youth and middle age was Archibald Campbell, Lord Ilay, later third Duke of Argyll (1682–1761). Smith's cousin and guardian William Smith was an employee of the Dukes of Argyll, and Smith entered their patronage network at an early age, perhaps during a visit in his Balliol days to one of the Argyll family estates in Adderbury, north Oxfordshire. Argyll was also a patron of Glasgow University, and Smith tried to meet him in 1751 on University business; he visited the ducal seat at Inveraray in 1759 or 1760. After a gap, Argyll was succeeded as Scottish political manager by two men of more modest origins: Alexander Wedderburn, later Lord Loughborough (1733–1805), and Henry Dundas, later Viscount Melville (1742–1811). Smith knew them both, the first intimately.

It was through the Argyll connection that Smith entered both political and noble circles. The politician Charles Townshend (1725–67), who according to Hume 'passes for the cleverest Fellow in England' (Hume to AS, 12.04.1759, *Corr.* # 31), was married to a sister of the second Duke of Argyll, Ilay's elder brother. Her previous husband had been the heir to Scotland's other grandest landowner, the Duke of Buccleuch. Townshend was therefore the stepfather of the young (third) Duke of Buccleuch. In 1759, when Smith came to Townshend's notice because of the publication of *TMS*, the Duke was a schoolboy at Eton. Townshend apparently first mentioned the idea of Smith acting as the Duke's tutor in 1759; in 1763 he made a firm invitation, which Smith accepted, giving notice of his resignation in November 1763. He proposed to pay back the student fees for the unexpired portion of his course, and if the students would not take their money back, to pay the money to the University for the substitute tuition. This offer is noted in the surviving University archives (GUA 26645; Ross 1995, p. 153). A detailed and picturesque story in a biography of Smith's intellectual Edinburgh friend Henry Home, Lord Kames, unfortunately published long after the event, has it that

> After concluding his last lecture . . . he drew from his pocket the several fees of the students, wrapped up in separate paper parcels, and beginning to call up each man by his name, he delivered to the first who was called the money into his hand. The young man peremptorily refused to accept it, declaring that the instruction and pleasure he had already received was much more than he either had repaid or ever could compensate, and a general cry was heard from every one in the room to the same effect. But Mr Smith was not to be bent from his purpose . . . [H]e told them this was a matter betwixt him and his own mind . . . 'You must not refuse me this satisfaction; nay, by heavens, gentlemen, you shall not;' and seizing by the coat the young man who stood next him, he thrust the money into his pocket and then pushed him from him. The rest saw it was in vain to contest the matter, and were obliged to let him have his own way. (Tytler 1807, i.278; quoted by Rae [1895] 1965, p. 170)

This is so illuminating about the author of *The Theory of Moral Sentiments* that one would like it to be true; and it is strongly suspected that Smith made substantial charitable donations towards the end of his life, which would be consistent with the behaviour reported here. And both Kames and his biographer (A. F. Tytler) belonged to Smith's Edinburgh literary circle, and used the same publishers. Tytler knew Smith and a letter from Smith to Tytler survives (*Corr.* # 254). On the other hand, Glasgow University *did* provide a substitute lecturer, and the rest of the session's lectures *were* delivered (because notes of them comprise *LJ(B)*). So if Tytler's story is true, it is difficult to make the sums add up. As one of the wisest Smith commentators, Jacob Viner, says of another encrusted story, *Si populus vult decipi, decipiatur* (Viner 1965, p. 47).[9]

Smith left for London in January 1764, where he met his new pupil. They then went to France, calling first in Paris, where Hume was at the time secretary at the British embassy, to pick up a letter of recommendation from the Ambassador (who unfortunately called him Robinson instead of Smith – *Corr.* # 83) before going to the slightly surprising destination of Toulouse, where Smith complained that they knew nobody and could not make themselves understood – 'I have begun to write a book in order to pass away the time' (*Corr.* # 82). Thus a spell in a boring provincial town gave rise to *WN*, although most of its essential themes were already in Smith's Glasgow lectures. Smith and Buccleuch, who had now been joined by his brother, had a more enjoyable side-trip to Geneva, to meet the great Voltaire, as did all enlightened people on the Grand Tour. At Geneva Smith first started to meet liberal Francophone intellectuals and mathematicians, an acquaintance which he strengthened when Townshend finally permitted the party to move to Paris, where they probably arrived at the end of 1765. There, Smith frequented the celebrated salons of the Enlightenment, especially those of Julie de l'Espinasse, protector of the gauche mathematician the Marquis de Condorcet; the grand Duchesse d'Enville, dowager of the Rochefoucauld dynasty; the atheist Baron d'Holbach; and the utilitarian philosopher C.-A. Helvétius (Ross 1995, p. 210; for Julie de l'Espinasse and Condorcet see McLean and Hewitt 1994, pp. 4–9). In particular, Smith came to know the two leading French economists, François Quesnay and A. R. M. Turgot. Quesnay was a doctor, who modelled the economy as a circulating system like the human body, and it was as a doctor that Smith called on Quesnay when he badly needed him in October 1766. Both Buccleuch (Scott) brothers contracted fever. The Duke recovered; his younger brother did not, despite the attentions of the three best doctors Smith could find.[10] The death of the Hon. Hew Campbell Scott ended the Duke's Grand Tour. Smith and the Duke returned to London, where Smith spent the first of his three short periods as a member of the council of economic advisers, as we might now say, to the UK government.

As a politician, Townshend was reckless and independent – a contemporary called him 'that splendid shuttlecock'. But from the early 1760s he seems to have consistently taken the view that the American colonists should bear a larger share of the costs of their defence. The Seven Years' War (1756–63) was essentially a war between the imperial powers of Britain and France, fought at the outer fringes of their empires, Canada and India, using, in part, proxy warriors such as Native Americans and Indian princes. The British victories in Canada under General Wolfe in 1759 removed a French tourniquet over American colonial expansion.

Before the war, the French had laid claim to the entire territory from the Great Lakes down the Ohio, Illinois and Mississippi valleys to New Orleans. Their key stronghold, on the Ohio River in modern Pennsylvania, was Fort Duquesne. On capture by the British it was renamed Fort Pitt in honour of the wartime Prime Minister Pitt the Elder. It is now Pittsburgh.

The British victory removed the tourniquet. But the expensive campaign, led by American-born British officers such as Major George Washington, was funded entirely by the British taxpayer, who benefited only indirectly. The direct beneficiaries were the colonists. Not only had the French tourniquet been removed, but British troops on the frontier protected the colonists' westward drive for new land from the Native American tribes whom they displaced, and who naturally fought the settlers to try to retrieve their land. Townshend wished to end the colonists' free ride. In July 1766 Pitt appointed Townshend Chancellor of the Exchequer. Townshend started to use Smith as a specialist adviser while Smith was still in France, as they worked together on the finances of the 'Sinking Fund', which was a scheme to balance the public debts incurred during wars with surpluses to be built up in times of peace. Chancellor Townshend's Sinking Fund was a direct ancestor of Chancellor Gordon Brown's 'Golden Rule' which requires that new debt may only be incurred to fund capital spending, not current spending. Townshend's calculations, corrected by Smith, show that the Sinking Fund was then building up too slowly to achieve this; therefore Townshend concluded that he needed to raise taxes, and raise the yield of existing taxes by reducing smuggling, in order to increase the tax yield by a total of £400,000 per annum. 'I will add to these a *real* American Revenue' (Townshend to AS, late 1766, *Corr.* # 302; stress in original).

Townshend presented his budget in March 1767, including his proposals for a *real* American Revenue. He would get his American revenue by imposing a duty on British goods landed in the colonies, including, ominously, tea. He took powers to impose these taxes directly on the state of New York, whose legislative assembly he suspended on the grounds that it had failed to pay its local militia costs.

Townshend's duties became a *casus belli*, leading to the Boston Tea Party (1773) and the outbreak of the American revolutionary war in 1775. Townshend did not live to see this, as he died suddenly in September 1767. But Adam Smith did. This led the economist C. R. Fay to comment 'in the last analysis it was professional advice which lost us [the UK] the first empire' (Fay 1956, p. 116). But was it Adam Smith's advice? And was it responsible for the loss of the American colonies? Smith scholars have taken opposing positions on these questions. Tiptoeing through the minefield, I tentatively suggest that *it probably was Smith's advice* that Townshend should tax the colonists. From his other writings it is amply clear that Smith shared Townshend's view that the colonists were taking a free ride on the public good of their defence, and that this should stop. This is crystal clear in advice which Smith gave to his old friend Wedderburn, when the latter was Solicitor-General, in 1778 (*Corr.*, Appendix B). It is also clear in the long chapter on colonies in *WN* (IV.vii, especially IV.vii.c.71–4).

However, *he would not have approved of the specific form that the Townshend duties took* for at least three reasons. First, the tea duties were an inefficient form of taxation. They do not conform to the maxims of taxation that Smith sets out in *WN* Book V, discussed later in this book. Second, they served Townshend's vested interest. He was a speculator on his own account in East India Company stock, even while serving as Chancellor of the Exchequer, a feat which managed to excite even contemporary commentators at a time when this sort of thing was commonplace (Thomas 2004). Second, the tea duties benefited the East India Company, because they helped to protect its monopoly of tea re-exportation to America. Third, they bypassed the American colonial legislatures, which should be responsible for funding the expenditure from which they benefit, and whose ambition should be encouraged by making them responsible for serious decisions rather than 'piddling for the little prizes which are to be found in what may be called the paltry raffle of colonial faction' (*WN* IV.vii.c.75).

Whether agreeing or disagreeing with his patron, Smith returned to his mother's house in Kirkcaldy in the summer of 1767 with a pension from the Buccleuch family that made him financially independent for the rest of his life. There he stayed for six years, taking his 'long, solitary walks by the Sea side' and feeling himself 'extremely happy, comfortable and contented' (*Corr.* # 103 to Hume 1767, quoted previously). Despite many humorous but persistent pleas from Hume (see Preface), Smith did not stir even as far as Edinburgh, which he could see every day on his sea shore walk, except when the mist came down.

As I write this, thirled to my office computer and making frequent visits to cyberspace, I marvel that Smith could have worked for six years in Kirkcaldy on *WN* with no libraries, no intellectual conversations and no recourse to the many social clubs of which he was a member or later joined.[11] Of course he had his Glasgow lecture notes, and possibly even earlier ones from his Edinburgh days; and of course the economic *theory* of *WN* required hard abstract thought for which the Kirkcaldy foreshore was as good a place as any. But *WN* is packed with facts – how did Smith come by them?

Partly by active correspondence with experts. The surviving letters of this period, which may be only a fraction of those that Smith sent and received, contain copious information and data which went into *WN*, about time-series for the price of corn, medieval Scots law and the circumstances surrounding the failure of the Ayr Bank in 1772 – in which the Buccleuch family probably lost a lot of money. But in 1773 Smith went to London, staying there until soon after *WN* was published, where he could talk to politicians, policy advisers and businessmen, and get access to the data that he required for his book. *WN* was a long time in coming, but it finally appeared in March 1776. Hume's letter of congratulation was less effusive than his letter on the publication of *TMS*, but warm none the less:

> Euge! Belle! Dear Mr Smith: I am much pleas'd with your Performance, and the Perusal of it has taken me from a State of great Anxiety. It was a Work of so much Expectation, by youself, by your Friends, and by the Public, that I trembled for its Appearance; but am now much relieved. Not but that the Reading of it necessarily requires so much Attention, and the Public is disposed to give so little, that I shall still doubt for some time of its being at first very popular. (Hume to AS, 01.04.1776, *Corr.* # 150)

Indeed there were no reports, this time, of bishops queuing up to buy Smith's book; but in fact it sold respectably for the rest of Smith's life (Sher 2004c).

THE BACKROOM POLICY ADVISER

While in London, Smith had become 'very zealous in American Affairs' – or so the Duke of Buccleuch told Hume. He would shortly again be in government service as a backroom adviser, but first he returned to Scotland for the latter part of 1776. He had had warning from Hume and others that Hume was unwell ('I weighed myself t'other day, and find I have fallen five compleat Stones. If you delay much longer, I shall probably disappear altogether' – DH to AS, 08.02.1776, *Corr.* # 149). Hume's long-drawn-out illness, which may have been bowel cancer or ulcerative colitis, was beyond eighteenth-century cure; but doctors advised him to take the waters, and he travelled to London and then Bath, meeting the northbound Smith at

Morpeth, Northumberland. The Bath waters did no good, and Hume arrived back in Edinburgh in July.

A revealing glimpse of the private Adam Smith comes from his letter describing Hume's illness to his friend the politician Alexander Wedderburn:

> I have nothing to tell you that will be very agreeable. Poor David Hume is dying very fast, but with great chearfulness and good humour and with more real resignation to the necessary course of things, than any Whining Christian ever dyed with pretended resignation to the will of God. (AS to Wedderburn, 14.08.1776, *Corr.* # 163)

Hume died on 25 August, having failed to get Smith to promise to oversee publication of his *Dialogues concerning Natural Religion*, which the prudent public Smith thought would be too inflammatory. However, Smith did ensure, as Hume had wished, that Hume's short autobiography *My Own Life* was published as soon as possible. As it was too short to make up a book on its own, Smith appended an affecting account of Hume's last days, which was in fact a very much toned down version of his letters to Wedderburn and others about Hume's illness. He sent a draft to Hume's brother, who approved it with minor alterations. Hume had told Smith that he was reading the Greek satirist Lucian's *Dialogues of the Dead*. The *Dialogues* are a set of sarcastic variations on the theme that all humans, whether rich, poor, beautiful, ugly, wise, stupid and so on are equal in death.[12] Smith tells us that Hume imagined himself pleading with Charon, the famously bad-tempered ferryman of the dead in Greek mythology, for a short delay before being forced to get on the fatal ferry.

> He then diverted himself with inventing several jocular excuses, which he supposed he might make to Charon, and with imagining the very surly answers which it might suit the character of Charon to return to them . . . 'But I might still urge, "Have a little patience, good Charon, I have been endeavouring to open the eyes of the Public. If I live a few years longer, I may have the satisfaction of seeing the downfall of some of the prevailing systems of superstition."[13] But Charon would then lose all temper and decency. "You loitering rogue, that will not happen these many hundred years. Do you fancy I will grant you a lease for so long a term? Get into the boat this instant, you lazy loitering rogue." '

Smith's account ends:

> Upon the whole, I have always considered him, both in his lifetime and since his death, as approaching as nearly to the idea of a perfectly wise and virtuous man, as perhaps the nature of human frailty will permit. (AS to W. Strahan, 09.11.1778, *Corr.* # 178)

Smith's audience caught the echo; modern audiences need to be told. The peroration of Smith's eulogy is a close copy of the last paragraph of Plato's dialogue *Phaedo*, recording the heroic death of Socrates, who stoically drank the fatal hemlock supplied by his executioners. In 1780, Smith ruefully told a correspondent that

> A single, and as, I thought a very harmless Sheet of paper, which I happened to Write concerning the death of our late friend Mr Hume, brought upon me ten times more abuse than the very violent attack I had made upon the whole commercial system of Great Britain. [In *WN*] (AS to A. Holt, 26.10.1780, *Corr.* # 208)

'As I thought a very harmless Sheet' is either naïve or disingenuous; probably the latter. Smith had worked hard and carefully on his eulogy, toning it down from the much more offensive (to Christians) wording of his letter to Wedderburn. As a former lecturer on rhetoric and belles-lettres, whose lectures Wedderburn had attended back in 1748, he surely knew exactly what he was doing when he repeated Hume's Lucianic dialogue and added his own Platonic one. He was signalling that both he and Hume found classical writings on the approach of death more consoling than Christian writings. However, on the side of the naïve interpretation is the fact that Hume's *Dialogues*, which had caused Smith much mental anguish because he was unwilling to carry out his friend's dying wish on the grounds that it would be too controversial, were published in 1779 to no controversy at all. Smith may have misjudged what caused most offence to the godly.

Smith spent most of the rest of his life in public service, while giving as much time as he could to plans to revise and (re)publish his works. At the end of 1776 he returned to London – in order, I would surmise, to resume the consultancy on American affairs that he had broken off on hearing of Hume's illness. Wedderburn had been appointed Solicitor-General in 1770 (and was promoted to Attorney-General in 1778). In the governments of Lord North, he was one of the principal makers of American policy. It would have been natural for him to consult his old tutor on difficult issues of public policy. A long memo headed in Wedderburn's hand 'Smiths Thoughts on the State of the Contest with America, February 1778' is generally regarded as authentic. It certainly reads and sounds like Smith, with his characteristic calm insubordination. It proposes a clear-headed but radical solution to the American war, which in 1778 looked like an Iraq or a Vietnam: a war that the hegemonic power of the day had found it easy to enter but hard to exit. I analyse Smith's solutions in Chapter 6.

In the same year Smith was appointed a Commissioner of Customs for Scotland. This post depended on patronage, and Smith for all his unworldly reputation was a skilled manipulator of patronage networks. He said that he had been appointed 'by the interest of the Duke of Buccleuch', and he probably also owed it to his friends Wedderburn and Dundas. But he certainly did not treat it as a sinecure. He told correspondents that it took him four solid days' work a week. He became a noted Edinburgh figure as he walked twice a day between his home, Panmure House in the Canongate, to the Custom House. His office was in the main part of the first building of classical Edinburgh, the Exchange opposite St Giles' Cathedral, the building that now houses Edinburgh City Chambers (Youngson 1966, p. 55). Some commentators have wondered why Smith, the scourge of inappropriate taxes, could become a Commissioner of Customs with a clear conscience. In *WN* he discusses how they can give perverse incentives to encourage smuggling. But I think there is an adequate answer in the 1767 discussions between him and Townshend. Whether or not Customs duties were a good tax – and with eighteenth-century technology they were one of the few taxes available to governments – they needed honest and efficient administration to maximise their yield. Smuggling was a major problem, and Customs and excise duties must be both designed and implemented in a way that would minimise smuggling and therefore maximise revenue at minimum cost. As he had written in *WN*:

> The high duties which have been imposed upon the importation of many different sorts of foreign goods, in order to discourage their consumption in Great Britain, have in many cases served only to encourage smuggling; and in all cases have reduced the revenue of the customs below what more moderate duties would have afforded. (*WN* V.ii.k.27)

Smith resumed his social life in Edinburgh, holding a salon on Sunday evenings in Panmure House which must have matched the Paris salons he attended in 1766 in intellectual standing, if not in the quality of food, drink or finery. Sir Walter Scott recalled that Smith used to walk round the table stealing sugar lumps from the basin, to the confusion and annoyance of his cousin-housekeeper Janet Douglas (quoted in Ross 1995, p. 310). He was saddened by the death of his mother in 1784 and that of his cousin-housekeeper in 1788 or 1789. He was delighted by his election as Rector of Glasgow University in 1787:

> No preferment would have given me so much real satisfaction. No man can owe greater obligations to a Society than I do to the University of Glasgow. They educated me, they sent me to Oxford, soon after my return to Scotland

> they elected me one of their own members, and afterwards preferred me to another office, to which the abilities and Virtues of the never to be forgotten Dr Hutcheson had given a superior degree of illustration. (AS to Dr Archibald Davidson, 16.11.1787, *Corr.* # 274)

In his last years, Smith made two more trips to London, the more important of them being in 1787. Some details of this trip remain obscure, and some have become encrusted with legends, as have most Smith anecdotes. But the broad outlines are clear. The dominant figure in British politics was now the astonishingly young Prime Minister William Pitt the Younger, son of the William Pitt of the Seven Years' War. Pitt the Younger first became Prime Minister at the age of twenty-four in 1783 and remained in power for the rest of Smith's life and the first half of the French Revolutionary and Napoleonic wars. Smith's friend Henry Dundas was Pitt's indispensable right-hand man, who sat at Pitt's side each evening organising British politics as they drank a bottle or six of port or claret (Hague 2004, pp. 220–1, 308).

Pitt was already a known admirer of Smith. He had promoted commercial treaties in order to bring about freer trade, and, in one of the few unsuccessful moves of his Prime Ministership, he tried to bring both civil rights and economic union to Ireland along the lines that Smith advocated in *WN*. His budgets were models of Smithian political economy, until the French wars started. In early 1787 Smith, by now in poor health, decided to take a break from his Customs duties in order to revise his books and attempt to publish his *Jurisprudence*, the part of the Glasgow lectures that would have been the missing link between *TMS* and *WN*. Dundas wrote to him in March 1787 to say 'I am glad you have got Vacation. Mr Pitt, Mr Grenville [Vice-President of the Board of Trade; Pitt's cousin and the other central player in politics] and your humble servant are clearly of opinion you cannot spend it so well as here', and invited Smith to stay in 'my Villa at Wimbledon . . . You shall have a comfortable Room and . . . we shall have time to discuss all your Books with you every Evening' (Dundas to AS, 21.03.1787, *Corr.* # 267).

The modern equivalent of such a letter might be one from the Prime Minister inviting the recipient to spend a few weeks at Chequers to explain his academic work to a nightly meeting in the company of the Chancellor of the Exchequer and the Foreign Secretary. Unsurprisingly, despite (or perhaps even because of) his dubious health,[14] Smith accepted the invitation, and put aside his publication and revision plans. Oral tradition, passed on by John Kay the caricaturist (who drew the cartoon of Smith on the cover of this book), has it that Smith came into a room at

Dundas's house where Pitt, Grenville and William Wilberforce were among the company. They stood up to greet Smith, who invited them to sit down. 'No,' said the Prime Minister, 'we will stand until you are first seated, for we are all your scholars' (Rae [1895] 1965, p. 405). On firmer ground is the fact, attested by a correspondent of Jeremy Bentham's, that Smith was 'much with the ministry; and the clerks at the public offices have orders to furnish him with all papers, and to employ additional hands, if necessary, to copy for him' (G. Wilson to J. Bentham, quoted by Ross 1995, p. 375). Smith had written the previous year to an opposition MP:

> I think myself much honoured by the slightest mark of Mr Pitts approbation. You may be assured that the long and strict friendship in which I have lived with some of his opponents, does not hinder me from discerning courage, activity, probity, and public spirit in the great outlines of his administration. (Quoted by Ross 1995, p. 376)

If Smith had had longer to live, a few months with the three most important Ministers of the Crown and the crème de la crème of HM Treasury fetching and carrying papers for him might have been quite beneficial to his academic work. But he did not have long. He had already told a correspondent that he was in his 'grand Climacteric,'[15] in 1787 (*Corr.* # 266); friends and acquaintances in London were worried by his appearance, although they thought that Hunter's surgery did him good. He returned to Edinburgh in August 1787 and probably never left again (not even to go to Glasgow for any event connected with his rectorship of the university). In the *Advertisement* to the sixth edition of *TMS*, which appeared in July 1790, Smith wrote that he still intended to publish his *Jurisprudence*, but that his 'very advanced age' made it unlikely that he would succeed. Smith therefore has nothing directly to say about the French Revolution, which broke out in 1789 and would soon lead to the horrible deaths of two of his best French friends, la Rochefoucauld and Condorcet. What the 1790 alterations to *TMS* may imply about Smith's views on France and revolution is contested, and I return to the subject in Chapter 6.

There is evidence that Smith faced death almost as stoically as Hume. An acquaintance wrote in late June 1790, 'His intellect as well as his senses are clear and distinct. He wishes to be cheerful, but nature is omnipotent. His body is extremely emaciated, and his stomach cannot admit of sufficient nourishment; but, like a man, he is perfectly patient and resigned' (W. Smellie, quoted by Rae [1895] 1965, p. 432). On 11 July, a Sunday, Smith asked Joseph Black and James Hutton to burn almost all his papers, which they did. His friends had come round for the usual soirée, but Smith said, 'I love your company gentlemen, but I believe I must leave you to go to another world'[16] (Rae [1895] 1965, p. 435). He died on 17 July, and is buried in Canongate churchyard, a few yards from his home.

It was the uneventful end to an outwardly uneventful life. Only in the events surrounding Hume's death had Smith's life risen to any dramatic climax. But it was his inward, intellectual life that mattered most. In his own lifetime, he had seen his economic doctrines adopted by leading politicians of both parties. His ethical doctrines, probably more important to Smith himself, percolated into public life in more devious ways; then, after his death, his economic doctrines came to be presented in a very partial way. The rest of this book is devoted to an attempt to recover the real, whole, Adam Smith, and to understand the implications of his thought for the present day. In Chapter 2, I describe the weak church and the weak state which alone made it possible for Smith's thought to emerge at all, but which set him a range of intellectual problems to solve in his two books.

NOTES

1. Of my Edinburgh school-leaving cohort of thirty, to the best of my memory two went to Oxford, one each to Glasgow and St Andrews and all the rest to Edinburgh University, where the first-year lecture classes contained great homogeneous blocks of students from each of the Edinburgh schools – a Heriot's block, a Royal High block, a Daniel Stewart's block, a Gillespie's block and so on. James Gillespie's High School for Girls is the original of the Marcia Blaine School for Girls in Muriel Spark's *The Prime of Miss Jean Brodie*.
2. In this book, I use the following labels for different Protestant factions, organisations and theologies. *Episcopalian* in a British context I treat as synonymous with *Anglican*: describing the Church of England, with a hierarchical structure including bishops (*episcopoi* – overseers – in Greek) and with the monarch of England/Britain/the United Kingdom as its supreme governor. *Erastianism* is the principle of support for a church whose supreme governor is head of state. Therefore all Anglican churches are Erastian (although not all Erastian churches are Anglican). *Presbyterian* churches, including the Church of Scotland established in 1690 and all the churches that seceded from it thereafter, are those with a Presbyterian form of government: that is, government by ministers and elders with formally equal status, and without bishops. *Calvinism* is the set of doctrines associated with Jean Calvin (1509–64), the founder of Presbyterianism. Calvinist

doctrines include Presbyterian Church government, but also other things, such as what Smith labelled an 'austere' set of morals. *Puritan*, *dissenting*, *Nonconformist* are all commonly used terms that include, but are not restricted to, Calvinist belief and Presbyterian church organisation.

3. *Cy pres*: 'As near as practicable: applied to a process in equity by which, in the case of trusts or charities, when a literal execution of the testator's intention becomes impossible, it is executed as nearly as possible, according to the general purpose' – definition from *Oxford English Dictionary* on-line edition at www.oed.com.
4. There is a story that Smith got into trouble at Balliol because he was found reading the work of the notorious atheist David Hume. But the source of the story is the early Victorian economist J. R. McCulloch, writing nearly a century after the (supposed) event. I think the story is too neat to be true. As, on Hume's own account, his *Treatise of Human Nature* fell 'dead born from the press' on publication in 1738, it is not very likely that either Smith or Balliol College found a copy in the early 1740s.
5. I assume that 'unaccountable supineness' is a scolding reference to the failure of the Edinburgh commercial class to repel Bonnie Prince Charlie in 1745.
6. The dank alleyway which is Fleshmarket Close, north of the High Street, still gives a vivid impression of what the shambles must have been like.
7. Alexander (Jupiter) Carlyle and his Victorian editor offer two variant anecdotes. In one, Hume paid a workman to paint 'St. David Street' on the empty street nameboard and the name stuck. In the other, Hume tells a scandalised servant who has seen the nameplate that 'many better men than me have been saints'. It would be nice if at least one of these stories were true. Carlyle [1860] 1990, pp. 289–90.
8. But surviving drafts show that he probably wrote out his lecture notes in full.
9. 'If the people want to be deceived, let them be deceived'. Viner is commenting on the claim that Smith took drafts of *WN* to Benjamin Franklin, Richard Price and others, and amended them in the light of their comments. I do not believe that one either.
10. One of the others was Dr Richard Gem (*Corr.* # 97). So interlinked were the Scottish, French and American Enlightenments that Gem later became the personal doctor, and political theorist, of Thomas Jefferson, who was American Minister in Paris 1785–9. See McLean and Hewitt 1994, pp. 55–7.
11. Smith was a member of, *inter alia*, the 'Select Society' of Edinburgh; Adam Ferguson's 'Poker Club', designed to campaign for a Scottish militia; a Fellow of the Royal Society (he was elected FRS in 1767, but did not take up his Fellowship until arriving in London in 1773); a founding Fellow of the Royal Society of Edinburgh; a member, while in London 1773–6, of 'The Club' formed to make an admiring circle for Dr Johnson – not something congenial to AS – and in his last years a congenial Sunday host of the Edinburgh literati. So he could be sociable when he chose to.

12. A free public-domain translation of the *Dialogues of the Dead* is at www.gutenberg.org/dirs/etext04/lcns110.txt.
13. In the Wedderburn version, this speech of Hume's runs 'Have a little patience only till I have the pleasure of seeing the churches shut up, and the Clergy sent about their business'. *Corr.* # 163.
14. While in London he was treated by the eminent Glasgow-born surgeon John Hunter. Ross 1995, p. 374.
15. 'A critical stage in human life; a point at which the person was supposed to be specially liable to change in health or fortune. According to some, all the years denoted by multiples of 7 (7, 14, 21, etc.) were climacterics; others admitted only the odd multiples of 7 (7, 21, 35, etc.); some included also the multiples of 9. Grand (great) climacteric (sometimes simply the climacteric): the 63rd year of life (63 = 7 × 9), supposed to be specially critical.' *Oxford English Dictionary* on-line edition, s.v. 'climacteric', sense B1. Smith was sixty-three at the time of writing this letter.
16. A more dramatically satisfying version is 'I believe we must adjourn this meeting to another place' (Rae [1895] 1965, p. 435), but this was not written down until after the more mundane version – it is in Stewart, *Account*, footnote to V.8, p. 328. As with Pitt the Younger, connoisseurs may make their own choice of last words (in Pitt's case between 'My country – how I leave my country!' and 'I could eat one of Bellamy's veal pies').

2

A Weak State and a Weak Church

Francis Hutcheson, Adam Smith and David Hume lived under a weak state and a weak church. If they had not, Smith and Hume might have been unable to publish their devastating demolitions of politics, economics and religion as they found them. Had they depended on the universities of Oxford or Cambridge rather than Edinburgh or Glasgow, they might have been silenced as effectively as their great predecessor John Locke. Locke fled to the Netherlands in 1683 as the political climate in England became more hostile to him and his friends, was expelled from his Oxford fellowship in 1684 and did not publish his great work in philosophy and politics until after the change of regime – the 'Glorious Revolution', which his work was seen to justify – in 1689. This chapter explores the institutions whose weakness gave the thinkers of the Scottish Enlightenment the space to write, but also a political and intellectual vacuum to be filled by better institutions.

THE STATE IN SCOTLAND

Scotland had never been a strong state. Poor, cold and not on the way to anywhere except Scandinavia, it had been neither the origin nor the target of any empire before 1707. It took roughly its present shape in the eleventh century, except that the northern and western islands were still under Scandinavian control for a further 300 years; and the Highlands and Borders were under nobody's effective control until the seventeenth century.

Lawless Scotland was always a challenge to the security of England. The much stronger government of England therefore tried to control all three of its troublesome peripheries – Scotland, Wales and Ireland. When Edward I tried to do so, he succeeded wholly in Wales, but only partly in Scotland. King John Balliol accepted Edward's overlordship, but William Wallace did not. Wallace defeated Edward's troops at Stirling in 1297. Wallace was later captured and executed, but the Scots won again under Robert Bruce at the decisive battle of Bannockburn (1314), very close to

Stirling. In 1320 the self-styled 'community of the realm of Scotland' produced the precocious Declaration of Arbroath as a political appeal to the pope. This early statement of national independence opened with a fictitious history of Scotland as a nation, and announced that 'as long as but a hundred of us remain alive, never will we on any conditions be brought under English rule'.[1]

However, talk is cheap; defence of the realm can be expensive. As Scandinavian empires shrivelled and English kings concentrated on French wars and civil wars rather than Scottish wars, Scotland faced no external threats for 200 years; however, successive short-lived kings and long regencies meant that the state remained weak. In the sixteenth century, with their French and civil wars over, English regimes again turned to protecting their northern frontier. They invaded Scotland in 1513 (the battle of Flodden); 1542 (Solway Moss); 1544–5 (the 'Rough Wooing'); 1547 (Pinkie); and Edinburgh (1572–3, by proxy). Scottish armies in the sixteenth century were as successful as the Scottish rugby team after 1990. Scotland received temporary protection from England in the Union of the Crowns in 1603, when James VI of Scotland succeeded to the throne of England by virtue of a shrewd dynastic marriage a century earlier. Shakespeare's *Macbeth* was written to honour this succession. It makes James VI and I one of the descendants of Banquo's son Fleance, who escapes assassination by Macbeth's agents. On arriving in London, James abandoned his earlier good intentions of revisiting Scotland frequently. He only returned once, in 1617 (Mitchison 1970, p. 163), and enjoyed boasting that he could govern Scotland by the stroke of his pen. That was much more congenial than tangling with Presbyterian clergymen, as he had had to do extensively while reigning as James VI of Scotland.

Had his successors known as well as he how to let sleeping dogs lie, they would have lived more peacefully and longer. As explained in the next section, the Scottish Reformation had taken an entirely different form to the English. Its Calvinist faction objected to bishops, whilst all the Stuart kings tried to (re)impose them. When Charles I tried, by introducing a new liturgy for the Scottish Church in 1637 without first consulting its General Assembly, a famous riot ensued in St Giles' Church in Edinburgh. A market stallholder called Jenny Geddes hurled her stool at the preacher, shouting (it is said) 'Daur ye say mass in my lug?'[2] The road from Jenny Geddes to civil war took only a year. And, as in rugby, the Scots won one of their occasional victories against the English. In the second Bishops' War of 1639–40 they occupied Newcastle upon Tyne after winning the battle of Newburn, which is not one of the battles that English schoolchildren learn about. To repel them, Charles had to call a mutinous parliament in order to raise the necessary taxes; what English historians call the Great Rebellion was under way. However, just as the Second World War started before 1939 if you are Chinese, so the Great Rebellion started before 1640 if you are Scots (or Irish). The apogee of Scottish power came in the Westminster Confession of 1643, when the Scottish minority on a Parliamentary committee purported to impose Calvinist doctrine on the churches of both countries. That Westminster Confession remains the official doctrine of the Church of Scotland (to the embarrassment of its present-day leaders). Adam Smith had to swear allegiance to it on taking office as a professor at Glasgow University. However, the Presbyterians backed the wrong (royalist) side in the second English civil war (1646–8), and the next English invasion of Scotland, under Oliver Cromwell's rule, restored the usual military situation at the Battle of Dunbar (1650). Cromwell believed that 'the Lord had delivered them into our hands' when the Scottish army was (it is said) ordered by its Presbyterian ministers to leave its safe high ground in order to attack the starving English army, which had been about to be evacuated by sea from Dunkirk-like Dunbar.

However, with the restoration of Charles II in 1660, the hardline Scots Presbyterians – 'Covenanters' – again became a guerrilla force, especially in south-west Scotland. They acknowledged no bishop, although Charles II had restored episcopacy. The flight of James II in 1688 gave the Presbyterians their opportunity. The new king and queen, William and Mary, arrived in England by Parliamentary invitation. James had escaped to France. His followers in the Scottish Estates also departed, to prepare for a military rising to restore him.[3] The remaining Whigs drew up a long Claim of Right, accepting William and Mary as monarchs on condition that they accepted the Presbyterian church as the national church of Scotland. The ensuing revolt of 'Bonnie Dundee' failed, as did the attempt of James to return to power via Ireland. Scotland under William and Mary remained, however, a poor and unhappy place. A mishandled attempt to enforce loyalty to the regime in the Highlands led to the Massacre of Glencoe (1692), whose brutality weakened support for the regime even though most Lowland Scots felt nothing but fear and loathing for the Highlanders. There was a succession of bad harvests. Most importantly, the creation and subsequent collapse of the 'Darien scheme' showed that Scotland was no longer viable as an independent state sharing its crown with another.

In 1695–6 Edinburgh merchants had launched 'The Company of Scotland trading to Africa and the Indes', incorporated under patent by an Act of the Scottish Parliament in June 1695. The Company of Scotland was intended as a trading company along the lines of the English East India Company. But, in the face of opposition from the English Parliament and executive, the focus of the Company changed, with the aim of creating a trading colony on the Isthmus of Darien (in what is now Panama). Faced with a threat to the East India Company's monopoly, in which many of them had a material interest, MPs and Lords in Westminster sought to cut off access to the capital market in London and across Northern Europe. The Board of Trade and Plantations was established in 1696 to set up a rival colony: 'This work seems to us to require all possible despatch, lest the Scotch Company be there before us, which is of the utmost importance to the trade of England' (quoted in Armitage 1995, p. 109).

The Westminster opposition was supported by King William, who sourly observed that 'I have been ill served in Scotland' (Insh 1932, p. 57), and is described as denouncing the project's supporters as 'raging madmen' (Devine 2003, p. 45). When the focus of the scheme turned to Darien, which encroached upon Spanish territory, it threatened to undermine William's ally in his war against Louis XIV. The Darien scheme collapsed, not only because of English executive and legislative obstruction, but also because of disease. The Scottish promoters lost all their money.

Darien showed thinkers on both sides that a united executive and legislature were needed. The Scots were not totally powerless, though, because William's successor Queen Anne looked likely to die with no surviving children and no close relative to succeed to the crown of either England or Scotland. The Scots made the most astute move they could, namely to announce that they reserved the right to nominate somebody other than the Elector of Hanover, already nominated by the English Parliament to succeed Anne as monarch. This would have revoked the Union of Crowns and reopened the security threat on the border, which the Bishops' War had shown was not an empty threat. Therefore the Union that was negotiated in 1706–7 had to contain concessions for both sides (McLean and McMillan 2005, Chapter 2).

The main concession demanded by the Scots related to the protection of the national church. Its establishment was confirmed in 1707, when the Scots negotiators insisted on adding an act for the protection of the Church of Scotland – drafted for the Scottish Parliament by the General Assembly of the Church itself. That Act remains part of the Acts of Union that constituted Great Britain in Smith's time, and still do to this day.

But while the Calvinist Presbyterians had executed a coup within the church, driving out the Episcopalians from their parishes, the coup did not extend to the state. The state moved south in 1707, leaving Scotland to be governed by a succession of London-based Scottish managers. Three of these were friends or acquaintances of Adam Smith. No monarch was again to visit Scotland until Sir Walter Scott stage-managed George IV's visit to Edinburgh in 1822.

The economic benefits of union to Scotland were mixed, with gains and losses. The west coast, as we have noted, gained spectacularly from the expansion of trade and the removal of the restrictions that had killed the Darien scheme. The east-coast trade, including that to and from Kirkcaldy, suffered at least relatively and possibly absolutely from the westward shift of Scottish trade. And, as Gilbert Elliot and his fellow promoters of a new town in Edinburgh had shrewdly noted (see Chapter 1), Edinburgh had suffered from the lack of a court and the lack of what we would now call the consequent multiplier effect of a nucleus of highly-paid people demanding luxury goods. I return to the question of how and why the gains came to outweigh the losses in later chapters.

The political outcomes were almost all benign. Under the Union of Crowns, government in Scotland was patchy and arbitrary, and subject to the whim of the executive. It was weak most of the time, but could be strong at the wrong time and the wrong way, as Jenny Geddes had pointed out. After 1707, it would be wrong to say that arbitrariness disappeared. In particular, on the few occasions when Scottish interests were directly opposed to English ones, they could simply be outvoted in Parliament. In the next section we shall see that this happened disastrously in 1712. However, on most matters of economics and politics, the interests of Scotland and of England were not directly opposed. Scotland was incorporated in a larger government. And it was a government which was, benignly for someone like Adam Smith, simply not there most of the time. The machinery of government – such as the administration of the Commission of Customs – ticked over more smoothly than it had ever done in poor, independent Scotland; the politics could be left up to the likes of Ilay (Argyll) and Dundas. Until Smith's death, Scotland remained a weak state. More strictly speaking, the Scots were experiencing life as the junior partner of a strong state.[4] After the Union they enjoyed the best of both worlds: they were largely left alone by Parliament (the Patronage Act 1712 turned out to be a rare exception) and so had the freedom to develop and innovate without much interference, but at least after 1746 they also enjoyed the stability and order that came from living under a strong administration. So in some ways their situation was not unlike that of a 'colony of a civilized nation' which Smith notes is so conducive to advancements in wealth and greatness in

WN IV.vii.b. Of course Scotland was not a colony. But much of what Smith says about the benign effects of distant government in the American colonies also applied in his own country:

> Thirdly, the labour of the English colonists is not only likely to afford a greater and more valuable produce, but, in consequence of the moderation of their taxes, a greater proportion of this produce belongs to themselves, which they may store up and employ in putting into motion a still greater quantity of labour. The English colonists have never yet contributed anything towards the defence of the mother country, or towards the support of its civil government. They themselves, on the contrary, have hitherto been defended almost entirely at the expense of the mother country. But the expense of fleets and armies is out of all proportion greater than the necessary expense of civil government. The expense of their own civil government has always been very moderate. It has generally been confined to what was necessary for paying competent salaries to the governor, to the judges, and to some other officers of police, and for maintaining a few of the most useful public works. (*WN* IV.vii.b.20)

It was not true that Scotland contributed nothing to British defence, but it contributed less than its population share of the cost, because it was the poorer partner in Great Britain. And the expense of its own civil government was very moderate so long as it was not absorbed in corruption and cronyism. Scotland was lucky in its political managers in Smith's time. All three – Ilay, Wedderburn and Dundas – appointed competent people, including Adam Smith, as their 'officers of police'.

However, Scotland became part of a strong and interventionist state in 1793, when Dundas, Pitt and others started to become seriously worried about pro-French 'sedition' in Scotland. Adam Smith was posthumously a victim of this, as we shall see.

THE CHURCH IN SCOTLAND

The Presbyterian Church of Scotland was founded by John Knox in the mid-sixteenth century, when Calvinist ideas first began to spread from Jean Calvin's Geneva; but its organisation is due to his successor Andrew Melvill, one of the authors of the *Second Book of Discipline* (1578). In 1575 Melvill started to campaign for the removal of bishops from the Scottish church, there 'being no superiority allowed by Christ among ministers'. The Presbyterians used the power vacuum in Scotland during the imprisonment of Mary Queen of Scots (1566–87) to establish their system of church government. But Melvill overreached himself, famously grabbing King James VI by the sleeve in 1596 to tell him that he was 'God's sillie vassall':

> And thairfor Sir, as divers tyms befor, sa now again, I mon tell yow, thair is twa Kings and twa Kingdomes in Scotland. Thair is Chryst Jesus the King, and his Kingdome the Kirk, whase subject King James the Saxt is, and of whase Kingdome nocht a king, nor a lord, nor a heid, bot a member!

Melvill announced that he and his friends were a deputation from the General Assembly of the Church of Scotland 'whame Chryst hes callit and commandit to watch over his Kirk'; 'the quhilk na Christian King nor Prince sould controll and discharge, but fortifie and assist, utherwayes nocht fathfull subjects nor members of Chryst'.[5] This was fundamentally different from the English Reformation concept of a national church. The Church of England was 'Erastian' – that is, under state protection. When Henry VIII declared himself the 'Supreme Governor' of the Church of England in the 1530s, he simply put himself – for political reasons – in the place of the pope. That need not imply any other change in church doctrine. After Henry, there were many faction fights in the Church of England (there still are). But almost all the factions accept that it is an established state church, with the monarch as its supreme governor, and its bishops holding seats in the House of Lords. English politicians and lawyers often manage to confuse England with Britain. In matters of church government this is bad law and bad politics because it fails to recognise that no faction of the Scottish church has argued for Erastianism since the defeat of the Episcopalians in 1690.

As previously noted, King James VI of Scotland became King James I of England in 1603. He and all his successors as kings (or Protectors) of Great Britain tried for ninety years to suppress the Presbyterian church, with its Calvinist notion of two kingdoms. The idea that there was a kingdom where the earthly king's writ did not run was anathema to Oliver Cromwell as much as to James VI and I, Charles I, Charles II, and James VII and II. None of them succeeded in extirpating Presbyterianism, although Cromwell came closest, at Dunbar.

The Calvinist faction organised a National Covenant in 1638, which bound the signatories to defend 'God's true and Christian Religion', which it defined as Presbyterian. They attempted to spread this to the whole of Britain by the Westminster Confession, which was accompanied by a Solemn League and Covenant binding them to impose Presbyterianism on England and Ireland. Thereafter the Presbyterian party, especially the extreme wing of it, became known as the 'Covenanters'.

In England, Cromwell ensured that the Covenanters got nowhere. Cromwell was a Puritan but not a Presbyterian; and as noted above the Scottish Presbyterians had backed the wrong horse (namely Charles I) in

1646. Nor did the Covenanters make headway in most of Ireland. In the north-east of Ireland, however, the former Catholic landowners and tenants had been displaced after a rebellion under Elizabeth. The formal Protestant 'Plantation of Ulster' that followed mostly involved loyal Anglicans, who became part of the (Anglican) Church of Ireland. However, outside the formal Plantation, the land of north-east Ireland was attractive to Scots, from the nearest part of the British mainland. It is only about fifteen miles from the nearest point in Scotland to the Ulster coast. In time these Presbyterians – 'Ulster Scots' is the useful American term for them – became the religious faction with the second largest following in Ireland. As already noted, Francis Hutcheson was one of them. The Ulster Scots, who had established Calvinist religion but never got a state monopoly for it, brought the praiseworthy (egalitarian, thrifty, earnest) aspects of Calvinism into politics without the bad (oppressive, sexually censorious, domineering).

THE AUSTERE AND LOOSE SYSTEMS

In Smith's Scotland, there were two main strands of Presbyterianism. In *WN* Smith himself called them the 'austere' and 'loose' systems: vivid, though not exactly complimentary, terms. It is worth quoting *WN* at some length here, because Smith shows himself to be a pioneer of religious sociology, and indeed of 'Chicago school' economic analysis of a non-economic phenomenon.

> In every civilized society, in every society where the distinction of ranks has once been completely established, there have been always two different schemes or systems of morality current at the same time; of which the one may be called the strict or austere; the other the liberal, or, if you will, the loose system. The former is generally admired and revered by the common people: the latter is commonly more esteemed and adopted by what are called people of fashion. (*WN* V.i.g.10)

The socio-economic reasons for this are as follows:

> In the liberal or loose system, luxury, wanton and even disorderly mirth, the pursuit of pleasure to some degree of intemperance, the breach of chastity, at least in one of the two sexes, etc., provided they are not accompanied with gross indecency, and do not lead to falsehood or injustice, are generally treated with a good deal of indulgence, and are easily either excused or pardoned altogether. In the austere system, on the contrary, those excesses are regarded with the utmost abhorrence and detestation. The vices of levity are always ruinous to the common people, and a single week's thoughtlessness

> and dissipation is often sufficient to undo a poor workman for ever, and to drive him through despair upon committing the most enormous crimes. The wiser and better sort of the common people, therefore, have always the utmost abhorrence and detestation of such excesses, which their experience tells them are so immediately fatal to people of their condition. The disorder and extravagance of several years, on the contrary, will not always ruin a man of fashion, and people of that rank are very apt to consider the power of indulging in some degree of excess as one of the advantages of their fortune, and the liberty of doing so without censure or reproach as one of the privileges which belong to their station. (*WN* V.i.g.10)

This passage reads like part of the natural history of religion that formed the now-lost first part of Smith's Glasgow lectures. In Smith's sociology of religion, the poor have a vested interest in supporting the 'austere' system because they would otherwise be ruined by the expenses of drink and fornication. The rich regard drink and fornication as luxury goods, which they can afford: indeed, 'superior goods' in later economic terminology. A superior good is one such that the richer you become the higher a proportion of your consumption it takes up.

This was an accurate and economical analysis of Scottish society. The 'austere', puritanical faction was strongest among the poor; the 'loose' faction, among the rich. After the Union, this led to divisive church power politics that have lasted until the present day. Rich Scots had reason to be afraid of the Covenanters. When they had seized power in the seventeenth century they had violently enforced their austere morality. In Edinburgh in 1650

> Much falsit and scheitting at this time wes daylie detectit by the Lordis of Sessioun; for the quhilk their wes daylie hanging, skurging, nailing of luggis, and . . . boring of tounges . . . And as for adulteries, fornicatioun, incest, bigamie, and uther uncleanes and filthynes, it did never abound moir nor at this time.[6] (Diary of John Nicoll, quoted by Mitchison 1970, p. 237)

This might have persuaded the Covenanters, but apparently did not, that hanging, flogging, nailing people's ears to the stocks and piercing their tongues did not (except the first) suppress fornication.

The Presbyterian settlement agreed in 1690 had put the appointment of parish ministers in the hands of the elders of the parish jointly with the heritors (that is, landowners with a right to take part). 'Austere' elders could, however, outvote 'loose' heritors. When the House of Commons came under Tory control in the Parliament of 1710, therefore, it enacted the Patronage Act 1712, which gave heritors the full power to nominate ministers (Devine 1999, pp. 19, 73). To the Covenanters, this was a flagrant breach of the Act of Union enacted only five years earlier. Seen in terms of Smith's socio-economics of religion, it was a powerful blow for the loose against the austere.

The war of the loose and the austere raged for the whole of Smith's lifetime. Glasgow was a stronghold of the austere; Edinburgh, of the loose. This is as Smith's socio-economics would predict. Glasgow was a manufacturing town; Edinburgh was not. Therefore a higher proportion of the population in Glasgow than in Edinburgh stood to be ruined by a week of drink and sex. The austere Presbytery of Glasgow attempted to prosecute Hutcheson for heresy, but failed. Even the Presbytery of Edinburgh pondered whether to try Hume, whose heresy was much more blatant than Hutcheson's. But in 1750, a group of ministers who were good friends of Smith and Hume took control of the General Assembly from their parishes around Edinburgh. These 'Moderates' were certainly a minority within the church, but they were physically close to Edinburgh, and they could control the church, and hold the fire and brimstone, until they in turn were unseated in a counter-counter-coup in 1843. The church had moved from hellfire to moderation in a century – it was to move back a century later.

Meanwhile, the austere faction had lost the power it had had in Edinburgh in 1650. Then it had had state power at its back – indeed it *was* the state power for much of the time. Now, the state in London had no interest in enforcing the decisions of kirk sessions or presbyteries in Glasgow or Ayr; nor did they even have the capacity to do so. And the austere faction did not even present a united front within the church. Some of them were so scandalised by the Patronage Act that they seceded; the seceders then split among themselves, and the monopoly of social control was lost even in 'austere'-dominated areas. This gave Smith a further bright idea. The section of *WN* quoted above continues:

> Almost all religious sects have begun among the common people, from whom they have generally drawn their earliest as well as their most numerous proselytes. The austere system of morality has, accordingly, been adopted by those sects almost constantly, or with very few exceptions . . . It was the system by which they could best recommend themselves to that order of people to whom they first proposed their plan of reformation upon what had been before established. Many of them, perhaps the greater part of them, have even endeavoured to gain credit by refining upon this austere system, and by carrying it to some degree of folly and extravagance; and this excessive rigour has frequently recommended them more than anything else to the respect and veneration of the common people . . . [When a poor man migrates from country to town, he] never emerges so effectually from this obscurity, his conduct never excites

> so much the attention of any respectable society, as by his becoming the member of a small religious sect. He from that moment acquires a degree of consideration which he never had before. All his brother sectaries are, for the credit of the sect, interested to observe his conduct, and if he gives occasion to any scandal, if he deviates very much from those austere morals which they almost always require of one another, to punish him by what is always a very severe punishment, even where no civil effects attend it, expulsion or excommunication from the sect. In little religious sects, accordingly, the morals of the common people have been almost always remarkably regular and orderly; generally much more so than in the established church. (*WN* V.i.g.11–12)

Unfortunately, 'the morals of those little sects, indeed, have frequently been rather disagreeably rigorous and unsocial', to which Smith proposes two remedies: the 'study of science and philosophy' and 'the frequency and gaiety of publick diversions' (*WN* V.i.g.12–14). These are public goods in so far as they correct the disagreeable rigour of religious austerity; therefore, Smith believes, the state has a legitimate role in paying for them.

As to the excessive 'zeal' of the austere, Smith saw that the eighteenth-century secessions of the Covenanters had rendered it harmless:

> But that zeal must be altogether innocent where the society is divided into two or three hundred, or perhaps into as many thousand small sects, of which no one could be considerable enough to disturb the publick tranquillity. (*WN* V.i.g, p. 793)

In other words, in religion as in the economy, a free market drives out monopoly power. This argument of Smith's in favour of 'a thousand little sects', and the remedy for their excesses, may surprise some devotees of the free-market Adam Smith Institute to which Gordon Brown drew attention. Smith's reasoning is exactly that used in the following decade by James Madison and Thomas Jefferson to disestablish the church, first in Virginia, and then, by the 'Establishment Clause' in the First Amendment to the US Constitution, throughout the United States.[7] The passage of Smith just quoted is remarkably close to Madison's argument against faction in *The Federalist* # 10, which Jack Rakove has shown was originally an argument for religious, rather than political, pluralism (Madison 1999, pp. 29–36; 160–7; McLean 2003). I examine these matters, including the Adam Smith Institute's Adam Smith, more fully in Chapter 6.

As already explained, this weakness of church and state gave Smith and Hume the space in which they could write and publish freely. It also impelled them to fill the vacuum left by the intellectual failure of hellfire moralism, and to think about first principles of government and economics. These are discussed in Chapter 3. But it is worth pausing to discuss Smith's evaluation of the Scottish church as an agency of social improvement.

Smith was probably a deist: that is, one who believed in a god who created the universe, but whose action was not required to explain how that universe developed. Divine intervention, Smith makes clear in his essay on the History of Astronomy, was a primitive belief that gave way to scientific hypothesis testing.[8] It is interesting, and, I think, significant, that Smith's comments about religious organisation come not in his book on ethics, the *Theory of Moral Sentiments*, but in his book on prudence, 'police',[9] government and economics, the *Wealth of Nations*. The only passage of *TMS* which expounds standard Christian (Protestant) doctrine, on the Atonement of Christ, was withdrawn in Smith's extensive revisions in 1790 and replaced by a short sarcastic passage that could have come from the pen of Hume (*TMS* Appendix II, esp. p. 400).

But in *WN* Smith has a lot to say about church organisation. He greatly prefers the Church of Scotland to the Church of England *for their respective effects on government and society*.

> In Scotland the establishment of the parish schools has taught almost the whole common people to read, and a very great proportion of them to write and account. In England, the establishment of charity schools has had an effect of the same kind, though not so universally . . .
>
> There is scarce perhaps to be found any where in Europe a more learned, decent, independent, and respectable set of men, than the greater part of the Presbyterian clergy of Holland, Geneva, Switzerland, and Scotland.
>
> In countries where church benefices are the greater part of them very moderate, a chair in a university is generally a better establishment than a church benefice . . . Where church benefices, on the contrary, are many of them very considerable, the church naturally draws from the universities the greater part of their eminent men of letters . . . In the former situation we are likely to find the universities filled with the most eminent men of letters that are to be found in the country. In the latter we are likely to find few eminent men among them . . . In England, accordingly, the church is continually draining the universities of all their best and ablest members . . . (*WN* V.i.f–g, quoted in V.i.f.55; V.i.g.37; V.i.g.39; Glasgow edition pp. 785, 810, 811)

Of all people, Smith's friend the Revd Hugh Blair, one of the leaders of the Moderate coup mentioned above, complained on the publication of *WN* that 'You are, I think, too favourable by much to Presbytery. It connects the Teachers too closely with the People; and gives too much aid to that Austere System you Speak of, which is never favourable to the great improvements of mankind' (H. Blair to AS, 03.04.1776, *Corr.* # 151). For the century that the Moderates ran the Church of Scotland, they made sure (not least through their control of the Presbytery of Edinburgh) that the Teachers were not connected too closely to the People. Smith and Hume both approved.

ADAM SMITH AND ROBERT BURNS

Nothing in the Scottish Enlightenment is more fascinating than the relationship between Adam Smith and Robert Burns (1759–96). Burns was an unsuccessful Ayrshire farmer who nevertheless managed to publish, by subscription, a volume of *Poems, chiefly in the Scottish Dialect* in Kilmarnock in 1786. This volume introduced Burns's style of irreverent, edgy satire to the world. The opening poem, *The Twa Dogs*, sets the tone. Using an already old literary device, Burns makes the peasant's collie Luath the hero, while not unsympathetic to Caesar, the nobleman's pedigree Newfoundland. The collection also includes an astonishingly rude poem about George III (*A Dream*); the first batch of Burns's satirical attacks on the 'austere' faction of Scottish Calvinism (*The Holy Fair* and *Address to the Deil*); and the first two of the poems which, as I shall argue in a moment, show the strong influence of Adam Smith on Burns (*To a Louse* and *Man was made to Mourn*).

After publishing the Kilmarnock Edition, Burns was lionised by the Edinburgh literati, including Adam Ferguson, at whose house in Sciennes Burns met the young Walter Scott (see Preface). Adam Smith joined the general acclamation of Burns, who was seeking subscriptions to fund an expanded edition of his poems (which became the 'Edinburgh Edition', published in 1787). Smith subscribed for four copies (Mizuta 2000, # 265). Unfortunately, the two men failed to meet. When Burns tried to track Smith down, bearing a letter of introduction from their mutual friend Mrs Dunlop of Stewarton, he found that Smith had just departed on his London trip in response to Dundas's invitation to spend some time discussing his work with the Prime Minister and the Foreign Secretary. Mrs Dunlop had written to Burns, sympathising with the problems of his farm and endorsing his proposal that he should join the army, but suggesting two alternatives. The first would be to take a farm in Orkney or the Northern Highlands. As to the second, she writes:

> Indeed, first when your Book [the Kilmarnock Edition] reached Edr., Mr Smith, Commissioner of the Customs, suggested a thing which he thought

> might be procured, and which he said was just what he would have wished for himself had he been in narrow circumstances – being a Salt Officer. Their income is from £30 to £40, their duty easie, independent, and free from that odium or oppression attached to the excise. He has through his life been a friend to unfriended merit, . . . both his *Theory of Moral Sentiments* and *Wealth of Nations* being much applauded. He was one of those [who] first held forth your name forcibly to the public at Edr., when very few had seen your Book, and my son told me was the person he heard take the most interest in your future prospects, wishing to procure you leisure to write . . . He lately complained that he had asked it, but could not get a sight of you. (Mrs Dunlop to R. Burns, 29.03.1787, in Wallace 1898, pp. 13–16)

She goes on to ask Burns to hand Smith the letter of introduction, asks to be remembered to Smith for his kindness to her thirty years earlier and advises Burns to ask Smith how to apply for a Salt Officership, saying that she will be glad to help. The last offer was presumably redundant, as the job would have been in the gift of Smith and his colleagues.

It is very heartening to learn that the author of *TMS* took his own advice and placed himself as an impartial spectator of Burns's plight, immediately coming up with a piece of excellent advice that, tragically, was not followed up. The life of a salt officer was presumably easier than that of an exciseman because salt was taxed wholesale at the point of production. So was whisky, but the points of production were numerous and illegal. Burns did later join the excise service (in spite of writing *The deil's awa' wi' th'exciseman*), but that saved neither his wealth nor his health, and he died aged only thirty-seven in July 1796.

The fact that Smith never met Burns is one of life's little tragedies. One wonders why Smith was not at the dinner at Ferguson's house. Smith and Ferguson had a relationship that was rocky at times, and this may have happened to be one of the bad times; alternatively, Smith's poor health may have discouraged him from trekking out to Kamschatka. Or, more simply, he may already have left for London. Dundas's invitation to Smith is dated 21 March 1787; Mrs Dunlop's letter of introduction was (presumably) enclosed with her letter to Burns dated 29 March 1787. Nevertheless, we know quite a lot, by direct evidence and by inference, about what each of them thought of the other.

As to Smith's attitude to Burns, the direct evidence lies in his subscription for four copies of Burns's collected poems, and in his remarks and actions reported by Mrs Dunlop. Why was Smith attracted to Burns? Recall that Smith might have become a professor of literature. He first delivered the lectures that have come down to us as *LRBL* in Edinburgh in 1748. He later gave or lent his notes to Hugh Blair (the Church of Scotland minister who thought Smith was too favourable to the Church of Scotland). Blair became Professor of Rhetoric and Belles-Lettres at Edinburgh in 1760. This was the first chair of English in any British university (Sher 2004b).

As a literary critic, Smith was mostly interested in prose. Only one of the thirty lectures in *LRBL*, # 21, is about poetry, and even that focuses on epic and dramatic poetry. Burns's great dramatic epic *Tam O'Shanter* was not published until 1791. Smith has less to say about the lyric, comic and satirical veins in which Burns wrote. But what he says is consistent with liking Burns's poetry. The great advantage of poetry, says Smith, is its conciseness. It can say in few words what in prose takes many. It can also be a more effective vehicle for ridicule than prose, because the poet can deliver pure ridicule in few words, without the explanations and exceptions that he might have to make in prose (*LRBL* # 21; ii.74–9). That description, from Smith's lectures delivered in 1763, perfectly fits some of Burns's poems that Smith would have read when he bought the Edinburgh edition, including (as to conciseness) *Green Grow the Rashes O* and (as to ridicule) *To a Louse* and *Death and Dr Hornbook*. It fits best of all the supreme masterpiece of Burns's satire, *Holy Willie's Prayer*, alas not published until 1799.

As to Burns's attitude to Smith, there are more clues. Writing to Robert Graham of Fintry, another Commissioner of Excise who Burns was hoping would become his patron, Burns says

> that extraordinary man, Smith, in his Wealth of Nations, find[s] my leisure employment enough. I could not have given any mere *man*, credit for half the intelligence Mr Smith discovers in his book. I would covet much to have his ideas respecting the present state of some quarters of the world that are or have been the scenes of considerable revolutions since his book was written. (RB to Robert Graham of Fintry, 13.05.1789, in Roy 1985, i.410. Letter # 341)

All the more is the pity that Burns never met Smith; he would certainly have indiscreetly passed on Smith's views about America and France to his next correspondent. At this point he had borrowed Graham's copy of *WN*, which he returned later in 1789. However, he later bought a copy of his own. This is a three-volume set now in Glasgow University Library, where I read it carefully, hoping to find annotations or underlinings that might tell us more about what Burns thought of Smith. Alas, there are none in Burns's hand. I think, however, that Book V – the part of *WN* where Smith discusses among other things education, the Scottish churches, the austere and loose systems of morals and the maxims of taxation – has been handled somewhat more than the rest of the book. Whether by Burns or a later owner, of course, I cannot tell.

There is also direct evidence that Burns owned, and approved of, *TMS*. His copy of the sixth (1790) edition is also in Glasgow University Library. I read it also, with the same negative results.[10] But this was not the first copy of *TMS* that Burns owned. In his commonplace book Burns wrote in 1783, 'I entirely agree with that judicious philosopher Mr Smith in his excellent theory of moral sentiments, that remorse is the most painful sentiment that can embitter the human bosom'. It is important to note that all editions of *TMS* from the fourth onwards – including the editions that Burns owned or saw – contained a new subtitle, so that the title-page now read:

> *The Theory of Moral Sentiments, or An Essay towards an Analysis of the Principles by which Men naturally judge concerning the Conduct and Character, first of their Neighbours, and afterwards of themselves.* (*TMS*, editors' introduction, p. 41)

In an early poem (not published in his or Smith's lifetime), *Epistle to James Tennant of Glenconner*, Burns writes

> I've sent you here by Johnie Simson
> Twa sage Philosophers to glimpse on!
> *Smith*, wi' his sympathetic feeling,
> An' *Reid*, to common sense appealing.
> Philosophers have fought and wrangled,
> An' meikle [much] Greek an' Latin mangled,
> Till, wi' their Logic-jargon tir'd
> And in the depth of science mir'd,
> To common sense they now appeal,
> What wives and wabsters [weavers] see an' feel

Smith did not use the term 'common sense' and Thomas Reid (1710–96), his successor in the Glasgow chair of moral philosophy, used 'common sense' as a technical term – roughly, the set of principles that are believed universally, the denial of which leads to contradiction – not the everyday understanding of the phrase that Burns probably had in mind. Smith did not support either Reid's appointment or his philosophy. Nevertheless, Burns has hit on the greater truth that Smith and Reid shared. He liked the egalitarian thrust of their morality. He sent another copy of *TMS* to his friend Riddell of Glenriddell with the inscription *Had I another Friend more truly mine / More Loo'd, more trusted, this had ne'er been thine* (Sources for this paragraph: documents collected in Glasgow University MSS 526/13/1).

Why does all of this matter? Because Smith and Burns were kindred spirits; and because Burns has transmitted Smith's thought to millions of people who may not have realised that it was Smith's.

They were kindred spirits because each of them makes clear in his own way how much he prefers the loose to the austere system of morals. Burns was indeed, as Smith says, one of those whose material interests would have been better served if he could have upheld the austere system. He was constantly in debt; he probably drank a lot (though, contrary to stories put about by some of the austere, he died not of drink but of rheumatic fever). He had several affairs with different women, and was unfaithful to his wife, Jean Armour, whose family tried to stop her from marrying him. He and his friends were arraigned by the local kirk sessions and presbyteries for 'fornication'. Burns took immortal revenge in *Holy Willie's Prayer* and many other satirical attacks on the 'Auld Licht' ministers and elders of Ayrshire. 'Auld Licht' was the contemporary term for what Smith calls the 'austere' moralists that is, the hellfire Calvinists who sought inspiration from Knox, Melville and the Covenanters. Many of them had seceded over the Patronage Act, which still further weakened their powers of social control over Burns and his friends.

This is not to say that Smith would have approved of all Burns's political views. Burns attacked privilege and the established order pretty indiscriminately. The Hanoverian kings reigned; well, he attacked the Hanoverians. William Pitt was Prime Minister; well, he attacked Pitt. Excisemen (such as Burns himself) were unpopular; well, he attacked excisemen. He was an undiscriminating enthusiast for the French Revolution, which he hailed directly in *A Man's a Man for a' that* (printed at the end of this book) and indirectly in *Robert Bruce's Address to his Troops at Bannockburn* ('Scots, wha hae' wi' Wallace bled / Scots, wham Bruce has aften led / Welcome to your gory bed, / Or to victorie.'). To attack the Hanoverian regime meant to extol the Jacobites. The devil, it is said, has all the best tunes. Burns took what were already stirring Jacobite folk-songs and verses and turned them into even more stirring poetry. His denunciation of the Act of Union and the Scottish negotiators of 1707, 'such a parcel of rogues in a nation', with its haunting modal tune, has become an unofficial Scottish nationalist anthem. Burns played a large role in creating a mythic Scottish history in which the good guys – Wallace, Bruce and Bonnie Prince Charlie – were constantly betrayed by the bad guys – the English and their treacherous Scottish allies. That mythic history was still in the air in my schooldays, since when *Braveheart* has given it another boost.

None of this would have appealed in the least to Smith or his Edinburgh fellow-clubmen. But some of it is a legitimate inference from arguments of Smith in *TMS*, as I shall argue later. When people say *O wad some Pow'r the giftie gie us / To see oursels as ithers see us*, the words are the words of Burns, but the thoughts are the thoughts of Adam Smith, expressed on the very title-page of *TMS*. When they repeat *The best laid schemes of Mice and Men / gang aft agley* (the peroration of 'To a Mouse') they are echoing Smith's attacks on 'the man of system' in *TMS*, discussed later, and his understanding of the unintended effects of economic change.

NOTES

1. The text of the Declaration is available, in the original Latin and in English translation, at www.geo.ed.ac.uk/home/scotland/arbroath.html.
2. Jenny Geddes is one of these cultural referents known to all Scots and no English. Robert Burns called one of his horses Jenny Geddes. Gordon Brown, in his eulogy to Robin Cook, delivered on 11 August 2005 from the very place at which Ms Geddes threw her stool, referred to 'this cathedral where famously one enraged citizen lacking Robin's eloquence and powers of persuasion spoke truth to power by hurling her seat at the preacher, with whom she disagreed'. In the next day's press, *The Scotsman*, *The Times* and the *Daily Telegraph* picked up his reference, according to a check I ran on the Lexis-Nexis search engine for the string 'Jenny Geddes'. But all three stories were filed by Scottish journalists.
3. This is the context of Sir Walter Scott's song, in my childhood learnt by all Scots schoolchildren:

   To the Lords of Convention 'twas Claverhouse spoke:
   Ere the Crown shall go down there are crowns to be broke
   So each Cavalier that loves honour and me
   Let him follow the bonnets of bonnie Dundee!

   Chorus
   Come fill up my cup, come fill up my can
   Come saddle my horses and call out my men
   Unhook the West Port and let us gae free
   For it's Up with the bonnets of Bonnie Dundee!

   'Claverhouse' and 'Bonnie Dundee' are the same person: John Graham, first Viscount of Dundee (?1648–89).
4. My thanks to Dennis Rasmussen for this happy phrase.
5. Diary of James Melvill, 1596, in Pitcairn (1842), pp. 369–70. *sillie*: plain, simple; *divers*: various; *sa*: so; *mon*: must; *Saxt*: Sixth; *whase*: whose;

nocht: not; *whame*: whom; *the quhilk na*: which no; *utherwayes*: otherwise [*sc.* they are].

6. *falsit and scheitting*: falsehood and cheating; *the quhilk*: which; *luggis*: ears.
7. 'Congress shall make no law respecting an establishment of religion, or prohibiting the free exercise thereof . . .'. US Constitution, First Amendment, ratified 1791.
8. Smith, *The History of Astronomy*, in *EPS* pp. 33–105. Note especially (p. 49): 'in all Polytheistic religions . . . it is the irregular events of nature only that are ascribed to the agency and power of the gods. Fire burns, and water refreshes; heavy bodies descend, and lighter substances fly upwards, by the necessity of their own nature; nor was the invisible hand of Jupiter ever apprehended to be employed in those matters'.
9. 'Police' had a much broader meaning in the eighteenth century than now. It is one of Smith's titles for the subject matter of *LJ* (*A* and *B*); and hence for *WN*, which is derived from those parts of *LJ*. The *Oxford English Dictionary* explains at *Police*, n., sense 3. a. *The regulation, discipline, and control of a community; civil administration; enforcement of law; public order*:

> The early quotations refer to France, and other foreign countries, and to Scotland, where Commissioners of Police, for the general internal administration of the country, consisting of six noblemen and four gentlemen, were appointed by Queen Anne, 13 Dec. 1714. This was app[arently] the first official use of the word in Great Britain. In England, it was still viewed with disfavour after 1760. A writer in the British Magazine, April 1763, p. 542, opines that 'from an aversion to the French . . . and something under the name of police being already established in Scotland, English prejudice will not soon be reconciled to it'.

10. Except that in a passage where Smith writes

> In all governments accordingly, even in monarchies, the highest offices are generally possessed, and the whole detail of the administration conducted, by men who were educated in the middle and inferior ranks of life, who have been carried forward by their own industry and abilities. (*TMS* I.iii.2.5)

someone has written 'Dundas' in the margin. Smith cannot have been thinking of Henry Dundas when he first wrote this passage, which was in the first (1759) edition of *TMS*, since Dundas was only a teenager at the time. But Dundas would certainly occur to a reader in about 1790 as an example of the sort of person Smith is writing about here. Unfortunately, not being a Burns specialist, I cannot tell whether the annotation is in Burns's handwriting. Burns's copy of *TMS* is RB 2905–6, and his copy of *WN* RB 2942–4, in Glasgow University, Rare Books Collection.

3

A Non-religious Grounding of Morals: Smith and the Scottish Enlightenment

THE LEGACY OF FRANCIS HUTCHESON

The weak church and the weak state had a double impact on the Scottish Enlightenment. They made it possible to exist at all. A generation before Hutcheson and Hume the threat of heresy or blasphemy trials had been very real. In 1693 the General Assembly of the Church of Scotland, which was entitled to pass binding law on its own account, had enacted 'An Act against the atheistical Opinions of the Deists'. Under this Act, the Scottish Privy Council searched bookshops for pamphlets containing deist or atheistical opinions. Their agents found pamphlets by an unfortunate student called Thomas Aikenhead,[1] who was convicted and hanged for blasphemy in 1697 (Broadie 2003, pp. 14, 34; Herman 2003 pp. 2–7). But the collapse of church and state power and intellectual authority that made the Enlightenment possible also forced its thinkers to develop alternative accounts of morals. Smith's version, in *TMS*, owed a great deal to his teacher Hutcheson, although Smith's moral theory is not the same as either Hutcheson's or Hume's.

Francis Hutcheson was – I think significantly – an Ulster Presbyterian. Although the Presbyterian church was established in Scotland in 1690, it has never been established in Ireland. Hutcheson's liberal outlook emerged early in life, in church controversies where he took the side of conscience against authority. While he was at Glasgow, the Presbytery of Glasgow, in its capacity as a church court, attempted but failed to prosecute him for heresy. His offence, according to his students, was to have taught that 'we have a notion of moral goodness prior in the order of knowledge to any notion of the will or law of God'. His students, who published a 'Vindication' of him in 1738, admitted that he had indeed taught that, but that the only alternative was to believe that if we had no notion of goodness apart from God's will, we would have no more to say in praise of God than that his will is consistent with itself:

> We count God morally Good, on this account, that we justly conclude, he has essential Dispositions to communicate Happiness and Perfection to his creatures . . . we must have another notion of moral Goodness, prior to any Relation to Law, or Will . . . Otherways, when we say *God's Laws are Good*, we make no valuable Encomium on them; and only say, God's Laws are conformable to his Laws or, his Will is conformable to his Will . . . So, when we say *God is morally good* or *excellent*, we would only mean, he is conformable to himself; which would be no Praise unless he were previously known to be good.

The authors of *A Vindication* hint that the attack on Hutcheson had been egged on by a senior member of the University and threaten retaliation:

> Other Students may fall a writing and printing against themselves or their Favourites, in Churches or in Colleges, and how can they complain, if others follow the Example set before them[?]

Apparently, one of the allegations against Hutcheson, that may have brought him before the Presbytery, was that he had said that

> The Government of the Church belongs to the Civil Magistrate . . . That all Heresies in Opinion should pass without any Censure – That Subscribing to a Confession should be banished out of the Church.

What he had really said, they went on, was quite different:

> Mr Hutcheson maintains that there are Powers of a religious Kind belonging to every Minister, and even some to every Christian, not derived from the Magistrate; But that it belongs to the Magistrate to take Care of the religious Notions of the People, to appoint proper Teachers and to support them . . . He also pleaded for universal Toleration by the State, toward all peaceable Subjects of whatever Religion, let the Church censure their Opinion as it pleases: And showed how this is reconcileable with the Magistrate's Care of Religion. (*A Vindication* quoted on pp. 7, 19, 14–15)

A Vindication is a remarkable document which ought to be better known. (There is a copy in the Special Collections of Glasgow University Library.) As it was published during Smith's first academic year, it is possible that he was one of the authors. Even if he was not, he would certainly have learnt of the controversy, and of the vigorous (and recognisably student-like, with its threats of retaliation against the other side) response of his senior classmates. And only forty years after Thomas Aikenhead had been hanged for saying the same things. Hutcheson's students had been well taught; his argument is impossible to circumvent. God cannot be the creator of morality unless that sentence is a tautology – 'morality is that which God tells us to do'. In other words, Hutcheson recognised the need to supply a ground for morals independent of religion. The same need struck the three greatest figures of the Scottish Enlightenment: David Hume, Adam Smith and Adam Ferguson. The three knew each other very well and moved in the same circles. Smith and Hume were very close friends. The relationship between Smith and Ferguson was patchier – at one stage Ferguson apparently believed that Smith had plagiarised his work; however, at another, Smith worked very hard to secure for Ferguson a tutorship of the same sort as Smith had held, in order to free Ferguson from his teaching duties as Professor of Moral Philosophy at Edinburgh.[2] Hume created a religion-free morality, and saw religion as a human artefact and belief in miracles as a miracle in itself. Ferguson and Smith both wrote what their mutual disciple Dugald Stewart first called 'conjectural history'. All three of them wrote about the natural history of religion – in other words, sociological studies of how and why humans feel a need for religious belief. The Revd Adam Ferguson, who had been a military chaplain before he became a professor, makes almost no mention of religion in his *History of Civil Society*, but his passing references seem to show that, like both Smith and Hume, he treated religion as a human artefact, which arose at certain stages of society to satisfy human needs to explain the supernatural (Ferguson [1767] 1995, pp. 48, 89, 192). Smith, Hume and Ferguson all visited France; Smith, like Ferguson, visited Voltaire, the doyen of sceptical humanism in France. All of these thinkers, rooted in Scotland, wrote for the world.

CLEARING THE GROUND: PART VII OF TMS

Like Hutcheson, therefore, Smith saw the need for a non-religious grounding for ethics. His method of providing one was in some ways similar to Ferguson's: they were both pioneers of historical sociology, as was Smith's student John Millar (Millar 1990). Their common method of conjectural history may have been inspired by Montesquieu. But Ferguson and (especially) Smith take it in entirely new directions.

We know quite a lot about the evolution of Smith's moral, political and economic thought. It began under Hutcheson in Glasgow – 'the never to be forgotten Dr Hutcheson', Smith called him when accepting an invitation to become Rector of Glasgow University (*Corr.* # 274, 1787 – see Chapter 1). Hutcheson postulated a common moral sense, innate among all humankind. This view was influential in America, transmitted by Hutcheson's writings and by his student John Witherspoon to *his* star student James Madison (McLean 2003, p. 19). It reappears unmistakably in the Declaration of Independence: *We hold these truths to be self evident: that all men are created equal.* It was reworked by Smith's Glasgow successor Thomas Reid, whom Robert Burns conflated with Smith (see Chapter 2). Smith actually rejected Hutcheson's 'common sense' ethics, but not his aim.

TMS and *WN* both derive from Smith's public lectures as Professor of Moral Philosophy in Glasgow. They both incorporate earlier material, and they both continued to be revised – *WN* until publication in 1776, and *TMS* extensively for the sixth edition published in 1790, the year Smith died. We shall later look briefly at the effect of the changes made in this edition. But the core of both is in Smith's lecture series. As John Millar explained, the second part of Smith's Glasgow public lecture covered 'Ethics, strictly so called, and consisted chiefly of the doctrines which he afterwards published in his Theory of Moral Sentiments' (see Chapter 1).

How then does Smith provide his non-religious grounding for morals? He had several forebears and contemporaries, and he carefully distinguishes his approach from all of them in Section VII (as it now is, after the extensive rearrangements of 1790) of *TMS*. Smith's Glasgow editors surmise that, although it comes at the end of the book, this section came at the start of Smith's lecture course, because it is a survey of the rival 'Systems of Moral Philosophy' whose problems Smith wished to highlight before advancing his own system. Therefore it makes sense to restore Smith's original putative order, and discuss this part of *TMS* first. Of the ancient systems of philosophy, Smith is clearly most sympathetic to the Stoics, whom he presents as not only 'stoical' in the modern English sense, but also as pioneer utilitarians:

> According to Zeno, the founder of the Stoical doctrine, every animal was by nature recommended to its own care, and was endowed with the principle of self-love, that it might endeavour to preserve, not only its existence, but all the different parts of its nature, in the best and most perfect state of which they were capable.
>
> The self-love of man embraced, if I may say so, his body and all its different members, his mind and all its different faculties and powers, and desired the preservation and maintenance of them all in their best and most perfect condition. Whatever tended to support this state of existence was, therefore, by nature pointed out to him as fit to be chosen; and whatever tended to destroy it, as fit to be rejected . . . Virtue and the propriety of conduct consisted in choosing and rejecting all different objects and circumstances according as they were by nature rendered more or less the objects of choice or rejection; in selecting always from among the several objects of choice presented to us, that which was most to be chosen, when we could not obtain them all; and in selecting too, out of the several objects of rejection offered to

> us, that which was least to be avoided, when it was not in our power to avoid them all. (*TMS* VII.ii.1.15–16)

In a passage deleted in the sixth edition, he goes on, 'The Stoics . . . appear to have regarded every passion as improper, which made any demand upon the sympathy of the spectator'. In a phrase, retained in 1790 and echoed by his letter to Wedderburn complaining about 'Whining Christians' (see p. 19), Smith says that the 'spirit and manhood' of the Stoics' doctrines 'makes a wonderful contrast with the desponding, plaintive, and whining tone of some modern systems' (*TMS* VII.ii.1.29).

Smith goes on to describe the systems that ground virtue in prudence (where he places the Epicureans) or in benevolence (where he praises his teacher Hutcheson as the most eminent), before proceeding to attack 'licentious systems'. These plural licentious systems boil down to one: Bernard Mandeville's *Fable of the Bees; or, Private vices, public benefits* (1714). Mandeville's argument is in his subtitle. If private vices (such as extravagant spending on personal luxuries) generate public virtues (such as national wealth), then they are praiseworthy. Smith concedes that Mandeville's system could not have become so notorious 'had it not in some respects bordered upon the truth' (*TMS* VII.ii.4.13). Mandeville was expounding what J. M. Keynes later labelled as the 'paradox of thrift'. However, Smith did not tackle Mandeville's economics until his second book.

Mandeville's book began life as a short doggerel poem, *The Grumbling Hive; or Knaves Turn'd Honest*, published in 1705 'in a Six Penny Pamphlet . . . ; and being soon after Pirated, cry'd about the Streets in a Half-Penny Sheet' (Mandeville 1732/1924, i. 4). *The Grumbling Hive* is so brutal that it makes Smith's later restatements of some of the same themes seem gentle by comparison. To begin with the hive of bees is prosperous and content. The bees have specialist tasks and their economy hums along:

> The Lawyers, of whose Art the Basis
> Was raising Feuds and splitting Cases
> Oppos'd all Registers, that Cheats
> Might make more work with dipt [mortgaged] Estates . . .
> They kept off Hearings wilfully
> to finger the refreshing Fee;
> And to defend a wicked Cause,
> Examin'd and survey'd the Laws,
> As Burglars Shops and Houses do,
> To find out where they'd best break through.

. . . Luxury
Employ'd a Million of the Poor,
And odious Pride a Million more
Envy it self, and Vanity
Were Ministers of Industry.

Trouble breaks out, however, when this hive of robbers sees the light and abandons its selfish behaviour. Suddenly the locksmith bees, fashion-arbiter bees, and lawyer bees are out of work:

The slight and fickle age is past;
and Clothes, as well as Fashions, last.
Weavers, that join'd rich Silk with Plate,
And all the Trades subordinate,
Are gone. Still Peace and Plenty reign,
And every Thing is cheap, tho' plain; . . .

The hive is decimated, so few bees remaining that it can no longer defend itself.

The Moral.
. . . So Vice is beneficial found
When it's by Justice lopt and bound;
Nay, where the People would be great
As necessary to the State,
As Hunger is to make 'em eat.
Bare Virtue can't make Nations live . . . (Mandeville 1732/1924, quoted on pp. i. 20, 25, 34, 37)

A society in which everyone saved thriftily would see less trade, and therefore, it seemed, less wealth, than one marked by conspicuous consumption, where the poor would have work thanks to the luxury, pride, vanity and envy of the rich.

The reception of *The Grumbling Hive* made Mandeville's name. Mandeville turned the poem into at first a short book, then a long one, and was just as savage in prose as in verse. Everybody who was anybody queued up to denounce *The Fable of the Bees*. Mandeville was arraigned by a grand jury and was nicknamed the 'man-devil'. According to Dr Johnson, every young man had a copy in the belief that it was a wicked book (Mandeville 1732/1997, p. xv). It was an effective way of disseminating a theory of (a)moral sentiments.

Mandeville clearly troubled Smith, as witness the amount of space he is accorded in *TMS*. The germ of his repudiation of Mandeville's economics is also in *TMS* but its full working-out came only in the theory of capital formation in *WN*. In fact, Smith's first publication on Mandeville antedates *TMS*. Writing a long review article for the *Edinburgh Review* in 1756, Smith urges his readers to look beyond Scotland to the exciting new writing being produced in France and Switzerland, drawing attention to J.-J. Rousseau's just-published *Discourse on the origins of inequality*. He says that *The Fable of the Bees* has

> given occasion to the system of Mr. Rousseau, in whom however the principles of the English author are softened, improved, and embellished, and stript of all that tendency to corruption and licentiousness which has disgraced them in their original author. (*Letter to the* Edinburgh Review, in *EPS* p. 250)

Mandeville and Rousseau both consider a state of nature before commercial society; but where Mandeville regards 'the primitive state of mankind as the most wretched and miserable that can be imagined: Mr. Rousseau, on the contrary, paints it as the happiest and most suitable to his nature' (*ibid.*). Smith steers a middle course. He agrees with Mandeville that commercial society generates more wealth (and therefore freedom) than any alternative, but is appalled by Mandeville's cynicism. To judge by the extracts he quotes from Rousseau's *Discourse*, he is also troubled by Rousseau's argument that the division of labour gives rise to unjust inequalities (Rasmussen 2005; *EPS* pp. 251–6). Smith's response to both Mandeville and Rousseau involves an appeal to what has become his most famous device, the *invisible hand*.

Smith writes in Book IV of *TMS* about the beneficial side-effects of the 'deception' that we admire the rich and their palaces, believing them to have a happier life than they really do:

> It is this which first prompted [mankind] to cultivate the ground, to build houses, to found cities and commonwealths, and to invent and improve all the sciences and arts, which ennoble and embellish human life; which have entirely changed the whole face of the globe, have turned the rude forests of nature into agreeable and fertile plains . . .

However, it is an illusion, because actually the rich do not consume any more of the essentials of life than the rest of us:

> The produce of the soil maintains at all times nearly that number of inhabitants which it is capable of maintaining. The rich only select from the heap what is most precious and agreeable. They consume little more than the poor, and in spite of their natural selfishness and rapacity, though they mean only their own conveniency, though the sole end which they propose from the labours of all the thousands whom they employ, be the gratification of their own vain and insatiable desires, they divide with the poor the produce of all their improvements. They are led by an invisible hand to make nearly the same distribution of the necessaries of life, which would have been made, had the

> earth been divided into equal portions among all its inhabitants. (*TMS* IV.i.10; pp. 183–5)

Why is this a response to both Rousseau and Mandeville? It responds to Rousseau because the opening sections of paragraph IV.i.10 echo Rousseau. Smith's reference to science and arts echoes the title of Rousseau's earlier ('First') *Discourse*, which had said that the progress of arts and sciences was bad for civilisations. The phrase about the rude forests and agreeable plains repeats Smith's 1755 translation of a phrase from Rousseau's 'Second' *Discourse on Inequality* (cf. *EPS*, pp. 252, 255; Rasmussen 2005). But whereas the paradoxical Rousseau argues that civilisation is bad for mankind, the staider Smith retorts, banally but correctly, that it is good. But this escape from Rousseau merely restates Mandeville's paradox; it does not solve it. To solve it, Smith needed to counter Mandeville's *economics*, which had to await *WN*.

However, Smith here introduces one of his master ideas, which recurs in both books. Scholars currently dispute whether the *invisible hand* is the cornerstone of Smith's system, or a passing satirical phrase. The former has been the conventional view, most vigorously challenged by Rothschild (2001, pp. 116–56). She points out that he uses the phrase only three times in his work. The first is an undeniably sarcastic comment in the *History of Astronomy*. Primitive religions, Smith says, attribute unusual events, but not regular and well-understood events, to 'gods, daemons, witches, genii, fairies'; they do not need 'the invisible hand of Jupiter' to explain the actions of fire, water or gravity, which they observe every day (*Astronomy* III.2, in *EPS* p. 49; Rothschild 2001, p. 116). Smith's second use of the invisible hand is in the passage from *TMS* just quoted. The third and last is in *WN*, in a chapter where Smith is discussing the futility of mercantilist restrictions on imports and exports. Even when a merchant prefers to support domestic rather than foreign industry for 'his own security',

> he intends only his own gain, and he is in this, as in many other cases, led by an invisible hand to promote an end which was no part of his intention. (*WN* IV.ii.9)

As Rothschild says (2001, p. 117), Smith 'is amused by the individuals who are led by . . . the hand they cannot see . . . He is also amused by philosophers who believe in systems of divine order'. The second remark is the more important, and it need not be *divine* order. Smith's profound insight is that order can arise spontaneously, unintended by either gods or humans. I return to this in Chapter 5.

To our eyes it is surprising that in *TMS* Smith says much about Mandeville, little about Thomas Hobbes and nothing about John Locke. The reason seems to be that Smith treated Hobbes and Locke as political rather than moral philosophers, belonging therefore in the book on Jurisprudence, which he never completed, and to the third rather than the second part of his Glasgow lectures. The perfect dovetailing of the end of *TMS* and the start of *LJ(B)* corroborates this. *LJ(B)* opens with a short discussion of Hobbes, whom Smith treats much more sympathetically than Mandeville, possibly because of Hobbes's 'utter abhorrence of the ecclesiastics' (*LJ(B)*, 2). Smith is cursory on Locke, whom he does not mention in *TMS*. In the two surviving sets of student notes on Smith's Lectures on Jurisprudence, Locke features only as one of the proponents of the fallacy that government can be derived from a social contract, and of the right to rebel if government fails to retain the consent of the governed (*LJ(A)* v.114–16; *LJ(B)* 94).

SYMPATHY AND THE IMPARTIAL SPECTATOR

Of his predecessors, then, Smith sympathises with the Stoics and with Hutcheson; recognises Mandeville as an opponent whose arguments need to be taken seriously; regards Hobbes's arguments as clever but impracticable because of the open fury they incited among clergymen; attacks thinkers who believe that there is a divine order to the universe; and overlooks Locke. Having done this ground-clearing, he erects his own moral doctrine. In *TMS*, as later in *WN*, Smith puts forward his own novel doctrine first, leaving the discussion of rival schools of thought, which came first in his lectures, to much later in the two books.

His key devices, introduced in Part I of *TMS*, are *sympathy* and the *impartial spectator*. Smith insists, perhaps unconvincingly, that *TMS* is a descriptive work of historical – or conjectural-historical – sociology, not a normative work telling people how they should behave:

> [T]he present inquiry is not concerning a matter of right, if I may say so, but concerning a matter of fact. We are not at present examining upon what principles a perfect being would approve of the punishment of bad actions; but upon what principles so weak and imperfect a creature as man actually and in fact approves of it. (*TMS* II.i.5.10)

Smith wishes to know what makes us recognise something as a *moral* sentiment, as opposed to any other kind. He answers that the first requirement is a kind of imagination which he calls sympathy. By that he does not mean sympathy in the ordinary English sense, but rather the capacity to see that the world could look different through another's eyes. Smithian sympathy is closer to what we call 'empathy'. To understand it, consider its opposite. The narrator of *The Curious Incident of the Dog in the Night-time* (Haddon 2003) is a fifteen-year-old boy with Asperger's Syndrome who is quite incapable of seeing the world, or himself, as others see them. He cannot tell a lie (because it involves mathematical contradiction), but nor can he recognise a moral sentiment. 'I know that they're working out what I'm thinking, but I can't tell what they're thinking. It is like being in a room with a one-way mirror in a spy film' (Haddon 2003, p. 29). In fact for Smith it is not a one-way but a conventional mirror. The impartial spectator is a person outside me who looks at me in order to evaluate my behaviour. By Book III of *TMS*, the impartial spectator has moved into my mind, to become my conscience. It is our capacity for sympathetic insight into others that allows us to take up the role of impartial spectator towards ourselves. I can mentally interrogate him in order to find out whether my behaviour is moral or not:

> [O]ur first moral criticisms are exercised upon the characters and conduct of other people . . . But we soon learn, that other people are equally frank with regard to our own . . . We begin, upon this account, to examine our own passions and conduct, and to consider how these must appear to them, by considering how they would appear to us if in their situation. (*TMS* III.i.5)

Robert Burns caught the idea exactly, and passed it on to millions who have never read *TMS*:

> O wad some Power the giftie gie us
> To see oursels as ithers see us!
> It wad frae mony a blunder free us,
> An' foolish notion:
> What airs in dress an' gait wad lea'e us,
> An' ev'n devotion! (*To a Louse*, final stanza)

Under the stern gaze of the impartial spectator, we would free ourselves from our own follies, including (but, as the lawyers say, not limited to) our airs in dress, gait and devotion.[3] Smith's philosophy, like Burns's poetry, is profoundly egalitarian.

THE SIXTH EDITION: MORALLY MORE RADICAL, POLITICALLY MORE CONSERVATIVE?

Smith continued to tinker with *TMS* for the rest of his life. In the second edition he introduced some refinements to his concept of sympathy, to meet damaging criticism from Hume and from Elliot of Minto. But the most substantial changes came in the sixth edition, published only a matter of weeks before Smith's death in 1790. He adds a new chapter to Part I on 'the corruption of our moral sentiments, which is occasioned by this disposition to admire the rich and great'. He expands Part III on 'the sense of duty' and contracts the only substantial discussion of conventional Christian theology in the earlier editions. He adds an entirely new Part VI on Virtue; and expands Part VII (the review of other systems of morality, discussed above) by bringing together scattered remarks about the Stoics in order to 'explain more fully, and examine more distinctly, some of the doctrines of that famous sect' (*TMS*, Advertisement to the sixth edition; Glasgow edition p. [3]). The cumulative effect of these changes is to make the work morally more radical and probably (though this is less clear-cut) politically more conservative.

The most amusing mark of Smith's increasing moral radicalism is his deletion of a long passage aligning his moral theory with the Christian theology of the Atonement. The passage ends 'the most dreadful atonement has been paid [by the death of Christ] for our manifold transgressions and iniquities'. For the page of which this is the peroration Smith substitutes a single, Humean, sentence:

> In every religion, and in every superstition that the world has ever beheld, accordingly, there has been a Tartarus as well as an Elysium; a place provided for the punishment of the wicked, as well as one for the reward of the just. (*TMS* II.ii.3.12)

In 1801 the Archbishop of Dublin published a book on the Atonement, in which he quoted the passage that Smith had, unbeknown to the Archbishop, deleted. 'A layman (and he too a familiar friend of David Hume)' had set out the doctrine of the Atonement 'as the natural suggestions of reasons. Yet these are the sentiments which are the scoff of sciolists and witlings' (Archbishop William Magee, *Works*, cited by Rae [1895] 1965, p. 428). As Rae goes on, 'the sciolists and witlings were not slow in returning the scoff' by pointing out that Smith had deleted the passage, signalling that he no longer believed in it. The discomfited Archbishop could only retort that the withdrawal must have been due to the baleful influence of the atheist Hume; but in fact Smith did not withdraw the passage until fourteen years after Hume's death. In earlier changes, however, there are small hints that Smith was becoming braver about his disagreements with Christian moral thought. Recall that in 1697 Thomas Aikenhead had been executed in Edinburgh for blasphemy. In Toulouse, in 1762, just before Smith's visit, a Protestant named Jean Calas had been tortured and executed on a false charge of murdering his son to prevent the son from adopting Roman Catholicism. The son had actually committed suicide. Smith recalls this scandal in one of the additions to *TMS* (III.2.11). In 1776 Smith was unwilling to promise to publish Hume's *Dialogues on Natural Religion*; and he had earlier been party to blocking Hume's accession to a chair in Glasgow, on prudential grounds (AS to W. Cullen, November 1751, *Corr.* # 10). It is as if the death of Hume enabled Smith to become bolder. As already noted, he published his eulogy comparing the death of Hume to that of Socrates in 1777; and his additions to the 1790 edition of *TMS* make it clearer than before that he preferred the morality of Stoicism to that of Christianity.

The new chapter on the corruption of morals also modifies Smith's thought. As noted, he had earlier argued that adulation of the rich, or at least of their lifestyle, was harmless, and even useful because it was a manifestation of the invisible hand that fostered economic growth. In the new chapter, however, Smith acknowledges the downside. Adulating the rich and despising the poor equally corrupt our moral sentiments; and they may lead politicians to take bad advice. In a remarkably rude story,

> When the duke of Sully [who had been an adviser to the Protestant King Henri IV of France] was called upon by Lewis the Thirteenth [his Catholic successor], to give his advice in some emergency, he observed the favourites and courtiers whispering to one another, and smiling at his unfashionable appearance. 'Whenever your majesty's father' said the old warrior and statesman, 'did me the honour to consult me, he ordered the buffoons of the court to retire into the antechamber'. (*TMS* I.iii.3.6)

It is not hard to imagine Smith wanting to say that to some buffoon of the court of George III when he was himself a policy adviser.

As to the political changes, scholarly attention has focused on chapter VI.ii.2, one of the added chapters on Virtue. Smith argues that 'the love of our own country seems not to be derived from the love of mankind', for if it were people would love France three times as much as Great Britain on the grounds that France was three times as populous (*TMS* VI.ii.2.4). This is held, I think rightly, to be an attack on the pro-French mathematician and moralist Richard Price, who had published a *Discourse on the Love of our Country* which states 'I have been spared to be a witness to two [the American and French] Revolutions, both glorious' (Price 1991, p. 195). If Smith's attack is indeed directed at Price, he must have written these sections, by his standards, very quickly, as Price's sermon was delivered in November 1789 and *TMS* came out in (at the latest) May 1790.

Better known is Smith's eloquent and apparently anomalous attack on 'the man of system': for what, one might well ask, was Adam Smith if not a man of system? Smith contrasts the man of system with 'the man whose public spirit is prompted altogether by humanity and benevolence'. By contrast, he says, the man of system

> seems to imagine that he can arrange the different members of a great society with as much ease as the hand arranges the different pieces upon a chess-board. He does not consider . . . that, in the great chess-board of human society, every single piece has a principle of motion of its own, altogether different from that which the legislature might chuse to impress upon it. (*TMS* VI.ii.2.16–17)

Is this really an attack on the French revolutionaries? It is true that some figures of the Revolution, such as Robespierre and St-Just, fit Smith's description perfectly; but they were unknown at the end of 1789, which is the latest possible date for this passage. Alternatively, the passage could be read as an attack on Richard Price and other English radicals such as Joseph Priestley, on Condorcet or on Rousseau, for whom Smith had probably lost the respect he expressed in 1756 (cf. *Corr.* # 93, on Rousseau's biting-the-hand-that-fed-him attacks on the genial David Hume). But Smith continues, 'It is upon this account, that of all political speculators, sovereign princes are by far the most dangerous' (*TMS* VI.ii.2.18). This makes the passage an attack not on the infant French Revolution, but on the 'enlightened despots' such as Frederick the Great of Prussia (d. 1785) or Catherine the Great of Russia (d. 1796).

Two important things, however, remain true of the 'man of system' passage. Firstly, it could be used after the fact to *create* a posthumous reputation for Smith as a hammer of the French Revolution. I discuss this in Chapter 6. Secondly, on a closer reading, it is perfectly consistent with Smith's deep argument about the force of spontaneous order. The man of system thinks he can move the rest of us around like chess pieces. We are not chess pieces; we have our own minds. These minds are narrow and feeble; but as we interact with one another, we are often (though not always) led as by an invisible hand to promote an end which was no part of our intentions. The 'man of system' passage shows how Smith was a precursor of the Austrian school of economics, which I discuss later.

In the next chapter, therefore, we explore where Smith thought the invisible hand worked benignly in the economy, and where it failed to overcome the visible hands of meddling politicians and economic agents; and we complete the story of Smith's reply to Mandeville.

NOTES

1. The following details on Aikenhead were posted on Wikipedia:

   > Aikenhead was indicted in December 1696, on evidence that he had told fellow students that Christianity was a 'rhapsody of feigned and ill-invented nonsense' and predicted that it would be 'utterly extirpated' by 1800. The case was prosecuted by the Lord Advocate, Sir James Stewart (grandfather of the future Jacobite economist [Sir James] Steuart) who demanded the death penalty to set an example to others who might otherwise express such opinions in the future. Aikenhead pleaded for mercy during the hearing and attempted to recant his views but was sentenced to death by hanging. On the gallows, he stated his belief that moral laws were devised by humans rather than divine.

   Retrieved from http://en.wikipedia.org/wiki/Thomas_Aikenhead consulted on 06.09.2005.
2. *Corr.* ## 138–42 and c-o.
3. Burns shares Smith's subversive habits. Does the last couplet mean that self-awareness would strip us of our *airs* in devotion (such as wearing fancy bonnets in church), or that it would strip us of devotion to a Christian God altogether?

4

Merriment and Diversion: Smith on Public Finance and Public Choice

ECONOMIC THEORY AND POLITICAL ECONOMY

The *Wealth of Nations* is many things, but two in particular: it is a treatise on economic theory and an economist's advice on public policy. The treatise on economic theory, with many digressions into history and current affairs, occupies Books I, II and III. Books IV and V are predominantly advice on public policy, although again containing many digressions into history and current affairs. They cover two policy domains where Smith had been intimately involved: the treatment of colonies (*WN* IV.vii) and taxation, public expenditure, public works and public goods (the whole of *WN* V).

From Smith's time until the mid-nineteenth century, the subject that he originated was usually called 'political economy' – for instance in the titles of the most important works of the next two generations, David Ricardo's *On the principles of political economy, and taxation* (1817) and Thomas Malthus's and J. S. Mill's books, both entitled *Principles of political economy* (1820 and 1848 respectively). Although Smith himself does not use the phrase in his title, his earlier rival Sir James Steuart does. Steuart's *Inquiry into the principles of political oeconomy* was published in 1767, and studiously ignored by Smith. Writing in 1772 about *WN* to his childhood friend William Pulteney, Smith says:

> I have the same opinion of Sir James Stewarts Book that you have. Without once mentioning it, I flatter myself, that every false principle in it, will meet with a clear and distinct confutation in mine. (AS to William Pulteney, 03.09.1772, *Corr.* # 132)

I discuss Steuart's allegedly false principles below. That Victorian monument the *Oxford English Dictionary* states that the phrase *political economy* is a translation of the French *économie politique*, and defines it as: 'originally the art or practical science of managing the resources of a nation so as to increase its material prosperity; in more recent [that is, late nineteenth-century] use, the theoretical science dealing with the laws that regulate the production and distribution of wealth' (*Oxford English Dictionary* on-line edition, s.v. *economy*, sense 3). The root meaning of *economy*, from the Greek, is *household management*. The French Physiocrats had coined *économie politique* to mean something like 'the management of the economy' in the modern sense. Smith says of them:

> This sect, in their works, which . . . treat not only of what is properly called Political Oeconomy, or of the nature and causes of the wealth of nations, but of every other branch of the system of civil government, all follow implicitly . . . the doctrine of Mr. Quesnai. (*WN* IV.ix.38)

Thus for Smith, political economy properly so called was identical with the subject-matter of his book. I speculate that not using the phrase in his title is one of Smith's ways of differentiating himself from Steuart and Quesnay.

Political economy has a pure and an applied side. The focus of this book is on Smith as an *applied* political economist – one who applies the principles of political economy to the design of institutions. Therefore his economic theory is not my primary concern. But of course it is a prerequisite for understanding the positions he took on public policy, so it makes sense to discuss it first.

THE ECONOMIC THEORY OF *WN*

Smith had been thinking about economics before Glasgow and continued to think about it afterwards. A so-called 'Early Draft' of *WN* (*LJ* pp. 561–84) probably dates to Smith's Glasgow years but he may have drafted it earlier. Dugald Stewart quotes from a 'short manuscript drawn up by Mr Smith' in 1755, containing 'many of the most important opinions in *The Wealth of Nations*' (Stewart, *Account*, in *EPS* pp. 321–2). Furthermore, says Stewart, Smith stated that the manuscript was in the handwriting of an amanuensis who left his service in 1749. This was in the context of charges of plagiarism, probably both by and against Ferguson, that were still raw in 1793; and the manuscript has disappeared. However, as one of Smith's two Glasgow student note-takers recorded him as saying, parts of Smith's thoughts on 'police' were 'too minute for a lecture of this kind' – that is, a course of lectures on moral philosophy. Accordingly, Smith spent twelve years, in France, then in Kirkcaldy and London, developing his ideas with great refinement and detail.

In France, Smith had met the leading French 'Physiocrats', François Quesnay and A.-R. Turgot. Turgot joined Smith in urging Hume not to prolong the dispute which the paranoid Jean-Jacques Rousseau had started against his befriender Hume. Smith had called on Quesnay's medical skills, unfortunately without success, to try to save the life of Hew Campbell Scott (see Chapter 1). Quesnay later sent Smith his collected works (Ross 1995, p. 215). Smith had planned to dedicate *WN* to Quesnay before the latter's death.

A rather silly argument about intellectual priority between the Physiocrats and Smith arose in the nineteenth century and has not entirely disappeared. Some people have alleged that Smith's ideas are derivative of the Physiocrats' – in particular, of Quesnay's master idea that ultimately the land is the only source of wealth. The publication of Smith's lecture notes, antedating his visit to France, should have put paid to that once and for all, but the argument still crops up from time to time. In France, as already noted, he first started work on 'a book in order to pass away the time' (*Corr.* # 82) during the boring eighteen months that he and Buccleuch spent in Toulouse, before he became personally well known to the Paris-based academicians. In Toulouse he must have noticed the contemporary political dispute about free trade in grain. In France, unlike Great Britain, there were internal barriers to free trade, caused partly by the interests of tax farmers and partly by a feeling that food should be retained in its region of production to prevent famine there, even if this caused famine elsewhere. The Physiocrats, above all Turgot and Condorcet, were passionately hostile to this regime, and denounced it furiously. But this work seems to have been independent of *WN*. Although Smith met Turgot, his and Condorcet's works on freeing trade in grain (known at the time as *la guerre des farines* – the flour war) are independent of Smith (Baker 1975, pp. 60–1; Rothschild 2001, pp. 78–82). Turgot was a politician and Condorcet what we might now label his special economic adviser (just as Smith was to be a member of the council of economic advisers to Townshend in 1767, to Wedderburn in 1778 and to Pitt the Younger in 1787). But the economic context was different. Smith did not have to solve the Frenchmen's problem of internal trade restrictions. These had been solved in Britain in 1707. He did have to deal with the tricky problem of colonial trade and taxation, which we discuss in the next section.

Smith summarised his view of the Physiocrats in *WN*:

> That system which represents the produce of land as the sole source of the revenue and wealth of every country, has, so far as I know, never been

> adopted by any nation, and it at present exists only in the speculations of a few men of great learning and ingenuity in France. It would not, surely, be worth while to examine at great length the error of a system which never has done, and probably never will do any harm in any part of the world. (*WN* IV.ix.1, p. 663)

He goes on nevertheless to examine the Physiocrats' 'error' for a further fifteen pages. '[P]robably never will do any harm' is a nice piece of Smithian irony. So much for the idea that Smith was the purblind follower of the Physiocrats.

Another, overlapping, idea is that Smith took, or even stole, his economic ideas from Sir James Steuart. Steuart, it is said, anticipated Smith's maxims ('canons') of taxation and had a more advanced doctrine of money, circulation and credit than Smith's.[1] Again, the publication of the two sets of *LJ* should have laid that one to rest. But, as the letter to Pulteney shows, Smith did see Steuart as a rival worth confuting. Who then was Steuart, and why did Smith seek to confute him without mentioning him by name?

Sir James Steuart (1713–80) came from a slightly higher, but broadly similar, social background to Smith. His forebears were Edinburgh lawyers (his grandfather prosecuted Thomas Aikenhead) and the family managed to amass some property in the disturbed late seventeenth century. He attended the burgh school of North Berwick and Edinburgh University. However, unlike Smith and his friends, Steuart became an ardent Jacobite while on his European travels. In 1745–6 he negotiated in France on behalf of Bonnie Prince Charlie, in an abortive attempt to get French military support for the Rising. In exile in France and Germany after the failure of the Rising, Steuart started to write his *Principles*.

Steuart returned to Scotland in 1763, and got the *Principles* published through the assistance of various people in a circle that overlapped Smith's, such as Professor Ruat, the Glasgow colleague of Smith's who had spent most of his time on the Snell litigation. It was difficult for Steuart to take an active part in discussing or disseminating his work, as he was not pardoned for his Jacobite activities until 1772. (Biographical facts are from Skinner 1998; 2004.) Therefore his *Principles* did not sell well in Britain, a fact which caused Smith some difficulty when he approached the same publishers about *WN*. However, in continental Europe and in the USA, Steuart's work was much better received – indeed, better than Smith's, until the mid-nineteenth century. Karl Marx, who admired Steuart, called his work a *Gesamt-System der bürgerlichen*

Ökonomie ('general system of bourgeois economics') in 1859 (cited by N. Kobayashi in Steuart [1767] 1998, Vol. I, p. lxxii).

It was surely Steuart's economic principles rather than his Jacobitism that Smith saw the need to confute. Smith worked in Scotland, a weak state. His compatriot Steuart wrote most of the *Principles* in the strongest state of the day, namely France. Steuart believed in a strong interventionist government; Smith did not. In his *History of Economic Analysis*, Joseph Schumpeter says of Steuart that, unlike Smith:

> he grouped all that really interests the public around the old-fashioned figure of an imaginary patriot statesman who in infinite wisdom watches the economic process, ready to interfere in the national interest. (Schumpeter 1954, p. 176)

Here are some of the things that Steuart would like the imaginary patriot statesman to do:

> We must encourage oeconomy, frugality, and a simplicity of manners, discourage the consumption of every thing that can be exported, and excite a taste for superfluity in neighbouring nations.
>
> [I]n a country entirely taken up with the object of foreign trade, no competition should be allowed to come from abroad for articles of the first necessity, and principally for food, so as to raise prices beyond a certain standard.
>
> [W]hen these [price] standards cannot be preserved and . . . prices get above them, public money must be thrown into the scale to bring prices to the level of those of exportation. (Steuart 1767/1998, i.II.xv, quoted on pp. i.279 and i.286)

Steuart goes on to discuss 'methods of lowering the Price of Manufactures, in order to make them vendible in foreign Markets' and the 'several Principles' of intervention in 'infant, foreign, and inland trade'. Broadly, these are that the statesman should lower export prices to make his nation more internationally competitive; should protect infant industries by excluding foreign producers of them; should send luxury production abroad so that the home market is not distracted by it; and, in inland commerce, should use tax transfers from producers to consumers to balance supply and demand (*ibid.*, pp. i.286–320). This reflects the economic policy he observed being practised in France before the Physiocrats – for instance, the controls on internal trade.

Smith thought this was all utterly wrong and dangerous, for reasons we shall examine in the next subsection. His basic economic ideas, therefore, did not come from the France of his travels, or of the Physiocrats, although many of his supporting illustrations did. They assuredly did not come from Sir James Steuart. I think that his basic ideas came from observing the world he saw about him; above all from a Scotland whose transformation in a generation since 1707 was as astonishing as the rise of the Asian tiger economies in the 1980s. Smith's most direct remarks about the Union come in a letter of 1760 to his publisher William Strahan, an expatriate Scot educated at the High School in Edinburgh:

> The Union was a measure from which infinite Good has been derived to this country. The Prospect of such good, however, must then have appeared very remote and uncertain. The immediate effect of it was to hurt the interest of every single order of men in the country. The dignity of the nobility was undone by it . . . Even the merchants seemed to suffer at first . . . The Clergy, too, who were then far from insignificant, were alarmed about the Church. No wonder if at that time all orders of men conspired in cursing a measure so hurtful to their immediate interest. The views of their Posterity are now very different. (AS to William Strahan, 04.04.1760, *Corr.* # 50)

Although not born until sixteen years after the Union of 1707, Smith had lived through the wrenching dislocations of the Union. Free trade with England had rapidly ruined some Scottish economic interests (including the 'trade . . . to France, Holland and the Baltic . . . almost totally annihilated' (*ibid.*; Kirkcaldy lost from the Union as Glasgow gained) and as rapidly promoted others. Speaking of the then proposed Union with Ireland in *WN*, Smith writes:

> By the union with Great Britain, Ireland would gain, besides the freedom of trade, other advantages much more important, and which would much more than compensate any increase of taxes that might accompany that union. By the union with England, the middling and inferior ranks of people in Scotland gained a compleat deliverance from the power of an aristocracy which had always before oppressed them. By an union with Great Britain the greater part of the people of all ranks in Ireland would gain an equally compleat deliverance. (*WN* V.iii.89)

That particular prophecy went badly wrong, because the Union of Ireland with Great Britain, effected in 1800, was dissolved in 1921, leaving the sulphurous and riven province of Northern Ireland behind. But this is because the Union did not take place on Smith's terms. Smith envisaged the disappearance of the Anglican Ascendancy in Ireland, which in his time lorded it over the much more numerous Catholics in the south and Presbyterians in the north of Ireland. Instead, King George III's refusal to grant Catholic Emancipation left a sullen and resentful majority in Ireland, who never accepted the legitimacy of the Union (McLean and McMillan 2005, Chapter 3).

Smith's perspective on Union for Britain and Ireland, and on economic growth, derives from the primacy that *WN* gives to the division of labour. *WN* begins with a bang:

> The greatest improvement in the productive powers of labour, and the greater part of the skill, dexterity, and judgment with which it is any where directed, or applied, seem to have been the effects of the division of labour. (*WN* I.i.1)

Smith goes on to develop an example which has become the best known part of *WN* (perhaps, one has to add cynically, because it is right at the beginning of a long and complex book). In the 'very trifling manufacture' of pins, a workman who did everything required from start to finish could 'scarce, perhaps . . . make one pin in a day, and certainly could not make twenty'. However, now that pin-making has been divided into eighteen distinct operations, even 'a small manufactory . . . where ten men only were employed' which Smith had observed could make about 'twelve pounds' of pins a day, numbering about 48,000; each person therefore in effect making about 4000 (*WN* I.i.3).

The division of labour is therefore capable of yielding extraordinary gains in productivity. These gains suffice to explain something that fascinated Smith, as it did many of his predecessors and contemporaries, notably including Locke, Montesquieu, Ferguson and Condorcet. This was the evolution of society from the hunter-gatherer communities that explorers were discovering in America and elsewhere, through the intermediate stages of shepherding and agriculture to commerce. Almost a century earlier, John Locke (one of whose jobs when he was in political favour was as secretary of the board responsible for the settlement of English colonists in the Carolinas and Georgia) had commented that 'a King of a large and fruitful Territory there feeds, lodges, and is clad worse than a day Labourer in *England*' (Locke [1690] 1988, II § 42, p. 297). Locke ascribes this to the lack of property rights in the hunter-gatherer communities of Native Americans. Smith agrees, but takes the argument much further into a full description of the characteristic institutions of each of the four stages of economic evolution. Much of this is in *LJ* rather than in *WN*, so it was not published in Smith's lifetime.

The first stage was the hunter-gatherer society. The Age of Hunters was an age of cooperation – because, without cooperation in the hunt, the hunters would starve. It was an age with minimal property rights, because there was no property to have rights in (*LJ(A)* i.27–35). The only exception was a large prey such as a wild boar or a whale. For these cases property rights in the kill had to be drawn up:

> In the same manner, at this day, the ships which go to the Greenland fishery share the whale that was wounded betwixt the ship who wounded and that which killed the whale. (*LJ(A)* i.40)

Hunter bands are small in size because 'in a short time any considerable number would destroy all the game in the country, and consequently would want a means of subsistence' (*LJ(B)*, 27). Smith's exemplars of the Age of Hunters were North American Indians, Tartar bands and Greenland fishermen.

Next came the Age of Shepherds, many of whose customs Smith deduces from what the Old Testament of the Bible tells us about Abraham and his contemporaries. The 'contrivance' that would come most naturally to hunters would be to tame some of their animals and settle down in one place (*LJ(A)* i.28). The Age of Shepherds needs much more extensive property rights than the previous age. For, if there is a band of shepherds who have tamed their flocks and an adjacent band of hunters who have not, what is to stop the hunters descending on the shepherds and stealing and eating all their sheep? 'Property, the grand fund of all dispute' is now needed. But because no shepherd can build up a stock of capital, property holdings in the Age of Shepherds are egalitarian. So, Smith supposes, are not only the customs for making laws – in a general assembly of the whole band – but also the laws that are made (*LJ(A)* iv.22–4).

The third stage is the Age of Agriculture. Smith occasionally acknowledges that this is all too neat, as when he admits that Native Americans, although mainly hunters, have some agriculture in the shape of corn and squash (*LJ(A)* i.29). But it helps him draw up his grand scheme of the evolution of inequality and of property rights. The Age of Agriculture marks the beginning of serious division of labour. Theft is not such a problem as in the Age of Shepherds, and therefore the punishments for it will not be so draconian. But there is much more, and more diverse, property to protect. Even the shepherds were allowed the private property of their huts, by local custom. As the Age of Agriculture progressed, so did property rights become more particular. Fields, originally owned in common, became parcelled up into individually owned plots. But individual ownership of a plot implies a need for individual defence of the plot – and hence arose more elaborate legal systems, and more elaborate political systems, including feudalism. Feudalism required a complex set of laws of inheritance and succession, including the rules to ensure that property was protected when the heir was a minor, and the special rules for celibate clergy (*LJ(B)* 159–61). The alternative (and to Smith, in this respect one of the country Whigs discussed below, morally superior) form of tenure was 'allodial',[2] as practised by German and Scandinavian tribes. An allodial lord would need to set up his own court to establish the property rights within his own manor (*LJ(A)* iv.119).

Finally comes the Age of Commerce, where the division of labour comes into its own:

> As men could now confine themselves to one species of labour, they would naturally exchange the surplus of their own commodity for that of another of which they stood in need. (*LJ(B)* 159)

People in the towns, which had been (as we might say but Smith did not) islands of capitalism in a surrounding feudal sea, became involved more and more in specialist trade, both with the surrounding countryside trading manufactured goods for food, and with one another. With the Age of Commerce comes the full panoply of property rights as it exists in a modern eighteenth-century society.

The account of the four stages of society is rich conjectural history. It is by no means unique to Smith. Something very similar appears in Condorcet's *Esquisse* (Sketch for the history of the progress of the human mind), written in 1793 as Condorcet hid from the revolutionary persecutors who would soon kill him. For Condorcet there are ten stages of progress, not four. Although Smith's account looks very similar to the classic Marxist account produced by Marx and Engels a century later, there are important differences. Marx and Engels cannot have known what Smith said in his lectures, which had not been rediscovered in their time. Also, while both Rousseau and the Marxists, in their different ways, stressed the disadvantages of capitalism, Smith celebrates the increase of wealth that the Age of Commerce makes possible. Later stages of *WN*, however, show that he is also interested in issues of distribution – and also issues of what Marx and Engels later labelled the 'alienation' brought on by the division of labour.

If the division of labour is the mainspring of economic growth, then economic growth is healthiest when the division of labour is permitted to the fullest possible extent. This is the basis of Smith's violent, although silent, objection to Steuart. All protectionist plans such as Steuart's involve interfering with the division of labour in so far as they redirect economic activity from the places where it can be carried on most efficiently to places where it is carried on less efficiently. The following lethal dart is surely aimed at Sir James Steuart:

> By means of glasses, hotbeds, and hotwalls, very good grapes can be raised in Scotland, and very good wine too can be made of them at about thirty times the expence for which at least equally good can be bought from foreign

> countries. Would it be a reasonable law to prohibit the importation of all foreign wines, merely to encourage the making of claret and burgundy in Scotland?. (*WN* IV.ii.15)

Accordingly, after discussing the division of labour, Smith moves on to point out that it is 'limited by the Extent of the Market' (from the title of I.iii). This immediately leads to the deduction that the greater the extent of the market, the greater the productivity and income improvement permitted by extending the division of labour. This was a natural conclusion for a Scotsman, who had observed an astonishing surge of growth in a few short years after 1746, to draw.

The rest of Book I of *WN* is devoted to the basics of (as we would now say) economic statics; Books II and III move on to comparative statics and dynamics. Smith discusses money as the lubricator of exchange. In Book I Chapter v, he argues that the 'real price of everything, what every thing really costs to the man who wants to acquire it, is the toil and trouble of acquiring it'. Therefore 'Labour . . . is the real measure of the exchangeable value of all commodities' (*WN* I.v.1–2). However, money sets nominal values, which are affected by changes in the supply of money. This leads on to a difficult discussion (I.vii) of the 'natural and market Price of Commodities' in which Smith tries (I think not very successfully) to reconcile his labour theory of value with a realistic observation of the function of money. It is because of the labour theory of value that some, especially those that follow in the footsteps of Karl Marx, have seen in Adam Smith a man of the Left. In this book I wish to show that Smith can indeed be called a man of the Left, but not for the labour theory of value, which I think leads into a blind alley of confusion.

Smith then goes on to distinguish the three sources of income, namely wages (the return to labour); profit (the return to capital); and rent (the return to land). Of these three sections, that on rent (I.xi) is much the longest and most complex. Smith is groping towards what we now call the Ricardian concept of rent, because it was first clearly expounded in Ricardo (1817). According to Ricardo, because land is inherently scarce, rents from land grow as population grows irrespective of any effort on the part of the landowner – indeed rent incomes may move in the opposite direction to wages, rent increasing as the return to wages (or capital) diminishes. Although the full Ricardian theory is not in Smith, there is enough for readers to see its truly radical implications:

> High or low wages or profit, are the causes of high or low price; high or low rent is the effect of it . . . The rent of land not only varies with its fertility, whatever be its produce, but with its situation, whatever be its fertility. Land

> in the neighbourhood of a town, gives a greater rent than land equally fertile in a distant part of the country . . . Good roads, canals, and navigable rivers, by diminishing the expence of carriage, put the remote parts of the country more nearly upon a level with those in the neighbourhood of the town. (*WN* I.xi.a.8–b.5)

This has heavy implications for the proper apportionment of tax and the proper scope of public expenditure: the landowners who held the great majority of seats in parliament in Smith's day were getting a windfall from roads and canals.

Book II of *WN* may be seen as Smith's answer to Mandeville. As noted in Chapter 3, Mandeville had argued in *The Fable of the Bees* that private vices such as extravagant spending on personal luxuries may generate public virtues such as national wealth. The converse implication is that saving may fail to generate wealth. The latter implication is what J. M. Keynes later called 'the paradox of thrift': namely, the possibility that the private sector wants to save more than it wishes to invest. There lies the paradox, seen by both Mandeville and Keynes: what is good for individuals can be bad for an economy. Like Sir James Steuart, Smith was troubled by Mandeville's paradoxes; if he were not, he would not have devoted so much space to Mandeville in *TMS*. Steuart's response to Mandeville is elaborate government control of where and when people may consume luxury goods. The brief extracts provided give a flavour of Steuart's ideas, which were much more in tune with the spirit of the age than Smith's. Governments passed what were called 'sumptuary laws' – that is, laws saying what their citizens could and could not consume – for all sorts of reasons, religious, social and economic.

Without mentioning either Steuart or Mandeville, Smith constructs his rival edifice in Book II. He opens by defining fixed and 'circulating' – we would now say 'working' – capital. Turning to macroeconomic aggregates, he then establishes that the net surplus in profits (and rents) generated by an economy in a year is the amount available for capital formation, after deducting the amount required for the circulation of money (the calculation of which was a thorny problem). There follows a long discussion on the role of banks as providers of capital. He ascribes the sudden spurt in Scottish growth in the twenty-five years before his book to the operations of those banks,[3] but warns that the principles of prudent banking are not yet firmly understood. He analyses the sad case of the Ayr Bank, about which he had sent and received several letters while writing *WN*. It had been set up to provide easy credit when other banks were restricting it; but its (to Smith) inevitable collapse exacerbated the crisis it had been created to alleviate.

In Book II, Chapter III 'Of the Accumulation of Capital, or of productive and unproductive Labour', Smith points out that not only domestic servants, but also kings, soldiers, sailors, 'churchmen, lawyers, physicians, men of letters of all kinds: players, buffoons, musicians, opera-singers, opera-dancers, &c' (*WN* II.iii.2) are unproductive in the sense that they do not produce capital or intermediate goods.[4] However, unlike the Physiocrats, who thought that only agricultural work was truly productive, Smith highlights capital formation by artisans: 'But the labour of the manufacturer fixes and realizes itself in some particular subject or vendible commodity, which lasts for some time at least after that labour is past' (*ibid.*). D. D. Raphael, the most acute of Smith commentators, has pointed to a passage in *LJ(A)* where Smith praises the self-improving artisan:

> One whose thoughts all center on one piece of work will be at pains to contrive how to do this in the cleverest and easiest manner. The inventions of the mill and the plow are so old that no history gives any account of them. But if we go into the work house of any manufacturer in the new works at Sheffiel[d], Manchester, or Birmingham, or even some towns in Scotland, and enquire concerning the machines, they will tell you that such or such a one was invented by some common workman. (*LJ(A)* vi.53–4; cf. Raphael 1985, p. 47)

Smith delivered that lecture only yards away from the laboratory where James Watt, mathematical instrument maker to the University of Glasgow, was working for Smith's best friend Joseph Black. As related above, Black had asked Watt to repair a model Newcomen engine. Between them, Black the theorist and Watt the hands-on technician worked out what was wrong with the engine. Watt soon patented the separate condenser, which would double the thermal efficiency of the Newcomen engine.[5]

Once Smith had a theory of capital formation, or if you will of endogenous growth, in place, he had restored harmony to his social and economic thought. Private vices were no longer public benefits if they crowded out capital formation.

The short Book III discusses 'the different Progress of Opulence in different Nations' – as topical a subject now as it was in Adam Smith's day. He is gearing up for an attack on 'the absurd speculations that have been propagated concerning the balance of trade' (*WN* III.i.1) to which he will return in Book IV. This is another attack on Steuart, among others. Popular economics, as popular now as in Steuart's time, holds that every nation should secure a favourable balance of trade, or of payments (the two concepts were not very carefully distinguished at the time). But of course that is as impossible as the blissful state of Lake Wobegon, where all the children are above average. Steuart's economics falls into contradiction. The rest of Book III considers cities as the engines of economic growth, with a long digression about the fall of the Roman empire. By the end of Book III Smith has built his system. It is time for him to move more directly to policy advice, which he does in Book IV under the guise of a critique 'of Systems of political Oeconomy'.

THE APPLIED POLITICAL ECONOMY OF *WN*

In a letter of 1780, the same one that expresses disingenuous surprise at the reception of his eulogy of Hume, Smith describes Book IV as a 'very violent attack . . . upon the whole commercial system of Great Britain' (AS to Andreas Holt, 26.10.1780, *Corr.* # 208). This attack occupies Chapters i to vi of Book IV. Smith opens by attacking the mercantilist fallacy that the wealth of a country is to be measured by the amount of money in it, which is closely allied to the fallacy that every country ought to export more and import less. Accordingly, he goes on to attack import substitution ('Of Restraints upon the Importation from foreign Countries of such Goods as can be produced at Home' – IV.ii), and in particular import barriers 'from those Countries with which the Balance is supposed to be disadvantageous' (IV.iii); he then turns his beady eye onto subsidies for domestic industry ('Of Drawbacks' and 'Of Bounties', IV.iv–v) before denouncing the 1703 commercial treaty between England and Portugal, which allowed access for English wool to Portugal in exchange for favourable terms for Portuguese wine in England. For Smith this was an obstruction to free trade rather than the promotion of it.

All of these sections of *WN* are as relevant today as when Smith wrote them. Politicians under pressure from domestic lobbies always yearn for protection. As I write in August 2005, the latest consequence of this is that millions of pounds worth of Chinese textile imports are stockpiled at EU ports because Chinese manufacturers and European retailers between them have committed the heinous offence of trying to sell 'too many' Chinese clothes to Europeans more cheaply than European manufacturers can produce them. Likewise, import substitution has been a seductive dead end for policy-makers in many countries, notably in Latin America where it was promoted by the Argentine economist Raul Prebisch (1901–86; cf. Yergin and Stanislaw 2002, pp. 232–44). Furthermore, politicians find bilateral trade treaties (such as the North American Free Trade Agreement) easier to understand and to promote than multilateral agreements (such as the World Trade Organisation). In the current decade, *The Economist* excoriates politicians nearly every week for preferring bilateral to multilateral trade agreements. The point is subtle, but Smith's discussion of the Anglo-Portuguese (Methuen) Treaty gets to the heart of it.

Subsidies to domestic industry need not emanate from self-interested lobbying, even though they usually do. In Smith's time, the Scottish Highlands were not only desperately poor and undeveloped, but were also a security threat to the British state. The support Bonnie Prince Charlie had received in 1745–6 showed how real the threat was. One response was to try to encourage industrial development there. To well-wishers, the herring industry seemed promising; and subsidising herring-fishing boats would have the spinoff benefit of training sailors who could be useful to the British Navy. Accordingly, the British government offered a subsidy of thirty shillings per ton on herring busses – the specialised boats for this fishery. In consequence, 'it has, I am afraid, been too common for vessels to fit out for the sole purpose of catching, not the fish, but the bounty' (*WN* IV.v.a.32). If Smith had been alive today to observe the Common Agricultural Policy of the European Union, he might wonder if anybody had bothered to read him in the intervening two centuries.

The longest section of Book IV is Chapter vii, on colonies, where Smith puts forward his heterodox ideas about American policy. As this is a large subject in its own right, I consider it separately in Chapter 6. After a final round-up denouncing the mercantile system, Smith turns to his critique of the Physiocrats (IV.ix), which has already been discussed.

To understand Book V, it is helpful to return to the point where *TMS* ends and *LJ* begins, mentioned in Chapter 3. The set of notes discovered in 1895, now known as *LJ(B)*, contains an elaborate copperplate title-page describing the contents as 'Juris Prudence: or, Notes from the Lectures on Justice, Police, Revenue, and Arms delivered in the University of Glasgow by Adam Smith Professor of Moral Philosophy'. The first page of notes continues, 'Jurisprudence is that science which inquires into the general principles which ought to be the foundation of the laws of all nations'. And, a little later in the same lecture:

> The four great objects of law are Justice, Police, Revenue, and Arms.
>
> The object of Justice is the security from injury, and it is the foundation of civil government.
>
> The objects of Police are the cheapness of commodities, public security, and cleanliness, if the two last were not too minute for a lecture of this kind. Under this head we will consider the opulence of the state.
>
> It is likewise necessary that the magistrate who bestows his time and labour in the business of the state should be compensated for it. For this purpose and

> for defraying the expences of government some fund must be raised. Hence the origine of Revenue . . .
>
> As the best police cannot give security unless the government can defend themselves against foreign injuries and attacks, the fourth thing appointed by law is for this purpose, and under this head will be shewn the different species of Arms with their advantages and dissadvantages, the constitution of standing armies, militias, etca.

Here is Smith's programme clearly set out.[6] *Justice* – the part never published, and we assume destroyed by Smith's executors just before he died – is narrowly construed as the institutions that protect the security of property and contracts. *Police*, *Revenue* and *Arms* all went into *WN*. But in the years between Smith leaving Glasgow and publishing *WN*, he hugely expanded the 'police' section – which is, essentially, most of Books I–IV – leaving 'revenue' and 'arms' each to occupy a small but important niche in Book V. It is convenient to discuss them in reverse order.

Arms

The argument between supporters of a standing army and of a citizen militia raged fiercely in Scotland, England and America in Smith's time. It was important both in political theory and in practical politics. Thinkers who may be grouped together as 'country Whigs' viewed a standing army as a standing threat to the liberties of the freeborn Englishman (or Scot, or American). The most important of these thinkers were Andrew Fletcher of Saltoun (1655–1716), Adam Ferguson, and Thomas Jefferson (1743–1826).

Andrew Fletcher is best known as the most eloquent Scottish opponent of the union of 1707. However, he spent most of his life outside Scotland. His *Discourse of Militias and Standing Armies* (Fletcher [1697] 1997) was written to oppose William III's retention of a standing army after the end of a war between England and the Netherlands. Fletcher argues that all standing armies in peacetime lead to tyranny; that 'the subjects formerly had a real security for their liberty, by having the sword in their own hands' (p. 18); and that that liberty should be restored by disbanding William III's army. The Revd Captain Adam Ferguson was a regular, not a militia, officer. Like Smith, he was out of Edinburgh when Bonnie Prince Charlie occupied the city in 1745. But their friends William Robertson, Alexander Carlyle and John Home – Moderates and literati – all offered to join an impromptu citizen militia to repel the Young Pretender. Ferguson later formed the Poker Club, its name, as he wrote, an 'Alusion to the use of that Instrument when fires like ours need to be Stirred' (Sher 2004a), to agitate for a Scottish militia. Its members were the same cast of convivial Edinburgh intellectuals and literati, including Smith.

Country Whig ideology had its most practical flowering in America. The revolutionary army was indeed a citizen militia (albeit with help from the regular French army) which defeated the standing army of the United Kingdom. The issue called forth some of Thomas Jefferson's finest writing, as we shall see in Chapter 6.

Smith's view of Arms therefore came as a severe disappointment to the other members of the Poker Club. He acknowledged the country Whig view that militias and liberty went together, but viewed a standing army as an inevitable accompaniment of a more advanced division of labour (*LJ(A)* iv.88; *WN* V.i.a). For Smith, as noted previously, society passed through four historical stages. The first was that of hunter-gatherers ('the lowest and rudest state of society'); the second, a society of shepherds; the third, an agricultural society; and the fourth, a commercial society. The nature and causes of the wealth of nations lay in this evolution. A commercial nation could take the division of labour, and hence the creation of wealth, to far greater length than any of its predecessors. But one necessary consequence, according to Smith, was the division of labour in warfare as in every other trade. War itself had become more specialised; but so had every other occupation. 'Military exercises come to be as much neglected by the inhabitants of the country as by those of the town, and the great body of the people becomes altogether unwarlike' (*WN* V.i.a.15). Therefore the only practical option, in a commercial state, is for the state to tax the people for the upkeep of a professional army. However, he notes prophetically that a militia which campaigns for several seasons may become as good as a standing army: 'Should the war in America drag out through another campaign, the American militia may become in every respect a match for [the British] standing army' (*WN* V.i.a.27). Indeed it did.

Adam Ferguson, the founder of the Poker Club, liked Smith's chapter on Arms as little as the Revd Hugh Blair liked his chapter on religion:

> You have provoked, it is true, the church, the universities, and the merchants, against all of whom I am willing to take your part; but you have likewise provoked the militia, and there I must be against you. (AF to AS, 18.04.1776, *Corr.* # 154)

Revenue

Smith's discussion of taxation and public expenditure is one of the finest parts of *WN*. In relying on ideas that were not formalised until cooperative game theory, he is indeed two hundred years ahead of his time. His fellow citizen Gordon Brown seems particularly struck by this part of Smith's thought. In his Edinburgh speech, Brown half-seriously announced that he kept Smith's maxims of taxation beside him while preparing the 2002 Budget.[7] The affinity goes much deeper, as will be discussed later.

The maxims of taxation are laid out in *WN* V.ii.b:

> I. The subjects of every state ought to contribute towards the support of the government, as nearly as possible, in proportion to their respective abilities; that is, in proportion to the revenue which they respectively enjoy under the protection of the state . . .
> II. The tax which each individual is bound to pay ought to be certain, and not arbitrary . . .
> III. Every tax ought to be levied at the time, or in the manner in which it is most likely to be convenient for the contributor to pay it . . .
> IV. Every tax ought to be so contrived as both to take out and to keep out of the pockets of the people as little as possible, over and above what it brings into the publick treasury of the state . . .

In Chapter 5 I shall look at some of the 'left-wing' credentials of Smith's maxims of taxation, even though they are a part of his thought that may seem to bring more comfort to the contemporary Right than Left. Here, though, there is space only to discuss maxim I. Smith not only says that taxation should be proportionate to income, but gives as his reason that the rich enjoy more revenue than the poor 'under the protection of the state' – a thoroughly egalitarian justification of proportionate taxation. He goes on to say that all the factors of production, Rent, Profit and Wages, should bear an equal proportionate burden, but gives reasons why he believes that land rents have been taxed too lightly. Indeed, anticipating later writers, including David Ricardo and Henry George, he goes on to say:

> Ground-rents seem, in this respect, a more proper subject of peculiar taxation than even the ordinary rent of land. The ordinary rent of land is, in many cases, owing partly at least to the attention and good management of the landlord. A very heavy tax might discourage too much this attention and good management. Ground-rents, so far as they exceed the ordinary rent of land, are altogether owing to the good government of the sovereign . . . Nothing can be more reasonable than that a fund which owes its existence to the good government of the state, should be taxed peculiarly . . . towards the support of that government. (*WN* V.ii.e.11)

As to public expenditure, Smith is equally radical. He and Hume worked out what we now call the theory of public goods. A public good is anything non-excludably supplied to everyone. If anyone gets the benefits of the Royal Navy, everyone does; you can neither practicably exclude anyone from its benefits nor charge anyone in Britain individually for naval services rendered. There are other goods which the market, left to itself, fails to provide. As Hume remarked in 1738,

> Two neighbours may agree to drain a meadow, which they possess in common: because . . . each must perceive, that the immediate consequence of his failing in his part, is the abandoning the whole project. But it is . . . impossible, that a thousand persons should agree in any such action; . . . each seeks a pretext to free himself of the trouble and expense, and would lay the whole burden on others. Political society easily remedies . . . these inconveniences. (Hume 1738/1911, Vol. II, p. 239; original Book III Part ii, Chapter 7)

The market fails to deliver some goods because, left to themselves, people rationally take a free ride. Therefore the state ('Political society') must provide what the market fails to.

According to Smith, the state should provide 'Defence, Justice, publick Works and publick Institutions' (*WN* V.i.a–e). All of these are either non-excludable public goods or, like Hume's meadow, are unprovided (or underprovided) in the market. Public works such as roads and bridges, and public institutions such as schools and universities, deliver both private goods to those who use them and the public good of a more mobile, educated and tolerant population. Schools and universities should be part-funded by the state, but independent (as in Scotland), not in the service of the established church (as in Smith's England).

But public provision does not necessarily imply provision by salaried public employees. Roads and bridges can be financed by turnpike tolls (though that too causes perverse incentives, which Smith discusses in *WN* V.i.d.1–10). Students should pay fees direct to their professors as they did to Smith himself (see Chapter 1). Oxford and Cambridge professors, who drew their salaries whether or not they did any teaching or research, did not impress the young Smith who taught himself for six years at Balliol.

THINKING LIKE AN ECONOMIST: ADAM SMITH AND PUBLIC CHOICE

Economists like to say, rather complacently, that *thinking like an economist* is the first prerequisite for a student of economics. Indeed, if you type that phrase into Google, you will reach the Economics 101 curriculum pages of a number of eminent academic economists.

To make matters worse, thinking like an economist sometimes seems to be just like thinking selfishly. In a famous experiment, Marwell and Ames (1981) tested an experimental public-goods game in classes of beginning graduate students. A public-goods game is a formalisation of Hume's meadow problem. Each citizen would rather the meadow was drained than not. But however many of the others volunteer to contribute to draining it, each citizen is strictly better off 'free-riding' than contributing. Free-riding means failing to cooperate in whatever collective effort is needed to drain the meadow, whether it be coming out with a shovel or making a financial contribution to pay a contractor. This sort of problem goes under the forbidding title of a 'generalised *n*-person prisoners' dilemma'. And in such a prisoners' dilemma, if played only once, the *dominant strategy* is to take a free ride. This is just another way of saying that, whatever proportion of the other players cooperate, you are strictly better off if you defect.

As Marwell and Ames's title indicates, they found that economics students consistently free-rode; students in the other social sciences consistently cooperated. This finding seems to be robust. Like many others, I have tried the Marwell and Ames experiment myself in mixed introductory classes, and have always got the same result as they did.

Does this mean that economists are consistently more selfish than other people? It may do, but it need not. What it must mean, as a minimum, is that an economist thinks through how people would rationally behave, given the incentives they face. It does not make any assumptions about what they want, beyond that whatever they want, they would rather have more of it than less; but that their relative desire for any one good declines as they acquire more of it. Upon those deliberately meagre foundations is built the whole of classical and neoclassical economic reasoning. Smith approved of parsimonious models which explain a lot with a little, as he says of the Copernican system in his *History of Astronomy* (IV.33–4, in *EPS* pp. 75–6).

Especially if you consider *TMS* and *WN* together, it is impossible to believe that Smith *advocated* selfish behaviour (though I return to this question in more detail in Chapter 5). What he does do is to think like an economist about the incentives facing politicians, economic agents and citizens. Here is Smith on trade associations:

> People of the same trade seldom meet together, even for merriment and diversion, but the conversation ends in a conspiracy against the publick, or in some contrivance to raise prices. It is impossible indeed to prevent such meetings, by any law which either could be executed, or would be consistent with liberty and justice. But although the law cannot hinder people of the same

trade from sometimes assembling together, it ought to do nothing to facilitate such assemblies; much less to render them necessary. (*WN* I.x.c.27)

The violence of Smith's attacks on mercantilism and vested interest is concealed behind his elegant yet plain style. Sometimes you need to read a passage twice to see how violent it is; sometimes not.

To found a great empire for the sole purpose of raising up a people of customers, may at first sight appear a project fit only for a nation of shopkeepers. It is, however, a project altogether unfit for a nation of shopkeepers; but extremely fit for a nation that is governed by shopkeepers. (*WN* IV.vii.c.63)[8]

The discipline of colleges and universities is in general contrived, not for the benefit of the students, but for the interest, or more properly speaking, for the ease of the masters. Its object is, in all cases, to maintain the authority of the master, and whether he neglects or performs his duty, to oblige the students in all cases to behave to him as if he performed it with the greatest diligence and ability (*WN* V.i.f.15).

And thus, place, that great object which divides the wives of aldermen, is the end of half the labours of human life; and is the cause of all the tumult and bustle, all the rapine and injustice, which avarice and ambition have introduced into this world. (*TMS* I.iii.2.7)

Smith's most violent attacks are reserved for those who have secured power on behalf of a special interest. The most flagrant conspiracies against the public, as he sees it, are those committed by the chartered monopoly companies such as the East India Company, which excluded others from their business and could therefore reap monopoly profits. The mercantilist, protectionist 'nation governed by shopkeepers' that he attacked saw the United States as simply 'a people of customers', to be taxed at the whim of the East India Company. It was to protect that company's monopoly of tea sales that the British government levied the taxes that led to the Boston Tea Party and spread to open revolt. Smith was not opposed to taxing the Americans, only to taxing them for the benefit of British special interests. In fact, in his policy advice to the British government, he firmly stated that the American colonists should be taxed to pay for the defence from the Native Americans and the French of which they were the sole beneficiaries. His most visionary scheme was for a peace with the United States, combined with ceding Canada and Florida – 'those splendid, but unprofitable acquisitions of the late [Seven Years, 1756–63] war' – back to France and Spain respectively. This would 'render our colonies the natural enemies of those two monarchies and consequently the natural allies of Great Britain' ('Smith's Thoughts on the State of the Contest with America', in *Corr.*, pp. 377–85, q. at pp. 382–3).

All of this illustrates that, for Smith, the enemy of freedom and prosperity was not government *per se*, but what we now label *rent-seeking* government (Tullock 1967; Krueger 1974). A rent-seeking society is one in which economic agents seek government policies that yield economic rents (that is, monopoly incomes) to themselves. A rent-seeking government is a government that is captured by rent-seeking interests. Rent-seeking interests are inevitable, if you believe Smith and his later followers such as James Madison and Mancur Olson (Madison *et al.* 1788/1987, # 10; Olson 1965, 1982). Rent-seeking government is not.

In Smith's hands, therefore, economics is a radically egalitarian discipline. Distinctions of status and power only obstruct liberty and economic growth. Merriment and diversion may cloak naked self-interest. Sir James Steuart, characterised by Schumpeter as conjuring up an imaginary patriot statesman who in infinite wisdom watches the economic process, ready to interfere in the national interest (see p. 64), fails to think like an economist. There may not be enough real patriot statesmen around for a Steuartian economy to work in the public interest.

NOTES

1. The seed was sown by Schumpeter's (1954, p. 184) notorious remark that *WN* 'does not contain a single *analytic* idea, principle, or method that was entirely new in 1776'. Under the authority of Schumpeter's ample cloak, this enables contrarians to argue that Steuart was more original than Smith, and understood some things that Smith failed to. It is easier to gain attention for the contrarian view that Steuart was original and Smith was not than for the plain vanilla view that Smith is an infinitely better economist than Steuart. I recommend to contrarians that they try actually reading Steuart and Smith in parallel. The names Salieri and Mozart come to mind.
2. *Allodium*: 'An estate held in absolute ownership without service or acknowledgement of any superior, as among the early Teutonic peoples; opposed to *feudum* or *feud*' – definition from *Oxford English Dictionary* on-line edition.
3. For corroboration, consider the very substantial role taken by the banks in financing the construction of classical Edinburgh: Youngson 1966 *passim*.
4. Typically of Smith's self-deprecating sarcasm, he includes himself with the kings, queens, churchmen and buffoons as unproductive.
5. The exact relationship between Smith and Watt remains elusive. In his capacity as (we might now say) Pro-Vice-Chancellor for Estates at Glasgow University, Smith investigated how much space Watt and the printer Robert Foulis were occupying, and whether it could be cut down (GUA 26650; Ross 1995, p. 146). On the other hand, Smith was a subscriber for one of Watt's other inventions, a copying machine (*Corr.* # 207: AS to W. Strahan, 26.10.1780).

6. *LJ(A)* and *(B)* are remarkable tributes to that Scottish education system that Smith praises so fulsomely in *WN*. The two sets of notes, taken by members of Smith's class in consecutive academic years, are very clear and coherent, and each serves as a validity check on the other. The later one is not copied from the earlier, because they report the lectures in a different order. Most of the students in Smith's class were boys aged between fourteen and seventeen – in modern British terms, between Key Stage 3 and AS (in England) or Higher (in Scotland).
7. Brown, Edinburgh Enlightenment Lecture transcript.
8. In the second edition Smith deleted 'nation that is governed by shopkeepers' and substituted the slightly less offensive 'nation whose government is influenced by shopkeepers'.

5

The Invisible Hand and the Helping Hand

Three of Gordon Brown's questions in the Edinburgh speech which set the framework for this book are:

> Is Smith, the author of the invisible hand, also the Smith of the helping hand?
>
> Or is the Smith of 'The Theory of Moral Sentiments' the Jekyll to 'The Wealth of Nations'' Hyde?
>
> Is it possible two centuries and more on from his famous work 'The Wealth of Nations' to find a way of reconciling his apparently contrasting views: that social behaviour is influenced by sympathy and that economic behaviour is motivated by self-interest?

The answers to the questions are closely linked. The second and third are really the same question, which I will tackle first in this chapter as it is desirable to get misconceptions out of the way first. So: is it correct that Smith believes that social behaviour is influenced by sympathy and that economic behaviour is motivated by self-interest? If so, does that mean that his two books, *TMS* and *WN*, in some sense contradict each other? The proposition that they do contradict one another was raised in nineteenth-century Germany, and became an academic industry of some size – known as *das Adam Smith-Problem*.

DAS ADAM SMITH-PROBLEM IST KEIN PROBLEM

The Adam Smith Problem, stated briefly, is that *TMS* appears to recommend and endorse sympathy, whereas *WN* appears to recommend and endorse selfishness. Therefore, it is argued, the two books are inconsistent. To understand how this took on its independent life as a 'problem' we need to pick up our earlier story about the changing reputation of Smith and *WN* as the eighteenth century gave way to the nineteenth.

Smith lived through the American Revolution and died in the first year of the French Revolution. He approved of some acts of the American rebels (such as their rejection of the taxes imposed by the shopkeeper government of Great Britain for the sole benefit of a monopoly trading company). He did not comment directly on others, which nevertheless flowed logically from the political thought of the Scottish Enlightenment. The Constitution, ratified just before Smith's death, and the Bill of Rights, ratified just after, derive unmistakably from the classrooms of Edinburgh, Glasgow and Aberdeen, though not specifically from Smith's own thought – with the interesting exception that James Madison's arguments for political pluralism began life as arguments for religious pluralism, and they are unmistakably Smith's arguments. Other aspects again Smith clearly disliked. As an adviser to the British government in 1767 and again in 1778, Smith thought that the Americans were taking a free ride on the defence of their western frontier, which the British were funding to the benefit of the Americans.

As to the French Revolution, Smith's attitude is hard to judge. He must have sent the final sections of his last work – the new material for the sixth edition of *TMS* – to the printer at the latest in around November 1789, when the French Revolution had not been under way for long enough for most people to be confident how it would turn out. Smith's friend Edmund Burke was already sure (and broadly right, after deducting his romantic excesses about Marie Antoinette) that it would turn out disastrously when he published his *Reflections on the Revolution in France* in 1790 (Burke [1790] 1993). These *Reflections* were a riposte to another admirer of Smith, Richard Price (although Smith did not reciprocate Price's admiration for him). So followers of Smith could, and did, take opposite views about the French Revolution. What is clear is that, when Francophobia spread across Pitt's Britain after war with France broke out in 1792, it was important for Smith's friends to distance him posthumously from France (this is discussed in Chapter 6). Thus was born the legend of Smith the anti-revolutionary.

It was Smith the anti-revolutionary promoter of capitalism that most nineteenth-century readers thought they were reading. These readers included the pioneer socialists, who first flourished in France and Germany. Smith became well known to German speakers quite quickly; already by 1800, there were two German translations each of *TMS* and of *WN* (Tribe 2002, p. 120). There is much to be said about Karl Marx's reading of Smith: notably that, although Marx seems to have thought Steuart a better economist, he admired Smith's labour theory of value and his account of the alienation caused by the monotony of factory work – the downside of the division of labour.

However, it was not Marx but a rival faction of socialists who first raised the 'Adam Smith Problem'. Bruno Hildebrand, an ethical (that is, idealist) socialist, complained in 1848 that *WN* was a hymn to selfishness. This misconception may have been partly due to a faulty translation, which garbled the 'invisible hand' passage of *WN* into praise of self-interest (Tribe 2002, p. 138). As the most extreme proponent of the Adam Smith Problem put it:

> Smith was an Idealist, as long as he lived in England [sic] under the influence of Hutcheson and Hume. After living in France for three years and coming into close touch with the Materialism that prevailed there, he returned to England [sic] a Materialist. This is the simple explanation of the contrast between [*TMS* and *WN*]. (W. Skarzynski, 1878, quoted by Oncken 1897, p. 445)

If ever a beautiful hypothesis was destroyed by an inconvenient fact, it is Skarzynski's. As early as 1897, Oncken could point out that the discovery of *LJ(B)* by Edwin Cannan in 1895 instantly destroyed the hypothesis that Smith changed his mind about selfishness when he visited France. *LJ(B)* shows that Smith had worked out the essential arguments of *WN* before he left Glasgow. To me the survival of the 'Adam Smith Problem' is truly a miracle – as miraculous as Hume described the belief in miracles as being. Frequent cross-references between the original *TMS* and *WN*, and the 1790 revisions to *TMS* would (and should) have shown that they are part of a consistent body of thought even if the linking evidence, first in *LJ(B)* and then in *LJ(A)*, had not turned up. Therefore, I believe that the notorious 'Adam Smith Problem' is exactly what his Glasgow editors have dismissed it as being: 'a pseudo-problem based on ignorance and misunderstanding' (Raphael and Macfie 1976, p. 20). Nevertheless, Gordon Brown raised it once again in his Edinburgh speech, and there are scholars who believe it is still a live issue (see, for example, Dickey 1986; Haakonssen 2002, p. xxiv). For the life of me I cannot see how or why.

The basic mistake made by those who believe that there is an Adam Smith problem is to assume that both books are directly normative: that *TMS* 'recommends' sympathy, and that *WN* 'recommends' selfishness. This is nonsense. Both books are analytic, albeit with normative implications. As a piece of analytical sociology, *TMS* asks 'What is a moral sentiment?' – what is it that makes us recognise something as a *moral* rather than any other kind of sentiment? Smith implies, or states, that better education, more frugality and (in *WN*, not *TMS*) religious pluralism would make people more moral. But it is not the task of the philosopher to make people moral, or mutually sympathetic, either in the ordinary use of that word or in Smith's extended use of it as a technical term. Recall that Smith makes this distinction in the text of *TMS* itself:

> [T]he present inquiry is not concerning a matter of right, if I may say so, but concerning a matter of fact. We are not at present examining upon what principles a perfect being would approve of the punishment of bad actions; but upon what principles so weak and imperfect a creature as man actually and in fact approves of it. (*TMS* II.i.5.10)

Admittedly, Smith is not entirely consistent; other parts of *TMS* are more normative.

WN is likewise an analytic inquiry. As its full title states, it asks what *causes* the wealth of nations. Smith answers: allowing the division of labour to generate endogenous growth, assisted by good institutions. The good institutions should include a good legal framework, efficient national defence, public works and the provision of public goods – or *Justice*, *Revenue* and *Arms* in Smith's own more elegant headings. Again, and in absolute harmony with *TMS*, Smith shows his taste for frugal egalitarianism. Frugality promotes capital growth, and therefore increases the wealth of nations (*contra* Mandeville). The 'prudent man' of *WN* is indeed the 'frugal man' of *TMS*. However, frugal egalitarianism is Adam Smith's *taste*, not his policy recommendation, nor indeed his moral recommendation. Frugality is a virtue, but it is a subsidiary virtue to sympathy and benevolence. Smith's policy recommendations attack institutions that destroy wealth, or liberty, or both, and promote institutions which do the opposite. Among the institutions that destroy wealth or liberty are rent-seeking bodies such as trade associations, chartered companies and magistrates and governments in so far as they are captured by those rent-seeking interests.

Therefore, the strong version of the Adam Smith Problem is certainly bogus. Smith does not 'recommend' sympathy in *TMS*, and he most certainly does not 'recommend' selfishness in *WN*. What about the weaker version: that social behaviour is *influenced* by sympathy and that economic behaviour is *motivated* by self-interest (my italics)? To answer this, we need to take a closer look at the notorious invisible hand and at the circumstances where Smith is prepared to suggest that governments should offer a helping hand.

SMITH AND THE INVISIBLE HAND

It is among philosophers and historians of ideas that the undead Adam Smith Problem continues to stalk through the common room. At least this has the spin-off benefit that it continues to produce interesting refutations. One such is the recent book by James Otteson, *Adam Smith's Marketplace of Life* (Otteson 2002). Otteson opens (pp. 3–11) by pointing out that in *TMS* sympathy is not directly a motive for action. It works indirectly by making the observer ask 'What would I wish to happen if I were in the position of the person in trouble whom I am observing?' The answer is typically 'I would like friends, acquaintances, even strangers, to help me.' Therefore sympathy leads to benevolence – to a helping hand, if you will. More generally, the impartial spectator principle generates rules of morality:

> As to love our neighbour as we love ourselves is the great law of Christianity, so it is the great precept of nature to love ourselves only as we love our neighbour, or what comes to the same thing, as our neighbour is capable of loving us. (*TMS* I.i.5.5)

Smith believes that, although morality is a human construct, humans have an innate moral sense. More than once, in passages in *TMS* to which Otteson draws attention, Smith insists that even the hardest criminal has feelings of remorse, which Smith attributes to the criminal's understanding of the impartial spectator's view of his actions (*TMS* III.2.9; V.2.1 – 'the sentiments of moral approbation and disapprobation, are founded on the strongest and most vigorous passions of human nature; and though they may be somewhat warpt, cannot be entirely perverted'; cf. Otteson 2002, pp. 240–57). There are no psychopaths in the world of *TMS*. Otteson argues that for Smith this innate sense of morality is God-given, and that Smith is therefore a deist in some fairly strong sense. I disagree. Smith's idea of an innate sense of morality is very like Noam Chomsky's sense of a deep language structure, innate in all humans (see, for example, Chomsky 1965). Whether or not Chomsky's argument is sound, it does not depend on God. Nor, I believe, does Smith's.

Smith is too optimistic about psychopaths. They do exist, just as people with autism and Asperger's syndrome exist. And in any case, Smith does not believe that benevolence alone makes the world go round. It is hard to feel as much benevolence for an unknown peasant in China as for my next-door neighbour; and it is not blameworthy not to do so. But there is a back-up: the principle of Hayek's spontaneous order, or if you will Smith's invisible hand. I treat these phrases as equivalent. This principle, according to Otteson, is the 'marketplace of life' that is a unifying theme in Smith. Indeed, it is not confined to *TMS* and *WN*, but also finds expression in Smith's essay on the first formation of languages, first published in 1761 and from 1767 onwards added as an appendix to successive editions of *TMS*. In this piece of 'conjectural history', as Dugald Stewart called it, Smith hypothesises that general nouns arise out of particular nouns by unplanned coordination: an easy solution, Smith thinks, to a dilemma that the 'ingenious and eloquent M. Rousseau of Geneva' had found insoluble. Where Rousseau thinks that the origin of generic words is inexplicable, Smith retorts, 'What constitutes a species is merely a number of objects, bearing a certain degree of resemblance to one another, and on that account denominated by a single appellation' (*Considerations concerning the First Formation of Languages* § 2, in *LRBL* pp. 204–5). Nobody (and no superhuman being) invented the rules of language; they are a matter of convenience, a spontaneous order, the result of an invisible hand.

Therefore, although Rothschild (2001), among others, is right to emphasise that the *phrase* 'invisible hand' appears only three times in the whole corpus of Smith's work, she perhaps underplays the underlying *concept.*

It is a very subtle concept, beyond the grasp of many people in Smith's time and since. We observe a complex form of human interaction – be it a moral code, a set of language rules or a set of economic relationships. As it is so complex, we infer that someone – a highly intelligent lawgiver, or a group of lawgivers, or perhaps a superior being – must have designed it. In Smith's day, that argument seemed to apply with even more force to the natural world. Shortly after Smith's death, the philosopher and theologian William Paley (1802) gave it its definitive form. If, never having seen a watch before, you found a watch lying in a field, Paley argues, you would realise that something so ingenious, all of whose cogs and springs combine to achieve the purpose of telling the time, must have had an intelligent designer. All the more, therefore, when you observe something marvellously complex in nature, such as the mammal (or for that matter the insect) eye, you are forced to conclude that it too had an intelligent designer. For Paley, the intelligent designer of nature is the Christian God.

Intelligent design versus *spontaneous order* – that dichotomy is fundamental in social and in natural science. In moral philosophy, Smith had learnt from Hutcheson and Hume that the idea that God directly wrote moral rules is empty, tautological or incoherent. *TMS* therefore presents a rival theory, which mostly argues for the spontaneous emergence of moral codes, though as just noted Smith retains a weakly deistic conception that moral ideas are innately implanted into all human beings.[1] In economics, Smith does not need even weak deism. There is no intelligent design behind economic exchange. Smith sets the scene by observing that

> Two greyhounds, in running down the same hare, have sometimes the appearance of acting in some sort of concert . . . [But] Nobody ever saw a dog make a fair and deliberate exchange of one bone for another with another dog. (*WN* I.ii.2; cf. Otteson 2002, p. 275)

Fair and deliberate exchange is a human invention. Leaving aside what does make greyhounds cooperate (a surprisingly tricky problem in evolutionary biology, not satisfactorily solved until the late twentieth century, by W. D. Hamilton and others[2]), Smith goes on to argue, in one of his most famous passages,

> It is not from the benevolence of the butcher, the brewer, or the baker, that we expect our dinner, but from their regard to their self-interest. We address ourselves, not to their humanity but to their self-love, and never talk to them of our own necessities but of their advantages. (*WN* I.ii.2)

This is so simple, and so profound, that I think that it alone suffices to rescue Smith from Schumpeter's (1954, p. 184) notorious charge of unoriginality. Economic exchange is an unforced bargain (assuming that I am not starving, and that the butcher, baker and brewer are not members of trading companies with monopoly rights, nor of a friendly society that meets every Tuesday night for merriment and diversion). When I buy meat from the butcher, I would rather have the meat than the money I hand over; the butcher would rather have my money than keep his meat for a higher bidder. The transaction does not take place unless each of us, *independently*, thinks, 'I am better off as a result of this transaction'. More than a century after Smith, this insight was formalised as *Paretian exchange*, named after the Italian economist and sociologist Vilfredo Pareto (1848–1923). Furthermore, and crucially, no government can do better than can private individuals in voluntary exchanges. No government official can possibly know either my schedule of preferences better than I do, or the butcher's better than he does. *Where there is no market failure* (a vital qualification, of which Smith was aware, and which I discuss in the next section), government intervention in market exchange cannot make things better, and may make them worse. Furthermore, nobody invented or designed this 'marketplace of life' – to return to Otteson's title phrase. Individual market transactions can arise through spontaneous coordination, or, if you prefer, an invisible hand, although the market needs to be secured by a regime of property rights.

To many people, even many sophisticated people, the idea that in any sense an economy works 'best' as the aggregation of unplanned spontaneous market transactions is as bizarre as the idea that the eye does not have an intelligent designer.[3] Yet the clear implication of Smith's reasoning is that unplanned market transactions – and *only* unplanned market transactions – will take us to a point on the Pareto frontier, which is defined as the set of points that share the property that nobody can be made better off without somebody else being made worse off. The invisible hand can get us to the Pareto frontier (if market failures can be corrected). It does not tell us where on the Pareto frontier we should be. To move from one place to another on that frontier may require the helping hand of government.

Smith did not write much about natural science – his main writings in what we would now call the philosophy of science are his essays on the history of astronomy and of physics. And, as he wrote a century before Darwin, he had no way of rebutting (even supposing that he would have wanted to) Paley's argument that the complexity of the eye can only be explained by intelligent design. Darwinian evolution and Mendelian genetics have between them shown that Paley's watch analogy fails to hold (Dawkins 1986). We cannot imagine a watch without an intelligent designer, but we can, and Darwinians say should, imagine the evolution of even eyes without positing an intelligent designer of them.

At one level, 'what would Smith have thought of Darwin?' is a silly game to play. At another, it is not, because Smith gives us a particularly clear clue in the first in time, and least noticed, of the three 'invisible hand' passages. Talking of pre-scientific societies, he says:

> Does the earth pour forth an exuberant harvest? It is owing to the indulgence of Ceres. Does the vine yield a plentiful vintage? It flows from the bounty of Bacchus. Do either refuse their presents? It is ascribed to the displeasure of those offended deities . . . Hence the origin of Polytheism, and of that vulgar superstition which ascribes all the irregular events of nature to the favour or displeasure of intelligent, though invisible, beings . . . For it may be observed, that in all Polytheistic religions . . . it is the irregular events of nature only that are ascribed to the agency and power of their gods. Fire burns, and water refreshes; heavy bodies descend, and lighter substances fly upwards, by the necessity of their own nature; nor was the invisible hand of Jupiter ever apprehended to be employed in those matters. But thunder and lightning, storms and sunshine, those more irregular events, were ascribed to his favour, or his anger. (*Astronomy* III. 2, in *EPS* pp. 49–50)

The implication is that the more of nature falls under a scientific explanation, the less need there is to invoke Jupiter, or any other god. Any invocation of a god always pushes back the question of interest to 'How and why was Jupiter created with the properties and attributes that you say he has: and how could you possibly know that your answer is correct?' By Smith's time, there was a scientific explanation of thunder and lightning, thanks to his acquaintance Benjamin Franklin. Now nobody need say the gods were angry to explain a thunderstorm. In Smith's time, the deep mysteries of how plants and animals assumed their wonderfully differentiated, and sometimes mutually dependent, forms were unsolved. It is plausible to infer from the *Astronomy* that, when a solution came along, Smith would have been glad to see the invisible hand of Jupiter marginalised yet further. I do not agree that Smith was an atheist; but I am prepared to accept that he might have been an atheist, or at any rate one who needed no hypotheses regarding God, if Darwin and Mendel had come along first.

SMITH AND THE HELPING HAND

Once we have disposed of the Adam Smith pseudo-problem, it is easy to see that Smith believed that people would often naturally offer a helping hand to those who needed it. Indeed, as we noted in Chapter 2, Smith seems to have behaved in just this way himself, according to Mrs Dunlop of Stewarton, who claimed acquaintanceship with both Smith and Robert Burns. On hearing of the poet's plight, Smith, who had already subscribed for four copies of Burns's collected poems, offered to get him a job as a Salt Officer, 'which he said was just what he would have wished for himself had he been in narrow circumstances' (Mrs Dunlop to Burns, 29.03.87 – see Chapter 2).

You cannot, however, rely on benevolence in economic relationships, and even self-interest by no means always benefits everyone. In the policy advice contained in *WN* (especially Book V), Smith offers a helping hand to the poor in two ways. The first is negative: his beady eye on rent-seeking conspiracies against the public leads him to see that in the power structure of the eighteenth century, these conspiracies are likely to be perpetrated by landowners, merchants and capitalists, at the expense of the poor. The second is positive. Smith's analysis of market failure justifies market-correcting state intervention in the economy. Some of this is to the benefit of the poor.

In *LJ* and *WN*, Adam Smith displays sympathy for working men and no particular sympathy for their employers. As noted above, he praises the machines of the Industrial Revolution 'invented by some common workman'. He regards the merriment and diversion of local merchants with the same beady eye as the monopolistic conspiracies of the East India Company, and regards the influence of each on government as pernicious. Many people are vaguely familiar with the 'nation of shopkeepers' passage I quoted above; but it really does repay reading three or four times so as to see just how venomous it is, especially in its original version.

When the Commons held a debate on a proposal to set a statutory minimum wage in 1795, both sides quoted Adam Smith in their support. Samuel Whitbread pointed out that Smith had written in favour of regulation tilted towards the workman, and more generally on behalf of high wages. Against him, Prime Minister Pitt called Smith in aid of his argument for removing restrictions on the free movement of the unemployed. They were both admirers, but Rothschild (2001, p. 63) concludes that 'Whitbread's Smith is in many respects closer to the "real" Smith, or the Smith of the real *Wealth of Nations*'. Samuel Whitbread did not get his statutory minimum wage in 1795; it arrived in the UK only with the National Minimum Wage Act 1998.

In his Edinburgh and Kirkcaldy speeches, therefore, Gordon Brown expressed his frustration at the 'capture' of Adam Smith by the right. Many politicians, scholars and lobbyists of the political right have claimed Adam Smith: for instance, in the UK, Margaret Thatcher[4] and the Adam Smith Institute; in central Europe, Vaclav Klaus, the Prime Minister, and later President, of the Czech Republic whose enthusiasm for an Adam Smith filtered through the lenses of Friedrich Hayek and the Mont Pelerin Society is well known.[5] In the USA, the most eminent historian of economic thought misrepresented Smith. Schumpeter (1954, pp. 182–94) revived an ancient controversy (see, for example, Kennedy 2005, pp. 241–8) when he attacked Smith as unoriginal. The strongest evidence for the capture of Adam Smith by the American right is the lavish support he gets from the Liberty Fund of Indianapolis – to which all scholars are in debt. As in earlier generations the official Soviet media and their overseas publishers subsidised remarkably cheap editions of Marx and Engels to spread the word, so does the Liberty Fund subsidise the magnificent Glasgow edition of the works of Adam Smith. The Liberty Fund, as its own statements and the other publications it sponsors make clear, is a staunchly conservative-libertarian think tank.

Gordon Brown's Adam Smith is a very different thinker from Margaret Thatcher's or Vaclav Klaus's. In 2003 Brown published a closely argued article about the roles of the state and the market. Originally given as a speech to the Social Market Foundation, it was later published in an academic journal (Brown 2003). It is not the most quoted of Brown's speeches since becoming UK Chancellor, but it ought to be. It repays close reading because it may not be until the second or third read-through that the reader will understand that Brown's views are a pure distillation from Adam Smith's views on 'police' and 'revenue'.

According to Brown,

> in almost every area of current controversy . . . the question is, at root, what are the best relationships between individuals, markets and government to advance the public interest . . . Take industrial policy. The essential question is whether . . . the state should replace market forces where they fail (the old

> Labour policy); whether the state should refuse to intervene at all even in the face of market failure (the old Tory *laissez-faire*); whether we should second-guess the market through a corporatist policy of supporting national champions (a policy I also reject); or whether, as I would propose, the best industrial policy for success in a global economy is to help markets work better . . . [E]ven when there is public sector provision, there can be contestability . . . [T]o have faith in markets cannot justify our sidestepping fundamental moral questions. (Brown 2003, pp. 266–7)

Brown went on to discuss 'Enhancing markets in the public interest' (which could be a gloss on the parts of *LJ* that were never published), 'the pursuit of equity' and 'the limits of markets' (likewise, a gloss on *TMS*) before moving away from these Smithian themes. Of course, I can be accused of selective quotation, but I hope these suffice to show that Brown's ideas are suffused with Adam Smith's. The opening section of Brown's Social Market Foundation lecture is a précis of the 'Revenue' section of Book V of *WN*. True, Smith does not use the word 'contestability'[6], but he certainly uses the concept, especially in his discussions of universities, canals and highways.

What exactly is the problem of market failure as it appeared to Smith? On the one hand, product markets can fail if they are deliberately obstructed by governments of shopkeepers, or by contrivances to raise prices and other conspiracies against the public. The labour market can fail if the magistrates, advised by the masters, obstruct combinations (that is, trade unions), or set maximum wages, or prevent people from moving around in search of work or benefits. All of these were common practices in Smith's time and they did not die out in the UK or other industrialised countries for a long time. In Third World countries they are still prevalent. The capital market can fail if the government regulates banks or the money supply in an inappropriate way. This sort of market failure is best addressed by a good structure of law, assigning property rights clearly and giving remedies for breaches of them. Smith did not set out his thoughts on this in final form. His book expanding the 'justice' segment of his Glasgow lectures was one of the 'two great works upon the anvil' that he told La Rochefoucauld in 1787 that he was still working on: namely, 'a sort of theory and History of Law and Government' (*Corr.* # 248). None of this saw the light of day; and whatever work was in progress at the time of Smith's death will have been among the manuscripts burnt by Black and Hutton on 11 July 1790.

Griswold (1999, p. 37) has argued that the theory and history of law and government was never published because it could not be written – because Smith's thoughts on these subjects were too imperfectly formed and perhaps even contradictory. Whatever may be true of law and government as a whole, this would not have been true on the narrower subjects of contract, tort and property rights. There are enough clues in *LJ* and in *WN* to establish what Smith thought about protecting property rights in the face of rent-seeking and other forms of positive market failure. Farmers have inadequate property rights in their land to have the correct incentive to improve it, when much of the benefit will go in increased rent to the landowner (*WN* III.ii.20). Under feudalism, urban merchants sought charters in order to protect their property rights in trade from depredation by feudal landlords, but this set up mutual hatred between the two groups:

> The princes who lived upon the worst terms with their barons, seem accordingly to have been the most liberal in grants of this kind [namely, charters and rights to build town walls] to their burghs. King John of England, for example, appears to have been a most munificent benefactor to his towns. (*WN* III.iii.8–9)

Modern commercial society is both fairer and more efficient than feudal society, because 'A tradesman to retain your custom may perhaps vote for you in an election, but you need not expect that he will attend you to battle' (*LJ(A)* i.118). Smith is hostile to primogeniture and entail,[7] because they obstruct free decisions about the transfer of property even after death – and the dead, who are not people, can have no rights. For the same reason, he is sceptical of the idea that a will should be binding (*LJ(A)* i.135–48; i.164–7).

Therefore we have a fair idea of the remedies that Smith proposed for the varieties of market failure that we might label market abuse. He wished to see deregulation, dismantling of monopoly rights and a fair and efficient law of contract and succession. The other sort of market failure – failure of economic agents to do things that would be mutually beneficial – was described in Chapter 4. As Hume had pointed out, two men may coordinate their activities to drain a meadow that they own in common (although even this is not always true, otherwise there would be no boundary disputes about garden fences). But a thousand commoners cannot practically coordinate their efforts, and therefore an improvement which would benefit them all fails to happen, unless 'political society' – that is, government – intervenes. As we have already noted, the list of government activities that Smith believes are sanctioned by this argument is quite long, and he devotes a substantial part of *WN* Book V to them. The first of these activities is national defence. This is a public good, although Smith does not explicitly couch his argument in those terms (*WN* V.i.a). But if anybody is protected by the Navy, everybody is: which means that nobody has an individual incentive to contribute. Indeed, so strongly does Smith promote the government role in national defence that he seems to contradict himself. In Book IV, Chapter ii, he calls the English Navigation Acts, which restricted trade to English ships in order to make English sailors more ready to fight in the Navy, 'the wisest of all the commercial regulations of England', because 'defence . . . is of much more importance than opulence'. On the other hand, as already noted, he is scornful of the bounty for herring busses that was introduced in part for the same purpose of training sailors, noting that it had led some venturers to fit out their boats to catch the bounty, not the herring (IV.v.a.32).

After defence, the next most important public good is 'the expence of justice'. In earlier sections of *WN*, as well as in *LJ*, Smith has given extensive reasons for believing that the privatised, or delegated, justice of feudal or allodial times was unfair and inefficient. Therefore justice is one monopoly that should be reserved to the sovereign. After justice come 'publick Works and publick Institutions'. Public works has the same meaning as today – infrastructures such as roads, bridges and canals. The only practicable way to construct a road or a canal is for the state either to build it directly (which Smith does not support) or to confer monopoly rights on the promoters to collect tolls. Thus, to this day, the tolls to be collected on certain bridges, like the Swinford toll bridge over the Thames near Oxford, are controlled by eighteenth-century Acts of Parliament. At Swinford the toll notices display the title of the Act empowering the tollkeepers to collect 5p from each car that crosses.

The main public institution that Smith discusses is education. We have already looked at this discussion, in the context of Smith's views on church and state, and on the superiority of elementary education in poor Scotland to that in rich England. Education, for Smith, serves multiple purposes. One is the improvement of the human capital stock; another is to spread scientific knowledge; yet another is to counter the monotony which the division of labour brings to the working life of the employee:

> The man whose whole life is spent in performing a few simple operations, of which the effects, too, are perhaps always the same, or very nearly the same, has no occasion to exert his understanding, or to exercise his invention, in finding out expedients for removing difficulties which never occur. He naturally loses, therefore, the habit of such exertion, and generally becomes as stupid and ignorant as it is possible for a human creature to become. (*WN* V.i.f.50)

Karl Marx did not discover the alienation of labour. Adam Smith was well aware of it, and his remedy, or at least palliative, is a liberal education, including the subsidising of cultural events (*WN* V.i.f.61). When the director of the Adam Smith Institute says 'We should privatize the BBC. The sale would earn a fortune for taxpayers, and we would all be spared the £126 annual licence fee',[8] he is not necessarily being faithful to his master.

The next, related, public good is regulation of religious doctrine, which is where Smith sets out his arguments against church establishment and in favour of pluralism. Finally, in what is surely a sarcastically short three-paragraph chapter (V.i.h), comes 'the Expence of supporting the Dignity of the Sovereign'. Whereas education merits thirty pages and religious instruction thirty-five, the public good of maintaining George III in monarchical style merits half a page.

PAYING FOR THE HELPING HAND

In a modern economy, taxation has at least two purposes. One is to pay for public goods (and for any other services that the state chooses to provide); the other is to redistribute wealth and/or income. We generally think of the second purpose as modern, dating back only to the foundation of the welfare state. In the UK, taxation for explicitly redistributive purposes can be dated back to the tax and public expenditure reforms of the Liberal government of 1906–14 (McLean and Nou 2005). But, in fact, Smith's discussion encompasses both purposes of taxation.

He opens, as noted, with four 'maxims with regard to taxes in general'. Each maxim is given in a single sentence, although a gloss on that sentence then follows. The headline sentences are:

> I. The subjects of every state ought to contribute towards the support of the government, as nearly as possible, in proportion to their respective abilities; that is, in proportion to the revenue which they respectively enjoy under the protection of the state.
>
> II. The tax which each individual is bound to pay ought to be certain, and not arbitrary.
>
> III. Every tax ought to be levied at the time, or in the manner in which it is most likely to be convenient for the contributor to pay it.
>
> IV. Every tax ought to be so contrived as both to take out and to keep out of the pockets of the people as little as possible, over and above what it brings into the publick treasury of the state.

I commented on 'maxim' or canon I in Chapter 4. Payment 'in proportion to their respective abilities' does not necessarily imply taxation as a fixed proportion of income for two reasons. The ability of a person living at subsistence level to contribute towards the support of the government is zero. Therefore any well-designed tax should have a zero rate for the poorest. Even if the rate is proportionate for all taxpayers other than the poorest, the overall impact of such a tax is 'progressive' in the public finance sense – that is, the average rate of tax is higher for the rich than for the poor. In so far as the proceeds are spent on public goods that benefit all equally, its impact is redistributive. But here comes Smith's second point. The part of maxim I that comes after the semi-colon is one of Smith's easily overlooked pieces of deep subversion. We all enjoy our revenue 'under the protection of the state'. If there was no state, there would be no protection of property rights; and the life of mankind would, as Hobbes memorably put it, be 'solitary, poor, nasty, brutish, and short' (*Leviathan*, Chapter XIII). Public goods such as defence and the legal system therefore protect more revenue of the rich than of the poor. Therefore there is a justification for taxing the rich more heavily than the poor – and Smith does make such a move when he suggests that ground-rents, which are unearned, should be taxed more heavily than other sources of income.

Maxim II warns against privatising tax-gathering. This had long been abolished in all parts of Britain, but was a prominent feature of public finance in France (not to mention biblical Palestine – that is why publicans[9] and sinners are grouped together in the New Testament). Successive French monarchs had delegated the right to levy taxes to tax-farmers in return for an up-front payment. Thus they gained ready cash to fight wars or build palaces, but at the expense of a continuing, and privatised, tax burden on the population. The Farmers-General built a wall round Paris to ensure that they collected their revenue. This naturally became a symbolic target of the Revolution (Schama 1989, pp. 71–9).

Maxim III privileges taxes on land or on houses (that is, in UK parlance, property rates), and also consumption taxes such as (modern) VAT. As Smith explains, rates are usually collected at the same time as rents, so that the taxpayer knows when to expect to pay them. Consumption taxes are voluntary to the degree that the taxpayer can choose to buy or not to buy the taxed article. This implicitly attacks consumption taxes on the necessaries of life, such as salt. But salt taxes were so temptingly easy to collect that they stayed in place for centuries (the *Sale e tabacci* signs above Italian shops are remnants of this regime still visible today). Robert Burns might have become a Salt Officer at Smith's suggestion. They also gave a powerful incentive to smuggling, which is in Smith's next point.

Maxim IV advocates economy in tax-gathering. Taxes may be expensive to collect in several ways, according to Smith. They may require numerous staff to collect them. They may 'obstruct the industry of the people' by deterring them from undertaking valuable economic activities. They may impose disproportionate penalties such as the draconian penalties in force against smugglers. The execution of a Fife smuggler in Edinburgh in 1736 provoked the Porteous riots, when a crowd said to contain many Fifers lynched the captain of the Edinburgh town guard in revenge (Ross 1995, p. 23). This system of taxes and penalties was doubly perverse according to Smith:

> an injudicious tax offers a great temptation to smuggling. But the penalties of smuggling must rise in proportion to the temptation. The law, contrary to all the ordinary principles of justice, first creates the temptation, and then punishes those who yield to it; and it commonly enhances the punishment too in proportion to the very circumstance which ought certainly to alleviate it, the temptation to commit the crime. (*WN* V.ii.b.6)

So speaks the son of the Kirkcaldy Collector of Customs and the future Commissioner of Customs for Scotland. Finally, bad taxes may 'subject . . . the people to the frequent visits, and the odious examination of the tax-gatherers'.

This shows that Dugald Stewart's summary of Smith's programme as 'easy taxes' – quoting a now-lost early document of Smith's – can be misleading. When he came to flesh out his account, Smith showed that by 'easy' he did not just mean 'low'. He meant 'as low as possible consistent with their purposes'.

It is entirely possible that Adam Smith shaped the UK tax schedule in one or two ways. He says that owner-occupied houses ought to be taxed according to the 'rent which an equitable arbitration might judge them likely to bring, if leased to a tenant' (*WN* V.ii.e.8). In a footnote to the third edition of *WN* he adds, 'Since the first publication of this book, a tax nearly upon the above-mentioned principles has been imposed' – which it was by Acts of 1778 and 1779, exactly at the time that Smith was active as an economic adviser to Alexander Wedderburn. The taxation of owner-occupied houses by their annual value was achieved by two taxes – domestic rates (abolished by Prime Minister Margaret Thatcher in 1990) and Schedule A income tax (abolished by Conservative Chancellor Selwyn Lloyd in 1961). If it is true that the 1778 and 1779 Acts were due to Smith, it is nicely ironic that two Conservatives, one of them a professed admirer of Smith, should have abolished taxation of imputed rent in favour of less satisfactory property taxes.

There was no income tax in Smith's day; and he objects to direct taxes on wage labourers on the grounds that either they would be passed on, through higher wages and higher prices, so that the true incidence would fall on the consumer, or they would lead to a fall in the demand for wage labour, and hence higher unemployment (*WN* V.ii.i.1–3). However, by 1798 Smith's admirer Pitt the Younger had run out of money to pay for the French wars. He therefore introduced the first income tax in his Budget of that year, when he said that income tax 'looks to the equality of the tax, and the general efficacy of the measure'. There was a sliding rate of zero on incomes below £60 a year, 1/20 (a shilling in the pound) on annual incomes between £60 and £200, and 1/10 (two shillings in the pound) on annual incomes above £200 (Hague 2004, pp. 433–4). This schedule fits with Smith's maxims as well as any income tax can. It exempts the working class and it is progressive, in accordance with the radical egalitarian interpretation of maxim I. Pitt's income tax was abolished at the end of the Napoleonic Wars. It was revived by another of the great figures in British public finance, Sir Robert Peel, in 1842, and has been with us ever since. It is not fanciful to see the hand of Adam Smith in the schedules and rates of income tax in the United Kingdom.

It is, I hope, already clear that a great deal of the philosophy and economics of Adam Smith is relevant to policy-making in the twenty-first century. I return to that in Chapter 7. But first, it is time to look systematically at the interactions between Smith and the Americans, and between Smith and the French.

NOTES

1. Therefore I disagree with both those such as Otteson (2002), who give a fairly strong role to God in Smith's thought, and those such as Minowitz (1993), who claim that Smith was an atheist.
2. For introductions see Dawkins (1976), Axelrod and Hamilton (1981) and Axelrod (1984).
3. Although one little irony, as has been pointed out, is that Christian conservatives tend to agree with Smith that the market does not have an intelligent designer, but at the same time agree with Paley that the eye does.
4. 'The Scots invented Thatcherism, long before I was thought of' – Margaret Thatcher, 1988, quoted by Young 1990, p. 528. Young thinks she may have been referring to Hume as well as to Smith, but I find this wildly implausible. David Hume and Margaret Thatcher really do not belong in the same room. I cannot think of any Scot other than Adam Smith that she may have had in mind – except perhaps Samuel Smiles (1812–1904), the apostle of Self Help from Haddington.

5. For Hayek's Adam Smith see Gamble 1996, pp. 25–32. For the Mont Pelerin Society see Hartwell 1995.
6. A market is *contestable* if an entrant has access to all production techniques available to the incumbents, is not prohibited from wooing the incumbent's customers and if entry decisions can be reversed without cost. This definition comes from W. J. Baumol, who first defined the concept. *Contestability* has not yet (July 2005) entered the *Oxford English Dictionary*, but has entered a briefing note from one of the UK's examination boards for advanced school students of economics. See www.edexcel.org.uk/ VirtualContent/70279.pdf.
7. Primogeniture means the exclusive right of the eldest son to inherit property. Smith believes that it is a reasonable rule for royal successions but not for property inheritance. Entail means fixing the line of descent of a property beyond the next generation.

   > There is no maxim more generally acknowledged than that the earth is the property of each generation. That the former generation should restrict them in the use of it is altogether absurd . . . [P]ersons not yet born he [the testator] can have no affection for. The utmost stretch of our piety can not reasonably extend to them. (*LJ(A)* i.165–6)

   Thomas Jefferson expressed the same view – independently, as he cannot have seen *LJ*. See Appleby and Ball 1999, pp. 593–8 ('The earth belongs in usufruct to the living' – letter to Madison, 06.09.1789).
8. Source: Dr Eamonn Butler, in Adam Smith Institute blog, 22.09.05, at www.adamsmith.org/culture/index.php/blog/individual/goodnight_auntie/.
9. The oldest meaning of *publican* in English is direct from Latin usage: 'One who farmed the public taxes; hence, a tax-gatherer'. This is the meaning found in the Authorised Version of the Bible. The meaning 'One who keeps a public house' is first attested only in 1728. Source: *Oxford English Dictionary* on-line edition, s.v. *publican*[1].

6

The French and American Smiths

SMITH ON AMERICA

In 1776, Hume wrote to Smith, 'The Duke of Bucleugh tells me, that you are very zealous in American Affairs'. He went on to say that he thought that Britain's difficulties with America were 'not as important as is commonly imagind' because business would not suffer as much as most people thought (*Corr.* # 149). On the latter point Smith agreed. But he was deeply involved – more deeply than has been generally realised – in helping to form British policy towards America. On the face of it, Smith's policy advice shows him to be no friend of the American colonies. But in other respects, his moral philosophy and economic theory was to be of great help to them.

We last observed Smith helping Chancellor of the Exchequer Townshend, the Duke's stepfather, with his tax policy in 1767 (see Chapter 1). In 1956 C. R. Fay accused Adam Smith of offering the professional advice that lost the American colonies to Great Britain. But Townshend was not Smith's only contact in government. Lord Shelburne was equally intelligent and an equally impossible colleague. He was a fellow minister with Townshend, although they did not get on well. Smith had known the family since 1758, when Shelburne had suggested that his younger brother should go to Glasgow rather than to Oxford, and that Smith should be his tutor. Smith took on this duty and discharged it conscientiously (*Corr.* ## 27–30). Hume later reported that Shelburne 'always speaks of you with regard' (DH to AS, 13.09.1763, *Corr.* # 75). Shelburne wrote that a journey from Edinburgh to London in Smith's company had made 'the difference between light and darkness through the best part of my life' (quoted by Fleischacker 2004, p. 21). In early 1767 Shelburne was the minister responsible for India as well as America. At the same time as helping Townshend over tax policy, Smith sent Shelburne a letter enclosing some travellers' tales of journeys in the South Seas, together with a proposal for a British expedition of discovery and some notes on Roman colonies, later incorporated in the chapter on colonies in *WN* (*Corr.* # 101). Nothing came of this, but it is reasonable to suppose that Smith continued to maintain contact with Shelburne on American policy after Townshend's sudden death later in the same year. In 1768 Smith thanked Shelburne for the 'kindness' he had shown to him in London; and in 1784 he presented him with a copy of *WN* (*Corr.* ## 113, 241).

Shelburne left the government in 1768 and did not return to government until 1782–3, when he was briefly and unsuccessfully Prime Minister. But his importance in this narrative is two-fold. As the patron of Pitt the Younger, he helped to create the political and intellectual bond between Smith and Pitt. And while in office, he drafted what became the Quebec Act 1774 (Watson 1960, p. 128). I am not aware that anyone has previously connected Smith with the Quebec Act, but the circumstantial evidence is strong. Shelburne was working on it while his links with Smith were at their strongest; it carries the mark of Smith the balance-of-power theorist; and it is entirely consistent with Smith's 1778 advice to another friend and minister, Wedderburn. Therefore I claim that Smith was probably involved in the ideas underlying it.

The Quebec Act 1774 has recently come to be seen as one of the most important *casus belli* of the American War of Independence. The Americans labelled it as one of the 'Intolerable Acts', and it appears in the Declaration of Independence:

> He [George III] has combined with others [Parliament] . . . for abolishing the free system of English laws in a neighbouring province, establishing therein an arbitrary government, and enlarging its boundaries, so as to render it at once an example and fit instrument for introducing the same absolute rule into these colonies. (Appleby and Ball 1999, pp. 103–4)

So what was this monstrous act? And if Smith was associated with it, does that merely prove twice over Fay's charge that Smith's professional advice lost America?

The British victory in Canada in the Seven Years' War (1756–63) had brought the whole of 'Quebec' – that is, the whole of the European settlements in Canada – under British control, exercised at first by direct rule and military proclamation. But it was already clear when Shelburne was minister that this was unsustainable. The people of this greater 'Quebec' remained mostly French-speaking and Catholic in religion. Britain could no more govern them directly than can the United States govern Iraq directly. Therefore the 1774 Act provided for an appointed legislature, and recognised the legitimacy of Catholic religion and French civil law in the province. This in itself enraged some of the militant Calvinists of New

England. But it was 'enlarging its boundaries' that was truly explosive. The act defined the southern boundary of Quebec as following the present US–Canadian border westwards as far as the north-western corner of Pennsylvania. But there it was to strike southwards along the Ohio River valley, passing just west of what the British had renamed Fort Pitt (later Pittsburgh) on capturing it from the French, until it joined the Mississippi, and up the Mississippi until it met the southern boundary of Hudson's Bay territory (then governed by a separate chartered company).[1]

In a series of recent papers, Norman Schofield has analysed how fundamentally this threatened the material and strategic interests of the American colonists (see, for example, Schofield 2002a, b). The Ohio and Mississippi valleys were the key to westward expansion of the American colonies. Politicians, including George Washington, were actively speculating in 'empty' land (that is, land inhabited only by Native Americans) west of the Appalachians, and states were making sometimes conflicting claims to incorporate these western lands in their territories. Before roads, the Ohio and Mississippi valleys were the trunk transport route for all goods – and troops – into or out of the western states. South of the new 'Quebec', Spain still claimed, albeit feebly, to control the Mississippi valley, and France controlled New Orleans at its mouth. The Quebec Act therefore completed a tourniquet on western colonial expansion. Schofield argues that this, rather than 'taxation without representation', was the tipping point for the colonists' resistance.

But why, then, did Smith, Shelburne and Prime Minister Lord North fail to anticipate that the Quebec Act would tip the colonists into war? Schofield suggests a possible answer. In 1774 it would have been hard for any rational observer to predict that the colonists would win a war of independence against the strongest military machine in the Western world. If they could rationally have predicted that they could not win, they would not have launched the war. So Schofield hypothesises (2002a, p. 13) that they received an early and secret signal of the French support that was to prove crucial for the ultimate American victory – and that they received that signal before 4 July 1776.

While advising successive governments about American policy, Smith was also busy writing what became the chapter on colonies in *WN* Book IV, Chapter vii. His friends were eagerly awaiting it, in the hope that his advice would be available in the worsening crisis. When it appeared, it cannot have been what anyone expected. Smith repeats his long-held view that the colonies cannot expect to take a free ride on their defence (IV.vii.b.20, quoted in Chapter 2). He argues that although the mercantilism underlying the relationship between Britain and its colonies in America (and India) is bad for everybody, it is not as bad as the regimes in the Spanish, Portuguese and (with one exception) French colonies. The one exception is the government of slaves. Slaves in Haiti (then the French colony of St-Domingue) are treated better than those in the southern English colonies, Smith argues, because France is an autocracy, where the government does not hesitate to interfere in owners' property rights if they treat their slaves badly. He illustrates this with an anecdote, recycled from his Glasgow lectures, about the emperor Augustus who forced a cruel slave-owner to free his slaves on the spot (IV.vii.b.54–5).

Smith leaves the discussion of slaves in the air, not exploring the multiple ironies that he has (surely deliberately) introduced. He moves on to some complimentary remarks about the colonists. They are more equal, both in general and in their state legislatures, than in the status-divided politics of Britain:

> Their manners are more republican, and their governments, those of three of the provinces of New England in particular, have hitherto been more republican too . . . The colonies owe to the policy of Europe the education and great views of their active and enterprising founders; and some of the greatest and most important of them owe to it scarce anything else. (IV.vii.b.51 and 64)

But the longest part of Smith's discussion is devoted to showing that mercantilism is bad for everybody: for the colonists, for Britain and for third countries. British mercantilism took the form of Navigation Acts and enumerated commodities. The former stipulated that only British ships might carry goods to or from the British colonies. The latter said that certain listed colonial products, including sugar, tobacco and cotton, may only be carried to Britain, from which they could be re-exported to the rest of the world.

The Acts had made the fortune of Glasgow after the Act of Union, and therefore in a sense had made Smith's own career. But he is unsparing. That they restrict colonial freedom is so obvious that Smith spends little time on that issue. Most of his discussion concerns the subtler losses incurred in Britain and the rest of the world. The legal monopolies of ships and trade create monopoly profits in those businesses. Therefore they draw excess capital to them, and starve other businesses of capital. Consumers have to bear the deadweight losses of tobacco being shipped indirectly and repackaged en route rather than being shipped directly to the country of consumption. A move to free trade would therefore make everybody better off.

Smith's most radical proposal must therefore have startled his readers.

> To propose that Great Britain should voluntarily give up all authority over her colonies, and leave them to elect their own magistrates, to enact their own

> laws, and to make peace and war as they might think proper, would be to propose such a measure as never was, and never will be adopted, by any nation in the world . . . If it was adopted, however, Great Britain would not only be immediately freed from the whole annual expence of the peace establishment of the colonies, but might settle with them such a treaty of commerce as would effectively secure to her a free trade, more advantageous to the great body of the people, though less so to the merchants, than the monopoly which she at present enjoys. (IV.vii.c.66)

If that was too radical, his alternative proposal was scarcely less so. He was dismissive of the American cry of 'no taxation without representation', observing that Guernsey and Jersey had lived perfectly happily with it for a long time. But, he went on, if some of the American colonies insisted on representation in Parliament, they should be offered it, with the carrot that the more their taxes raised, the more seats in Parliament they would be offered.

> Instead of piddling for the little prizes which are to be found in what may be called the paltry raffle of colony faction; they might then hope, from the presumption which men naturally have in their own ability and good fortune, to draw some of the great prizes which sometimes come from the wheel of the great state lottery of British politicks. (IV.vii.c.75)

In a much told, but little understood, story, Smith's friend Sir John Sinclair of Ulbster went to Smith in great alarm on hearing the news of the British defeat at the battle of Saratoga in 1777. The [British] nation must be ruined, said Sinclair. 'Be assured, my young friend', replied the imperturbable philosopher, 'there is a great deal of ruin in a nation' (Sinclair 1837, p. 37). By this Smith meant that the British defeat was not the end of Britain.

He exhibits the same cool detachment in his 'Notes on America' prepared for Wedderburn the following year. He goes through the possible conclusions of the American war. Option I, the 'complete submission of America', is inconceivable even if the military tide turns in Britain's favour, because the 'ulcerated minds of the Americans are not likely to consent to any union even upon terms the most advantageous to themselves'. Smith again puts forward the idea of American representation in Parliament, but concedes that only 'a solitary philosopher like myself' can see the advantage of it. Option II, an American victory, would bring the advantages he had spoken of in *WN*. Britain would no longer have to pay for the defence of America. A Machiavellian suggestion is that in the event of an American victory Britain should

> restore Canada to France and the two Floridas[2] to Spain; we should render our colonies the natural enemies of those two monarchies and consequently the natural allies of Great Britain. Those splendid, but unprofitable acquisitions of the late [1756–63] war, left our colonies no other enemies to quarrel with but their mother country.

But American victory (let alone the ingenious idea of handing back Canada and Florida) 'would not, in the eyes of Europe appear honourable to Great Britain'. Smith sees only two other options: III, the 'restoration . . . of the old [that is 1763–76] system', which might be tolerable if there was a secret agreement between the British and American elites that it would be gradually dismantled – but it would be hard to keep such an agreement secret; and IV, 'the submission or conquest of a part, but a part only' of the rebel colonies. He saw that as the likeliest, and worst, option, because of the military burden. Luckily, British incompetence, the success of American citizen militias and the French intervention on the American side brought about Smith's option II instead of IV. He was not a British government adviser at the peace negotiations of 1783, so that the clever idea of ceding Canada to France and Florida to Spain did not see the light of day until the memorandum was rediscovered in the 1930s. (All quotations in this paragraph are from the memorandum in *Corr.*, Appendix B, pp. 380–5.)

SMITH IN AMERICA

Adam Smith's political views therefore brought limited comfort to either side. His broader philosophical views, and more broadly still those of the Scottish Enlightenment more generally, would make a great contribution to American thought and to institutional design. The specifically Smithian parts were egalitarianism and religious pluralism. The more broadly Scottish parts contributed an oppositionist, 'country Whig' tone to American constitutionalism. Part of that involved the right to bear arms and support for state militias.

Of those who created the institutions of the United States, two were distinctively Smithian: James Madison and Thomas Jefferson. One was distinctively a follower of Sir James Steuart, and therefore an opponent of Smith's economics: Alexander Hamilton. I discuss them in that order.

James Madison's Adam Smith

Since the pioneering work of Douglass Adair, written in the 1940s but not published in book form until more recently, the debt of the American

Framers to the Scots has been recognised. Wills (1978) brought it to wider attention but his claims go much too far. Adair wrote much about the influence of Hume on Madison. So far as I am aware, only one writer (Fleischacker 2002, 2003) has drawn attention to the influence of Smith on Madison. But it is crucial – and it bears more on religion than on economics, although it certainly bears on both.

James Madison (1751–1836) was small and scholarly.[3] Brought up in the plantation economy of foothill Virginia, he disliked the hunting and drinking culture of his peers. He attended the College of New Jersey (later Princeton) from 1769 to 1772. This choice, unusual for a Virginian, may have been due to the reputation the College already had as a hotbed of opposition to the British colonial regime, under its Scottish evangelical head John Witherspoon. Witherspoon belonged to the opposite church party to Hutcheson and Smith. He was certainly an exponent of Smith's 'austere' system of morals rather than the 'loose' system of Hutcheson, Smith and Burns. However, he had a Covenanter's hatred of externally imposed religion, which he transmitted to Madison. He was later to sign the Declaration of Independence.

On his return to Virginia, Madison campaigned for religious pluralism. Whereas white settlement in the New England states, Pennsylvania and Maryland had been organised by religious dissenters, Virginia, the Carolinas and Georgia were 'official' British plantations named after British monarchs[4] and with the Anglican Church established in the English manner. Madison's support for the large minority of Baptists in the state helped to secure his first election to the state constitutional convention in 1776. He served in government for most of the time until his retirement from the Presidency in 1817. His finest moments did not include his presidency, where his administration stumbled into the unsuccessful War of 1812 against the British, but they did include:

- his promotion of religious freedom in Virginia
- his work in the Constitutional Convention of 1787 and his justification of the Constitution in his numbers of the *Federalist* in 1788–9
- his role as floor manager of what became the Bill of Rights in the First Congress (1789–91)

In all of this he was encouraged by his best friend, Thomas Jefferson.

Madison was the main author of the 'Memorial and Remonstrance against Religious Assessment' (1785) which led to the Virginia Declaration of Religious Freedom the following year and then, by means of Madison's floor management, to the 'Establishment Clause' of the First Amendment to the US Constitution, which states, 'Congress shall make no law respecting an establishment of religion, or prohibiting the free exercise thereof'. The Establishment Clause, still a central and much-debated feature of the US Constitution, embeds Adam Smith's preference for religious pluralism. The arguments that led to it were Scottish and/or Smithian. We can track them through successive documents: the 'Memorial and Remonstrance', 'Vices of the Political System of the United States' (1787) and the *Federalist* No. 10 (1788).

The 'Memorial and Remonstrance' comprises fifteen objections to a bill that would have provided state support for religious teachers. The most important are Nos 1 and 2, which might have been written by Andrew Melvill (or John Witherspoon), and No. 7, which might have been written by Adam Smith:

> 2. Because if Religion be exempt from the authority of the Society at large, still less can it be subject to that of the Legislative Body . . . The Rulers who are guilty of such an encroachment, exceed the commission from which they derive their authority, and are Tyrants . . .
> 7. Because experience witnesseth that ecclesiastical establishments, instead of maintaining the purity and efficacy of Religion, have had a contrary operation. During almost fifteen centuries has the legal establishment of Christianity been on trial. What have been its fruits? More or less in all places, pride and ignorance in the Clergy, ignorance and servility in the laity, in both, superstition, bigotry, and persecution. (Madison 1999, pp. 30–2)

'Vices . . .' was one of two research notes which Madison wrote for himself and fellow Virginia delegates while preparing for the Constitutional Convention in 1787. It underlay the 'Virginia Plan', also authored by Madison, which set the agenda for the first six weeks of the Convention's debates. The Virginia Plan envisaged a stronger federal, and weaker state, government than the Constitution as finally agreed by the delegates. By the time we come to 'Vices', the voice of Andrew Melvill has fallen silent, but that of Adam Smith has become louder, and speaks of the economy as well as of religion.

> All civilized societies are divided into different interests and factions, as they happen to be creditors or debtors – Rich or poor – husbandmen, merchants, or manufacturers – members of different religious sects . . . &c &c. In republican Government the majority however composed, ultimately give the law. Whenever therefore an apparent interest or common passion unites a majority what is to restrain them from unjust violations of the rights and interests of the minority, or of individuals? . . . When indeed Religion is kindled into enthusiasm, its force like that of other passions, is increased by the sympathy of a multitude. But enthusiasm is only a temporary state of religion, and while

> it lasts will hardly be seen with pleasure at the helm of Government. (Madison 1999, pp. 76–8)

The *Federalist Papers* were organised by Alexander Hamilton (1755–1804) in an attempt to persuade the state convention of New York to ratify the draft constitution. Madison, who was only Hamilton's third choice as co-author, had to produce the first of his numbers, No. 10, in a great hurry to fill the next available slot in the New York newspapers. So he turned to 'Vices', and polished it and edited it to form what has remained the most famous of the eighty-five numbers. He further downplays his religious arguments, because they are less relevant in this context than in 1785. But they are still there as Madison argues that the solution to faction is an 'extended republic'. And even the non-religious part of his argument echoes Smith.

Here is Smith on factionalism in the American colonies:

> It [a union with Britain] would, at least, deliver them from those rancorous and virulent factions which are inseparable from small democracies, and which have so frequently divided the affections of their people, and disturbed the tranquillity of their governments, in their form so nearly democratical. In the case of a total separation from Great Britain, which, unless prevented by a union of this kind, seems very likely to take place, those factions would be ten times more virulent than ever. (*WN* V.iii.90)

Madison shared Smith's diagnosis, though not his remedy:

> A religious sect, may degenerate into a political faction in a part of the confederacy; but the variety of sects dispersed over the entire face of it, must secure the national councils against any danger from that source: A rage for paper money, for an abolition of debts, for an equal division of property, or for any other improper or wicked project, will be less apt to pervade the whole body of the union, than a particular member of it . . . (Madison 1999, p. 167. For the reasons for treating the *Federalist* # 10, rather than ## 45–51, as representing what Madison really thought, see Kernell 2003; McLean 2003)

The most Smithian aspect of Madison's thought is that he, too, thinks like an economist. Consider the following three examples:

- [T]he most common and durable source of faction has been the various and unequal distribution of property. Those who hold and those who are without property have ever formed distinct interests in society (The *Federalist* # 10: Madison 1999, p. 162).
- In the compound republic of America, the power surrendered by the people, is first divided between two distinct governments, and

then the portion allotted to each, subdivided among distinct and separate departments. Hence a double security arises to the rights of the people. The different governments will control each other; at the same time that each will be controled by itself (The *Federalist* # 51: Madison 1999, pp. 296–7).

- 'Mr MADISON considered it as a primary object [of what became Article II.1 of the US Constitution, dealing with the Electoral College] to render an eventual[5] resort to any part of the Legislature improbable. He was apprehensive that the proposed alteration [namely throwing the choice of a President, if no candidate had a majority in the Electoral College, into the House rather than the Senate] would turn the attention of the large States too much to the appointment of candidates, instead of aiming at an effectual appointment of the officer [that is, the President], as the large States would predominate in the Legislature which would have the final choice out of the Candidates (Speech at the Convention, 5 September 1787, in Madison's own report: Farrand 1966, 2:513).

Suppose we were to divide social scientists into Smithians and Steuartians (although Adamites and Jamesians might be neater). Adamites believe that institutions should be designed around the expectation that people will pursue their rational self-interest, but that they should be given incentives to behave sociably; and that order results from good institutional design plus spontaneous coordination. Jamesians believe in trusting legislators to act in the public interest. Then Madison was wholly Adamite, Jefferson was more naïvely Jamesian and Hamilton was almost entirely Jamesian.

Thomas Jefferson's Adam Smith

The multifaceted Thomas Jefferson (1743–1826) was deeply influenced by both the Scottish and the French Enlightenments. Born into the same planter class as his neighbour and friend Madison, he attended the College of William & Mary in Williamsburg, Virginia, where

> It was my great good fortune, and what probably fixed the destinies of my life that Dr. Wm. Small of Scotland was then professor of Mathematics . . . Fortunately the Philosophical chair became vacant soon after my arrival at college, and he was appointed to fill it per interim: and he was the first who ever gave in that college regular lectures in Ethics, Rhetoric & Belles letters. (Jefferson, *Autobiography*, in Jefferson 1984, p. 4)

Small was a graduate of Marischal College, Aberdeen, who had arrived in Virginia in 1758. On his return to Britain in 1764 he settled in Birmingham, where he joined the circle of scientists and engineers that clustered around James Watt's business partner Matthew Boulton. According to his entry in the *Dictionary of National Biography* (Lane 2004), he had met Watt in Glasgow; he also knew Smith's close friend Joseph Black. The title of his William & Mary lecture series exactly echoes that of Smith's two Glasgow series and of their Edinburgh precursors. Therefore it is reasonable to assume that the student Jefferson was at only two removes from Adam Smith's lectures.

Jefferson's career was entwined with Madison's throughout their lives. He was the main author of the Declaration of Independence, and he worked with Madison on the Virginia campaign against establishment, asking late in life for his tombstone to be inscribed 'Author of the Declaration of American Independence, of the statute of Virginia for religious freedom, and father of the University of Virginia', which it is. In 1784 he was chosen to be American Minister in France, where he remained until September 1789. There he met the leading lights of the Enlightenment, including Condorcet, and saw the opening scenes of the Revolution, which he admired. (Jefferson had a blind spot for riot and bloodshed.) The four years that Jefferson spent in France were the most intellectually fruitful of his life. His political theory is an amalgam of the Scottish and French Enlightenments. On return he became Secretary of State in Washington's first administration, but fell out with Secretary of the Treasury Hamilton. Jefferson and Madison became leaders of the 'Republican' opposition to Hamilton's 'High Federalism', until he won the hotly contested Presidential election of 1800. He served two mostly successful terms, before retiring as a politician to remain a superb scholar and a disastrously inept plantation owner for the rest of his life.

While serving as President, he recommended *WN* to a correspondent as 'the best book to be read' on 'the subjects of money & commerce, unless Say's Political Economy can be had' (TJ to J. Norvell, 14.06.1807; cf. also TJ to J.-B. Say, 01.02.1804; Jefferson 1984, pp. 1176 and 1143). Say was the leading French disciple of Smith. So what did Jefferson make of Smith, specifically, and of the Scottish Enlightenment more generally?

An interesting pointer here is his library. The most learned, but also the most hopelessly in debt, of the American Founding Fathers sold his library to the US Congress in 1815, so that it became the nucleus of the Library of Congress. Jefferson compiled a catalogue of his library, which was lost – and some of the books were destroyed in a fire in 1851. The catalogue was rediscovered only in 1989 (Gilreath and Wilson 1989). It shows that Jefferson owned most of the key books of the Scottish Enlightenment, including the works of Hutcheson, Ferguson and Lord Kames. He owned a copy of *WN*, together with one of the Mandeville's *Fable of the Bees* and Hume's *Essays*. But Jefferson did not own (or at least, did not sell to Congress in 1815) *TMS*, nor what are now seen as Hume's big philosophical works, his *Treatise of Human Nature* and his two *Enquiries*. For the most part, Jefferson's ideas are generically Scottish rather than specifically Smithian. He believes in the deistic, common-sense account of morality offered by Hutcheson and Reid and absorbs the oppositional, 'country Whig' ideology shared to a greater or lesser degree by all the Scots except Hume. (Jefferson, unlike Madison, does not approve of Hume.)

One much anthologised item is the last thing Jefferson ever wrote – a letter of June 1826 to the Mayor of Washington, DC, stating that he would be unable to attend the fiftieth anniversary Fourth of July celebration there due to ill health:[6]

> May it [American independence] be to the world, what I believe it will be (to some parts sooner, to others later, but finally to all,) the signal of arousing men to burst the chains under which monkish ignorance and superstition had persuaded them to bind themselves, and to assume the blessings and security of self-government . . . All eyes are opened, or opening, to the rights of man. The general spread of the light of science has already laid open to every view the palpable truth, that the mass of mankind has not been born with saddles on their backs, nor a favored few booted and spurred, ready to ride them legitimately, by the grace of God. (TJ to Mayor Roger C. Weightman, 24.06.1826, in Appleby and Ball 1999, p. 149)

In a fine act of literary detection, Douglass Adair (1974, pp. 192–202) showed that the image of 'saddles on their backs' comes from the dying speech of Col. Richard Rumbold, a former Cromwellian – and associate of the Levellers – sentenced to death for his participation in Monmouth's rebellion against King James II in 1685. Jefferson knew that this letter was *his* dying speech. It is the manifesto to posterity of Jefferson the opposition Whig, like so many of the American revolutionaries seeing the revolt against the British Crown as the country against the Court. The rest of his imagery is distilled Enlightenment thought. 'Monkish ignorance and superstition' is pure Voltaire, Hume or Smith.[7] The country Whigs came to power in the United States under Jefferson and his friends, and enshrined their ideology in the Bill of Rights – the first ten amendments of the US Constitution. The (very Smithian) guarantees of freedom of religion in the First Amendment have already been quoted. As the Establishment Clause is a beacon for American liberals, so is the Right to Bear Arms for American conservatives. The Second and Third Amendments now seem to belong to a different ideological universe entirely from the First. The Second Amendment states:

> A well regulated Militia, being necessary to the security of a free State, the right of the people to keep and bear Arms, shall not be infringed.

However, the Second Amendment is merely the logical culmination of the militia campaign of Fletcher and Ferguson.

Alexander Hamilton's Adam Smith

However, in one aspect of his life and work, Jefferson *was* a Smithian, thinking like an economist. The rift between him and Madison (who came to be known as the Republicans) and Hamilton (who led the extreme – 'high' – wing of the Federalists)[8] arose over economic policy and spilt over into constitutional matters. Jefferson and Madison believed that the foundation of the state should be the 'virtuous farmer'. This was in part a borrowing of country Whig ideology, and in part a reflection of their economic base, which was rural, southern and western. Hamilton believed in actively promoting industry and trade. This aligned his economic interest with the towns, such as they were, and the commercial states of New England and the Mid Atlantic region.

In economic policy, Hamilton followed Sir James Steuart rather than Adam Smith. He wanted to see an active policy of encouraging manufacture. This was equally aligned with *his* commercial and industrial base, which lay from New Jersey northwards to the New England states. The conflict with Jefferson and Madison broke out over Hamilton's 'Report on the Public Credit' of January 1790.[9] Hamilton wished to achieve a Smithian end by non-Smithian means. The end was to restore the public creditworthiness of the United States, which was well below junk-bond status. It had failed to repay the debts, both domestic and foreign, that either the individual states or the United States had incurred in fighting the revolutionary war. Hamilton proposed that the debt should be repaid at par to its current holders; and that the United States should assume the debt liabilities of the individual states. This would be funded out of future economic growth and taxation of imports and luxuries (especially, therefore, of luxury imports).

To the Virginians Madison and Hamilton, several difficulties arose. One was that many of the original holders of domestic debt – that is, Revolutionary War soldiers who had been given credit notes in lieu of pay – had sold their credit notes at deep discounts to speculators. If debt was repaid at par as Hamilton proposed, the speculators rather than the original debt holders would benefit – indeed, would make a huge profit. Secondly, the Virginians thought that the assumption of state debts punished prudent Virginia which, they argued, had honoured its debts, and rewarded the governments of feckless states that had failed to repay their debts. The Smithian part of Jefferson's response was the political part. Madison had argued in the *Federalist* 10 that one of the expected divisions of interest was between debtors and creditors. Jefferson believed that debtors far outnumbered creditors – he was in a position to know, as he had massive debts himself that he never repaid. However, the creditors had disproportionate power in Congress, and purchasers of Revolutionary war paper had a direct interest in enacting a highly profitable payment to themselves.

The Virginian debtors had plenty of self-interest at stake too. However, Jefferson had a good point. It was very easy for those with a vested interest to buy seats in the legislature in order to promote a conspiracy against the public. Whether or not it happened with Revolutionary debt, it unquestionably happened after the Civil War – the 'Gilded Age' – when Congress was directly bought by crooked railway speculators in a simple bargain. In exchange for Union Pacific stock, Congress voted monopoly rights to the Union Pacific to form the eastern leg of the transcontinental railroad, and to sell off land next to the tracks for profitable homesteads. (Sources for these paragraphs are Ellis 1998, 2001; Jefferson 1984; Sloan 1995; Bain 2000.)

With its rapid growth since 1800, interrupted only by the Civil War, its openness to migrants and its relatively small welfare state, the USA has become the heartland of the right-wing interpretation of Adam Smith. But that is because the left-wing credentials of Smith were imperfectly transmitted and lost with the founding generation.

SMITH ON FRANCE

Smith was a critical friend of the French Enlightenment. He was probably an enemy of the French Revolution (although there is no proof). The French Revolution had, however, a strange double effect on Smith. It helped to bury the reputation of Smith's radicalism, both in France and in the anglophone world. It substituted a new dialogue of 'left' and 'right'. Those words were invented during the French Revolution. The National Assembly evolved out of an assembly called by King Louis XVI. In royalist (and for that matter Christian) tradition, the place of honour was on the king's right hand. Therefore the king's nobles (most likely to be his friends) sat on the right. The king's ordinary citizens (least likely to be his friends) sat in the less honourable place on the left.[10] These positions were maintained when the king had gone. The terms 'right' and 'left' thus acquired their current meanings. It may be anachronistic, therefore, to call Adam Smith a man of the left. But his egalitarianism was as strong as that of the most egalitarian of the French left.

Smith's personal engagement with the francophone Enlightenment in both France and Switzerland has already been described (see Chapter 1). His general intellectual outlook, and analysis of the wrongs of society, resemble those of French Enlightenment figures quite closely. His solutions are distinct. Like Voltaire, Holbach and Condorcet, he was disgusted by religious intolerance. Voltaire mocked it (and Smith occasionally copied or quoted his satire; see, for example, *TMS* III.2.35). Holbach and Condorcet were militant atheists. Smith was a religious pluralist. Like Quesnay, Condorcet (again) and Turgot, he saw that state intervention in the economy is wealth-destroying. The term *laissez-faire* (in full, *laissez faire, laissez passer*) is generally attributed to the early physiocrat Vincent de Gournay (1712–59); it does not appear, in any variant, in *WN*. The earliest quotation in English, in the *Oxford English Dictionary*, in which 'laissez-faire' is used in its usual modern sense, dates back only to 1887. The Gournay version indeed refers to conditions in France, not Scotland. In France, either the king or a tax-farmer could stop you passing from place to place until you had paid a tax. In Great Britain, that had been swept away by the Act of Union. Adam Smith is not a simple exponent of *laissez-faire*. His subtle and complex relationship with Turgot and Condorcet is well discussed by Emma Rothschild (2001). Although he admired them, it was not unqualified admiration, as the chapter on the Physiocrats in *WN* (Book IV, Chapter ix) shows. This has been discussed in Chapter 4.

As to the French Revolution, there are few clues. The only surviving letter either to or from Smith in the last two years of his life to discuss France is one from P.-S. Dupont de Nemours, a friend of Turgot, Condorcet and Jefferson. Dupont sends Smith a copy of his pamphlet on the recent Anglo-French commercial treaty. He speaks of the 'storms to which you see our kingdom is prey', but continues that they

> are not as harmful as they appear . . . We are progressing rapidly towards a good constitution . . . You have very much hastened this useful revolution, [and] the French *Economists* have not harmed it (*Corr.* # 277, 19.06.1788; my translation).

No reply from Smith has survived. Smith was working very hard and by his own admission very slowly on the revisions for the sixth edition of *TMS*. Some of these revisions may relate to the French Revolution. One seems to be an explicit criticism of the dissenting minister and mathematician Richard Price, who had preached a sermon 'On the Love of Country' welcoming the Revolution. These new passages contain a well-known but rather strange denunciation of 'the man of system . . . so enamoured with the supposed beauty of his own ideal plan of government, that he cannot suffer the smallest deviation from any part of it' (*TMS* VI.ii.2.17; pp. 233–4). It is rather strange because Smith himself was nothing if not a man of system, both in his writings and in his personal habits. But he never set out an ideal plan of *government* except on matters of taxation and public expenditure, where he had been very systematic indeed. Cautious as ever, Smith refused to allow the new edition to be published in Edinburgh, only in London – perhaps because he feared attacks by Calvinist ministers (Ross 1995, p. 395).

These slight clues lead Smith scholars to conclude that Smith was rather alarmed by the French Revolution – as well he might have been, since it involved violence from the outset. Not, of course, violence on the genocidal scale of the Terror of 1793–4, but brutal violence none the less: the Terror was 'merely 1789 with a higher body count', in Simon Schama's (1989, p. 447) caustic summary. On the other hand, Smith was no friend of the *ancien régime*. All his French friends were reformers, and Smith is highly critical of French taxation policy and the forced labour of the *corvée* in several places in *WN*.

But Smith was wise to be cautious. The immediate reaction to his death was cool except among his close friends and, perhaps dangerously, in France (Ross 1995, pp. 408–9; Rothschild 2001, p. 53). By 1792, Britain was at war with Revolutionary France. By the following year, Revolutionary France seemed to be an appalling monster, where terror was the order of the day at home and military conquest abroad. If reaction in Britain seems extreme, it might be helpful to imagine the reaction in modern Britain or the USA if, say, a murderous fundamentalist regime with nuclear weapons came to power in Iran or North Korea. It was in the year of terror 1793 that Smith's friend Dugald Stewart wrote the first biography of Smith. Stewart himself explained in later editions of this memoir that in 1793 'the doctrine of a Free Trade was itself represented as of a revolutionary tendency' (in *EPS* p. 339). This understated the case. The Scottish legal authorities prosecuted various pro-French intellectuals for sedition. The evidence against Thomas Muir of Huntershill, according to the prosecution, was that 'He said, that their taxes would be less if they were more equally represented'. This earned Muir fourteen years' transportation. The Scottish judge Lord Craig attacked Stewart directly, forcing him to formally recant his views and to state: 'I shall ever regret that I dishonoured some of my pages by mentioning with respect the name of Condorcet' (both q. Rothschild 2001, p. 56).

Therefore Stewart was at pains to stress Smith's respectability – and drew the attention of the persecuting Lord Craig to the memoir as evidence of both his own and Smith's innocence of sedition. He played down the radical and played up the conservative parts of Smith's thought. Quoting a manuscript of 1755, now lost,[11] Stewart states that Smith then said

> Little else is requisite to carry a state to the highest degree of opulence from the lowest barbarism, but peace, easy taxes, and a tolerable administration of justice; all the rest being brought about by the natural course of things.

Smith's work

> aimed at the improvement of society – not by delineating plans of new constitutions, but by enlightening the policy of actual legislators. Such speculations . . . have no tendency to unhinge established institutions, or to inflame the passions of the multitude.

Stewart went on to quote from the additions to the sixth edition of *TMS* just mentioned – a fact that tends to strengthen the hypothesis that they were added to distance Smith from the French Revolutionary 'system'. Or, more cautiously, that even if *Smith* did not intend the passage to be read in this way, it was very convenient for *Stewart*, who had Lord Craig breathing down his neck, to insist that the 'man of system' passage showed that Smith hated the French Revolution. Unlike the man of system, quoted Stewart from the new passage in *TMS*,

> The man whose public spirit is prompted altogether by humanity and benevolence, will respect the established powers and privileges . . . of the great orders and societies into which the state is divided.

Stewart goes on to complain that Smith's chapter on taxation in *WN* is 'more loose and unsatisfactory' than the rest (Stewart *Account* in *EPS*, quoted on pp. 322, 311, 318, 323. Stewart's quotation from *TMS* sixth edn is from VI.ii.2.16, p. 233).

Up to a point, Professor Stewart. Emma Rothschild has pointed out (2001, p. 58) that this section of Stewart's *Account* follows the legal form of a defence counsel's speech in a sedition trial. Stewart's judgment of the chapter on taxation is a matter of opinion (though it is a startling opinion); as to the rest, he tells the truth, but not the whole truth. Yes, Smith was a quietist, always worried that Hume was going too far, always willing to enlighten the policy of actual legislators, always cautious about what he said in public. But we know that he was much less cautious in private ('Whining Christians'). And of course his advice is for anybody, not merely actual legislators but also those who wish to become legislators in their place.

At the same time, the enthusiastic support of Prime Minister Pitt the Younger for Smith bolstered his respectability. This mantle of respectability spread from Smith's views on taxation and public expenditure (almost certainly the part of his work that Pitt honoured most highly) to all of them, and at the same time coloured them with Pitt's opposition to revolutionary France.

SMITH IN FRANCE

The other side of the coin is that many of the generation of intellectuals who understood and admired Smith were wiped out in the Revolution. La Rochefoucauld was dragged from his carriage and lynched by a mob in front of his wife and mother in September 1792 (Schama 1989, p. 679). Condorcet died in 1794, by suicide or from exhaustion, while in hiding from the agents of the Committee of Public Safety who would have guillotined him without trial if they had found him (McLean and Hewitt 1994, pp. 30–1). Condorcet's widow Sophie de Grouchy was a notably courageous survivor. She published a translation of *TMS* in 1798, appending eight 'Letters on sympathy' of her own. These were addressed to her brother-in-law P.-J.-G. Cabanis, who wrote that Smith's analysis was 'incomplete', and that Sophie de Grouchy had completed what Smith left incomplete, through 'simple rational deliberation' (1802, quoted by Faccarello and Steiner 2002, p. 73. The *Letters* have now been published separately for the first time: Condorcet [1793] 1994). To a French intellectual, the idea that sympathy develops autonomously by spontaneous coordination, rather than rationally, was unacceptable (Condorcet [1793] 1994, p. 152; Faccarello and Steiner 2002, p. 72).

Furthermore, even the Condorcet circle, including Dupont when not writing to Smith, regarded Turgot as the real economic genius: 'where Smith has added to it [Turgot's economic treatise] there is a lack of exactness and even of argument' (Dupont 1782, quoted by Faccarello and Steiner 2002, p. 90). Condorcet was the most cosmopolitan of intellectuals. But even he could not suppress national pride in France as the home of all scientific advance (Letter to Garat 1785, translated in McLean and Hewitt 1994, p. 11). Where Condorcet led, lesser intellectuals followed. Smith was, unfortunately, not French; therefore, unfortunately, he could not be an intellectual of the front rank. Condorcet chided Smith for 'having taken too little account . . . of the irresistible force of reason and truth' (1786, quoted by Faccarello and Steiner 2002, p. 90). Most French scholars preferred the economics of Steuart to those of Smith. Steuartian unlike Smithian, economics, justified extensive state intervention in the economy, at least so long as it was done by wise men such as (nowadays) the graduates of the *Ecole Nationale d'administration* – the *énarques* who dominate both economic policy-making and business leadership in France. There was a minority strand in French thought, launched by Jean-Baptiste Say, that propagated the Smithian idea of spontaneous order, and hence of economic liberalism (Faccarello and Steiner 2002, pp. 112–16). But the opposite, statist, tradition is deeply rooted in France, both on the left and on the right.

NOTES

1. Texts of the Quebec Act 1774 are available in numerous places on the Web, includingwww.solon.org/Constitutions/Canada/English/PreConfederation/qa_1774.html.
2. 'The two Floridas' were East and West Florida. East Florida was most of the present state of Florida. West Florida was the western Florida panhandle plus the Gulf Coast areas of Alabama and Mississippi, stretching as far as New Orleans, still under French control.
3. He was the shortest President of the USA to date. Abraham Lincoln was the tallest.
4. Virginia from the 'virgin queen' Elizabeth I; the Carolinas from Charles (Latin *Carolus*) II.
5. 'Eventual' here means 'possible' (like *éventuel* in French).
6. Jefferson and his fellow-revolutionary John Adams, the last two surviving signatories of the Declaration of Independence, were actually both to die on that same day, 4 July 1826.
7. Hume wrote sarcastically of 'the whole train of monkish virtues'; Smith, in *TMS*, of the 'futile mortifications of a monastery' (*TMS* III.2.34–5 and note).
8. Both names are extremely confusing. The Jefferson 'Republicans' formed the core of what later became the Democratic Party. The Hamilton 'Federalists' were really nationalists, wishing a larger role for the federal government and a smaller role for the states than had the authors of the *Federalist Papers* ten years earlier. In 1787 the opposite of 'Federalist' was

'Anti-Federalist'. In 1800 the opposite of 'Federalist' was 'Republican'. The modern Republican Party was not founded until 1856, as an anti-slavery movement.

9. A Web text of the Report is at www.wwnorton.com/college/history/archive/resources/documents/ch08_02.htm.
10. See the etymology in *Oxford English Dictionary* on-line edition at www.oed.com, under 'centre', sense 15.
11. There is a helpful discussion of this document, the plagiarism charges that it rebutted and its disappearance in the Appendix to Kennedy 2005 (pp. 241–8).

7

Adam Smith Today

In this chapter I attempt to pick up all the threads that I have deliberately left loose so far. Probably, Smith was no great sympathiser with the French Revolution. But his writing supports all three of the slogans of that revolution. He was in favour of liberty, of equality and of the one that is most usually ignored nowadays, namely fraternity. Therefore the first half of this chapter reviews what Smith has to say to us on each of those three subjects.

Adam Smith's work is without doubt what Thucydides wanted his history to be: κτημα ες αιει ('a possession for ever'). Therefore thinkers and politicians of all stripes – from Marxists to libertarian conservatives – have a claim on him. Each can legitimately find support in Adam Smith for their positions. In the second half of this chapter, however, I want to argue that what we might now call a social-democratic reading is truest of all to the historical Adam Smith. By a social-democratic reading I mean a left-of-centre but non-Marxian reading. I conclude by looking at the uncanny similarities between the ideas of Adam Smith and those of Gordon Brown – Langtonians[1] both.

SMITH ON LIBERTY

Adam Smith was both an economic and a social liberal. An economic liberal believes that non-interference with the market usually produces the most efficiency, where efficiency is defined as maximising output per unit of input. A social liberal believes that people should usually be allowed to get on with their own lives as they wish, so long as they do not adversely affect the lives of others.

The two sorts of liberalism are obviously related, but neither one implies the other. Economic liberalism is primarily about efficiency, whereas social liberalism is primarily about freedom. In modern politics they often appeal to quite different people. Economic liberals are often social conservatives, and *vice versa*. People who believe that the state should get out of the market often believe strongly that the state should police morals. Those who are horrified at that are often also horrified by what they see as the consequences of the market, which they frequently hold responsible for pollution or Third World poverty.

At the core of Smith's economic liberalism is his belief in spontaneous order – in the invisible hand if you must (although I share the anxiety of those who think that a passing metaphor should not stand for the whole theory). I suggested above that a passage in Book I of *WN*, where Smith says that you never observe voluntary exchange among dogs but only among humans, and that furthermore you get your dinner by an exchange with the butcher, the baker and the brewer which is in the interest of both sides, is his most fundamental insight. On it are built the whole of modern microeconomics and modern welfare economics.

There are two main schools in modern economics, and Smith is the ancestor of both. *Austrian economists* are radically subjective. Almost all economists are methodological individualists. That is, they believe that only individuals act. Aggregates like classes or national economies do not act because they are not people. Most schools of economics, however, believe that statements can nevertheless be made about some of these aggregates, for instance that an economy is in equilibrium or not, or that all the transactions necessary to bring it to the Pareto frontier have, or have not, taken place. Austrians deny even such properties as these to aggregates like an economy, and still more to aggregates like 'the working class' or 'the capitalist class'. They get their name because the leading figures in the movement – Carl Menger in the nineteenth century and Friedrich von Hayek in the twentieth – hailed from Austria. An Austrian economist starts from the perspective that only each individual can know his or her preference scale. They accept, on the grand scale, Smith's criticisms in the 1790 additions to *TMS* of the man of system who believes that humans are chess pieces that the thinker can move across the board, forgetting that they have the power to choose. Hayek takes the phrase 'spontaneous order' from his contemporary Michael Polanyi and makes it Smith's (and his fellow Austrians') central insight. However, to do that, he has to ignore the whole mechanism of the self-aware, sympathetic, impartial spectator of *TMS* (Hayek 1988; Petsoulas 2001, pp. 2, 150).

It is obvious that the radical subjectivism of Austrian economics rules out all government planning on the basis of politicians, bureaucrats or planners knowing what is best for us better than we do ourselves. Less obviously, it also rules out most of the assumptions made by mainstream economists, such as that individuals maximise their utility subject to a budget constraint. To an Austrian, 'maximising one's utility' is far too purposive a description of what we do as we grope our way through life.

How then do Austrian economists know if or when an economy is working efficiently? They assume that individuals participate in the market by trying it. We engage in a trade if it brings us at least enough benefit for it to be worth our while. If not, we walk away from it. Austrian economists are therefore the fiercest of all enemies of market regulation. Nobody can find out what works best for each market participant except by trying it. Smith's early maxim

> Little else is requisite to carry a state to the highest degree of opulence from the lowest barbarism, but peace, easy taxes, and a tolerable administration of justice; all the rest being brought about by the natural course of things

stands beside his late attack on the man of system, representing him, to speak anachronistically, at his most Austrian. (see Chapter 6)

Whereas Austrian economists shun mathematical models of the economy, *general equilibrium theorists* revel in them. The main founder of general equilibrium analysis is taken to be the Swiss economist Léon Walras (1834–1910), although the basic ideas are in Smith and Ricardo. Walrasian economics, to begin with, is not too different from Austrian economics. Both envisage a trial-and-error process (called *tâtonnement* in general equilibrium literature) to establish the market price for each good. Equilibrium analysis starts by establishing the point at which each individual market is in (so-called partial) equilibrium. A market is in equilibrium if it clears; that is, there is neither excess supply (unsold goods, unemployed workers or capital) nor excess demand (unsatisfied wants). The big bang is to extend partial equilibrium analysis of each market (such as the labour market, the capital market, the goods market) to a general analysis of all markets at once. As introductory textbooks like to put it, the economy is like a water bed. Any transaction anywhere on the bed affects the whole surface of the bed. But establishing the conditions for general equilibrium is very non-introductory indeed. The two main contributors to general equilibrium theory, Kenneth Arrow and Gérard Debreu, both won the Nobel Prize in Economics (in 1972 and 1983 respectively) in part for this work.

Austrian and general equilibrium analysis are the two most sophisticated models of the market economy; both, I have suggested, are due to Adam Smith. However, Smith was anything but a naïve market liberal, or market fundamentalist as people now say. As extensively shown in earlier chapters of this book, Smith has a lively appreciation of market failure. He knew that markets could fail in various ways. One was by contrivances to raise prices or conspiracies against the public. A related one arose from unequal access to power, so that whenever legislatures regulated wage rates their counsellors were always the masters and never the men. The other sort of market failure, which Hume was probably the first to understand, is the failure of voluntary transactions to secure public goods such as defence, land drainage or scientific knowledge. For Smith, the state has a role in correcting both sorts of market failure.

Because he never completed his *Jurisprudence* we don't know Smith's full answer to the problem of defeating collusion and market-rigging. But from passages in *LJ* and *WN* we know substantial parts of it: good contract law, cheap and efficient access to justice, abolition of restrictive legislation such as primogeniture and entail. His answer to the failure of the market to deliver public goods is in Book V of *WN*, as discussed in earlier chapters. The state should provide public goods such as defence, utilities and scientific knowledge; it should provide, or part-provide, education; and it should oversee but not directly provide spiritual public goods – the direct provision of these should be left to the market in sects.

Smith's economics, therefore, anticipates two great economists of the twentieth century: Joseph Schumpeter (1883–1950) and Mancur Olson (1932–98). He is Schumpeterian in his belief that spontaneous order creates growth through creative destruction. He is Olsonian in his understanding of market failure, collusion and the underprovision of public goods. What Smith observed in the Scotland of his day was, in later terminology, endogenous growth facilitated by the creative destruction (cf. Schumpeter 1942, Chapter VII) of capitalism. The economic interests that had been protected up to 1707 lost their protection, and suffered thereby. But this was more than offset by the economic interests that prospered – and whose prosperity had not been anticipated in 1707. Smith gives the instance of the meat trade, which not only prospered but caused the value of formerly valueless land in highland and southern Scotland to rise (*WN* I.xi.b.8 and I.xi.m.13; note that the Dukes of Buccleuch are the largest landowners in southern Scotland). The meat trade, which features nowhere in the economic clauses of the Act of Union (McLean and McMillan 2005, Chapter 2), was an unexpected engine of economic growth. The industries that *are* mentioned in the Act (coal and salt) did not expand spectacularly in Smith's time. The east-coast trade with the Netherlands, which Adam Smith could observe every day in Kirkcaldy and from which his father had collected customs duties, probably declined with the post-Union opening of west-coast trade.

All of these were spontaneous; organised or anticipated growth failed to happen. And we know what Smith thought about government or charitable attempts to promote useful industries in the desolate rebellious

Highlands: 'it has, I am afraid, been too common for vessels to fit out for the sole purpose of catching, not the fish, but the bounty' (*WN* IV.v.a.32).

But what enabled the creative destruction of capitalism in eighteenth-century Scotland to succeed? Precisely the weak state and the weak church under which Smith had grown up. The difference between Scotland after 1707 and Ireland after 1800 was that in the former (only) the old institutions of social domination were destroyed and traders could work their creative destruction without institutional hindrance. We have seen that Smith wished the same for Ireland: he says so in the chapter on colonies in *WN*. But his dream (which was also Pitt's dream) crashed when George III vetoed Catholic emancipation in Ireland in 1801, leaving the old structures of minority Anglican Ascendancy domination in place. When Smith spoke of people of the same trade seldom meeting, even for merriment and diversion, without planning a contrivance to raise prices or a conspiracy against the public, he saw institutions in exactly the light that Olson was to see them in his *Rise and Decline of Nations* (Olson 1982). Olson has acknowledged that Smith was 'extraordinarily sensitive to the varying capacities of different groups to organize to obtain the advantages of monopoly' (Olson 1976, p. 107).

Olson writes:

> There was extraordinary turmoil [in Britain] until a generation or two before the Industrial Revolution (and this probably played a role in opening British society to new talent and enterprise), but since then Britain has not suffered the institutional destruction, or the forcible replacement of cities, or the decimation of social classes, that its Continental counterparts have experienced. The same stability and immunity from invasion have made it easier for the firms and families that advanced in the Industrial Revolution and the nineteenth century to organize or collude to protect their interests. (Olson 1982, p. 84)

Accordingly, for Olson, Britain was the ideal type of what he called 'institutional sclerosis'. Sclerotic democratic polities were those where free institutions had grown up for a long time in restraint of trade. In a democracy, the law cannot hinder people of the same trade from sometimes assembling together even for merriment and diversion, but the conversation often ends in a conspiracy against the public. This is equally true of associations of land, of labour and of capital. But both Smith and Olson are most exercised by the pernicious effects of organisations of capital. (For more on Olson see McLean 2000.)

Olson was a member of the public-choice school of economists. Public choice has been defined as 'the economic study of nonmarket decision making, or simply the application of economics to political science'

(Mueller 2003, p. 1). On this definition, Adam Smith was surely the greatest pioneer of public choice (although Mandeville, Hume and Hobbes deserve a bow as well). Smith applies economics to political science by observing what it is rational for political agents to do: trade associations, American colonists or holders of East India Company stock, for instance. Where it is possible to create an incentive structure that will make political outcomes efficient without government intervention, Smith recommends one. The most startling example is his proposal to Wedderburn to offer Canada back to France and Florida back to Spain, so that the Anglophone settlers in the American colonies would have a direct incentive to pay for their own defence and to renew their alliance with Great Britain. Where it is not possible to give political actors the correct incentives, Smith recommends government action, for instance in defence and education.

One part of Smith's economic liberalism which was highly controversial in his own time was his attitude to international trade. Most earlier writers on economics, up to and including Steuart, had argued that each nation must try to secure a balance of trade, or of payments, or both, in its favour. This was truly Lake Wobegon economics, for it would require every nation to have an above average balance in its favour. But it was very popular in Smith's time, and remains so. Many politicians never raise their economic thought beyond the belief that exports are good and imports are bad – from which they go on to conclude that protecting home industries and putting up tariffs or quotas against imports are good economic policy. The economics of Sir James Steuart still thrive in the economic policies of even supposedly free-market countries and blocs. The United States subsidises home steel and farm production. Japan protects its rice industry. The European Union subsidises farming and tries to keep out Chinese textiles. These policies depend on elementary misunderstandings of economics.

More subtly, Smith is opposed to bilateral trade treaties. The Methuen Treaty of 1703 between England and Portugal, in which the Portuguese government agrees to admit English woollen goods and the English government in exchange agrees to admit port wine to England, 'has been . . . much commended'. However,

> Such treaties, however, though they may be advantageous to the merchants and manufacturers of the favoured, are necessarily disadvantageous to those of the favouring country. A monopoly is thus granted against them to a foreign nation; and they must frequently buy the foreign goods they have occasion for, dearer than if the free competition of other nations was admitted. (*WN* IV.vi.2–3)

It may be said that the English do not make port and the Portuguese do not make woollen goods, and hence Smith's objection is unfair. But his point is quite general. Any bilateral treaty excludes third parties. Therefore, even if each party is a 'favouring country', it loses in relation to third-party trade, compared to a regime of free trade. Bilateral, or restricted, trade treaties are omnipresent in the modern world – the North American Free Trade Area has three members, for instance, and the European Union has twenty-five. Even though these trade agreements improve the flow of trade within the member states, they may prejudice it with the outside world. The Chinese bra affair of 2005 showed this eloquently.

If Smith's reasoning is sound, then it is sound even when the agreement is between rich nations and poor ones. As I write, there is a powerful current of opinion that says that world free trade is unfair to the poor (see, for example, Klein 2000, Hertz 2001). One of the leading British aid charities, Christian Aid, has launched a Trade Justice Campaign. In a section of its website headed 'The Slavery of Free Trade', Christian Aid writes:

> Free trade means a country's economy is run without government intervention. It is a policy that rich country governments and international institutions are forcing poor countries to accept.
>
> Free trade is imposed on poor countries through:
>
> - agreements between two or more countries
> - conditions and 'economic advice' given to poor countries in return for loans from the International Monetary Fund (IMF) and the World Bank
> - agreements at the World Trade Organisation.
>
> The effects of free trade can be seen across the developing world. Millions of poor people's livelihoods are being threatened, and their governments are powerless to prevent it (www.christian-aid.org.uk/campaign/trade/basics.htm).

This would get very short shrift from Adam Smith. The acid test is whether millions of poor people's livelihoods would be better under protectionism than under free trade. For Smith, this can very rarely be true. He has little patience with even the most respectable argument for protection – the 'infant industry' argument advanced by Steuart.

Indeed, Christian Aid and other charitable NGOs would find Smith an uncomfortable companion on other grounds. The anti-slavery campaigner William Wilberforce, who met Smith in 1787, regarded him as an ally and admired his work. On slavery, Smith reciprocated. On other charitable issues he did not. The Highlands of Scotland were then as destitute as much of Africa today. Wilberforce was rebuffed when he tried to get Smith's support for a charitable plan to set up fishing villages in the Highlands. Wilberforce wrote to one of the society's officials:

> Dr Smith, with a certain characteristic coolness, observed to me that he looked for no other consequence from the scheme than the entire loss of every shilling that should be expended in it, granting, however, with uncommon candour, that the public would be no great sufferer, because he believed the individuals meant to put their hands only in their own pockets. (W. Wilberforce to J. H. Brown, 14.09.1787, in Wilberforce 1840, I, 40, quoted by Ross 1995, p. 377)

Why the characteristic coolness? Smith at least acknowledges that private charity is better than a government scheme. But charitable giving on behalf of the Highlanders may not get them what they most need, of which only they can be the best judges. This is Smith the Austrian economist speaking, and in some guises it can sound hard-hearted. On the other hand, he was proved largely right in the case of Highland fisheries. The only Highland fishing ports set up at this time that have survived are Wick on the north coast and Ullapool on the west. And Ullapool had to wait for twentieth-century pleasure craft, holiday homes and the Lewis ferry before it became prosperous. The general implication that donors may give charitable money in wasteful ways has alas proved true on all too many occasions as well.

So much for Smith's economic liberalism. His social liberalism follows from his adoption of part but not all of his Scottish Protestant inheritance, spiced up by his admiration for Stoical self-command. The threats to liberty that seem most to concern him, in *TMS*, are those that come when poor people become ambitious for the goods or the place of the rich:

> Are you in earnest resolved never to barter your liberty for the lordly servitude of a court, but to live free, fearless, and independent? There seems to be one way to continue in that virtuous resolution; and perhaps but one. Never enter the place from whence so few have been able to return; never come within the circle of ambition; nor ever bring yourself into comparison with those masters of the earth who have already engrossed the attention of half mankind before you. (*TMS* I.iii.2.7)

But the poor have as much personal freedom as the rich:

> In the most glittering and exalted situation that our idle fancy can hold out to us, the pleasures from which we propose to derive our real happiness, are almost always the same with those which, in our actual, though humble station, we have at all times at hand, and in our power. Except the frivolous pleasures of vanity and superiority, we may find, in the most humble station, where there is only personal liberty, every other which the most exalted can

> afford; and the pleasures of vanity and superiority are seldom consistent with perfect tranquillity, the principle and foundation of all real and satisfactory enjoyment. (*TMS* III.3.31)

Once again we sense the affinity between Adam Smith and Robert Burns. The poem in the Kilmarnock Edition of 1786 most admired at the time seems to have been 'The Cottar's Saturday Night'.

> From scenes like these, old Scotia's grandeur springs,
> That makes her lov'd at home, rever'd abroad:
> Princes and lords are but the breath of kings,
> 'An honest man's the noblest work of God;'
> And certes, in fair virtue's heavenly road,
> The cottage leaves the palace far behind.

Now deeply out of favour for its sugary sentimentality, the poem is an idyllic picture of the happiness of the poor but honest labourer, which could have been – and perhaps was – a versification of this passage of *TMS*. For Smith then, as for Burns, the freedom that mattered most was the freedom to live your own life in your own way, free from the inquisitions of church, state, landlord or feudal superior. Smith's social liberalism is therefore closely linked to his egalitarianism, to which I now turn.

SMITH ON EQUALITY

Smith's radical egalitarianism, I have argued above, derives from his acceptance of half the heritage of Andrew Melvill combined with his contempt for the other half. It is necessary to stress one more time how different is the Protestantism of the Calvinists (together with the other radical sects of the sixteenth and seventeenth centuries such as Baptists (or Anabaptists), Independents or Congregationalists, and Quakers) from the Erastian Protestantism of the Church of England. The radical sects rejected religious hierarchy, arguing that the message of Christ is equally accessible to all believers, whether by individual reading of the Bible or individual revelation direct from God. There was no room in this vision for bishops, still less for a head of state with any authority in religious matters. This is fundamental doctrine of the post-1690 Church of Scotland, as accepted, for example, by Hutcheson – if we are to believe the report in *A Vindication*.

In the century before Smith, the idea of the moral and political equality of all mankind was new (or at least recently renewed) and startling. In Smith's time, most people probably agreed with Shakespeare's *Troilus and Cressida*: 'Take but degree away, untune that string / And, hark! what discord follows'. In Greek philosophy, both Plato and Aristotle believed in hierarchy and rule by the morally (or intellectually) superior. The ancient philosopher whom Smith discusses at greatest length, and obviously likes best, is the slave Epictetus, one of the leaders of Stoicism.[2] The ideal of equality of humankind is of course derivable from Christianity, but it had had little prominence in western Christianity before the mid-sixteenth century. Only the Christians of the Reformation, and then mostly the more extreme reformers, including Calvinists, Anabaptists and Quakers, took it seriously. But then, by 1596, we have Andrew Melvill grabbing the king's sleeve to argue his point of view the more forcibly (see Chapter 2). It is in 1647, during the English Civil War, that we hear the political implications of Reformed egalitarianism for the first time. The officers of Cromwell's army are debating the future republican constitution of Great Britain in Putney Church, to the south-west of London. General Ireton asks what the 'Levellers', the most radical faction of the army, mean by their demand that 'every man that is an inhabitant is to be equally considered' in parliamentary representation. Col. Thomas Rainborough replies:

> For really I think that the poorest he that is in England has a life to live as the greatest he; and therefore truly, sir, I think it's clear that every man that is to live under a government ought first by his own consent to put himself under that government. (Sharp 1998, p. 103)

Smith was not greatly concerned with political egalitarianism. Of Locke's reworking of the Leveller doctrine that government is legitimate only if it has the people's consent, Smith said (remarkably forthrightly) in one of his Glasgow lectures:

> God knows it is but a very figurative metaphoricall consent which is given here. And in Scotland still more than in England, as but very few have a vote for a Member of Parliament who give this metaphoricall consent. (*LJ (A)* v.134)

Smith never had a vote himself, although he became a senior government adviser. He was much more concerned with *moral* egalitarianism. A key passage early in *TMS* runs:

> And hence it is, that to feel much for others and little for ourselves, that to restrain our selfish, and to indulge our benevolent affections, constitutes the perfection of human nature; and can alone produce among mankind that harmony of sentiments and passions in which consists their whole grace and propriety. As to love our neighbour as we love ourselves is the great law of Christianity, so it is the great precept of nature to love ourselves only as we

> love our neighbour, or what comes to the same thing, as our neighbour is capable of loving us. (*TMS* I.i.5.5, p. 25)

This illustrates multiple things about Adam Smith. It subtly hints that he places Stoic ethics ('to love ourselves only as we love our neighbour') above Christian ethics, while not appearing to deny the truth of Christianity. It conveys the fundamental economic idea of reciprocity, of exchange in the 'marketplace of life' (Otteson 2002). Further, it describes a moral sentiment while also giving a guide to life which Smith himself admired. Like his great friend David Hume, he was a very frugal man. To love oneself only as one loves his neighbour is morally desirable, but it also freed Smith, as it freed Hume, from any awkward dependence on others. In 1754, Hume had been censured by the Faculty of Advocates in Edinburgh, whose librarian he was, for buying two allegedly pornographic French books for the library. Hume described his ingenious reaction in a letter to Smith, which it may not be fanciful to imagine Smith had in mind while writing the above section of *TMS*:

> But being equally unwilling to lose the Use of the Books and to bear an Indignity; I retain the Office, but have given Blacklock,[3] our blind Poet, a Bond of Annuity for the Sallary. I have now put it out of these malicious Fellows power to offer me any Indignity; while my Motives for remaining in this Office are so apparent. (Hume to AS, 17.12.1754, *Corr.* # 19)

Thus *TMS* sets out a system of egalitarian and post-Christian ethics which attract moralistic and frugal politicians of the Left to this day. Smith's egalitarianism, frugality and plainness all merge in a notable letter to his publisher about arrangements for publication of the third edition of *TMS*:

> The *Dissertation upon the Origin of Languages* is to be printed at the end of the *Theory*. There are some literal errors in the printed copy of it which I should have been glad to have corrected, but have not the opportunity, as I have no copy by me. They are of no great consequence. In the titles, both of the *Theory* and *Dissertation*, call me simply Adam Smith without any addition before or behind. (AS to his publisher William Strahan, 1766 or 1767, *Corr.* # 100)

This was too egalitarian even for his fellow-Scot Strahan. Despite Smith's instructions, the third edition retains the title LL.D. after Smith's name.

But the history of the Covenanters showed Smith and his Edinburgh Moderate friends that the Calvinists in power could be as great a threat to equality as to liberty. The part of Melvill's inheritance that Smith entirely rejects is the idea of the Kirk as the agent of social control. Recall that as recently as 1697 the Kirk had arranged for Thomas Aikenhead to be hanged for blasphemy. The dark side of Calvinism was the belief that its followers were God's elect. If they were God's elect, then of course they could treat those who were not God's elect as they pleased. In the generation after Smith, these dark recesses of the Calvinist mind would be explored by two of the greatest Scottish writers – Burns in *Holy Willie's Prayer* and James Hogg in his electrifying *Private Memoirs and Confessions of a Justified Sinner* (Hogg [1824] 1969), which is still capable of terrifying the reader. Hence, once again, the importance for Smith of having thousands of little sects, many of them austere, but none of them able to impose the terrifying discipline of the elect upon society at large.

SMITH ON FRATERNITY

Fraternity is a natural and obvious implication of the impartial spectator. Recall that editions of *TMS* from the fourth onwards, therefore including Burns's copies, carried the expanded title 'The Theory of Moral Sentiments, or An Essay towards and Analysis of the Principles by which Men naturally judge concerning the Conduct and character, first of their Neighbours, and afterwards of themselves'. From this it follows that once we are capable of seeing ourselves as others see us, we are naturally drawn to sympathise – in the ordinary sense as well as Smith's extended sense – with the plight of others.

In *WN*, Smith acknowledges that fraternity has a down side (think of the merriment and diversion of fraternal bands of tradesmen). But I read his remarks about the poor as inspired by a spirit of fraternity. He explicitly endorses combinations of employees (trade unions, in modern terminology), while attacking combinations of masters (trade associations or guilds):

> It is not, however, difficult to foresee which of the two parties must, upon all ordinary occasions, have the advantage in the dispute, and force the other into a compliance with their terms. The masters, being fewer in number, can combine much more easily; and the law, besides, authorizes, or at least does not prohibit their combinations, while it prohibits those of the workmen. We have no acts of parliament against combining to lower the price of work; but many against combining to raise it. In all such disputes the masters can hold out much longer. A landlord, a farmer, a master manufacturer, a merchant, though they did not employ a single workman, could generally live a year or two upon the stocks which they have already acquired. Many workmen could not subsist a week, few could subsist a month, and scarce any a year without

> employment. In the long run the workman may be as necessary to his master as his master is to him; but the necessity is not so immediate.
>
> We rarely hear, it has been said, of the combinations of masters, though frequently of those of workmen. But whoever imagines, upon this account, that masters rarely combine, is as ignorant of the world as of the subject. Masters are always and everywhere in a sort of tacit, but constant and uniform combination, not to raise the wages of labour above their actual rate. (*WN* I.viii.12–13)

This is to anticipate Olson's insight that trade associations contribute more to democratic sclerosis than trade unions because they have fewer potential members, and therefore fewer potential free-riders. Later in the same chapter of *WN*, Smith makes a point that has been rediscovered by modern students of Third World poverty – namely, that the very poor have multiple children in the reasonable belief that few of them will survive:

> Every species of animals naturally multiplies in proportion to the means of their subsistence, and no species can ever multiply beyond it. But in civilised society it is only among the inferior ranks of people that the scantiness of subsistence can set limits to the further multiplication of the human species; and it can do so in no other way than by destroying a great part of the children which their fruitful marriages produce.
>
> The liberal reward of labour, by enabling them to provide better for their children, and consequently to bring up a greater number, naturally tends to widen and extend those limits. It deserves to be remarked, too, that it necessarily does this as nearly as possible in the proportion which the demand for labour requires. If this demand is continually increasing, the reward of labour must necessarily encourage in such a manner the marriage and multiplication of labourers, as may enable them to supply that continually increasing demand by a continually increasing population. (*ibid.*, 39–40)

THE MARXIAN SMITH

It follows from the passages just quoted that a socialist, even Marxian, reading of Smith is by no means absurd. Mancur Olson's analysis of the differential power of producer groups is in a sense Marxian. A policy is a public good, therefore any policy, even one that benefits only an interest group, will not come about unless members of that interest group join the lobby for the policy, and do not free-ride on the lobbying efforts of others. Olson shows that groups comprising relatively few producers – such as trade associations and above all landowners – find it easy to form combinations to overcome their internal collective action problems and get the legislature to legislate in their class interest. The dispersed and weak interests of labour find it much harder to do so. The germ of that argument is in Adam Smith, for instance in the passages just quoted. Therefore if it is legitimate to see Olson as a post-Marx Marxian, it is legitimate to see Smith as a pre-Marx Marxian.

Secondly, as noted above, Smith, like Marx after him, sees two sides to the division of labour. It increases wealth in aggregate. But it may make the lives of factory workers monotonous and brain-killing. This is part of what Marx later called the 'alienation' of labour. Smith's remedy is publicly financed, brain-enlivening education and culture.

But it was for his role in the labour theory of value that Smith was honoured in Soviet Russia:

> Adam Smith has always been an officially recognised author in Russia, irrespective of political regime and ideological doctrine, though only his economical doctrine became widely known . . . Soviet ideologists used Smith's work in their attempt to establish principles for the understanding both of capitalism and the construction of socialism . . . When the construction of the market economy [in Russia] was embarked upon in the 1990s it provoked a new wave of interest in the famous work of Adam Smith. (Artemieva 2002, pp. 162–3)

Smith did not originate the labour theory of value. It can be traced back to Locke's argument, in the *Second Treatise of Government*, that property rights arise when men mix their labour with an object found in nature. The Protestant Locke believes that originally God gave the earth to humankind in common. However,

> Though the Earth, and all inferior Creatures be common to all Men, yet every Man has a *Property* in his own *Person*. This no Body has any Right to but himself . . . Whatsoever then he removes out of the State that Nature hath provided, and left it in, he hath mixed his *Labour* with, and joyned to it something that is his own, and thereby makes it his *Property*. (Locke [1690] 1988, II. § 27)

Smith has, confusingly, not one but two labour theories of value.

> The value of any commodity, therefore, to the person who possesses it, and who means not to use or consume it himself, but to exchange it for other commodities, is equal to the quantity of labour which it enables him to purchase or command. Labour, therefore, is the real measure of the exchangeable value of all commodities.
>
> The real price of everything, what everything really costs to the man who wants to acquire it, is the toil and trouble of acquiring it. What everything is really worth to the man who has acquired it, and who wants to dispose of it or exchange it for something else, is the toil and trouble which it can save to himself, and which it can impose upon other people. What is bought with

> money or with goods is purchased by labour as much as what we acquire by the toil of our own body. (*WN* I.v.1–2)

Most of this passage insists that the real price, or value (Smith uses both words), at which you can *acquire* something is the value of the *other people's* labour that has gone into making it. But in the last sentence of this extract he seems to swing back to Locke's idea that the value of the things we make is measured by the amount of *our own* labour that we have put into it. Making these two quantities equal one another is known in Marxian economics as the transformation problem, which is generally held to be hard or impossible to solve within a Marxian framework.

Marx's *Theories of Surplus Value*, sometimes known as Vol. 4 of his *Capital*, was never completed nor published in his lifetime. It explores the prehistory of the concept of surplus value which he sees as the cornerstone of his economic theory. Surplus value means the part of the workers' labour power which is surplus to the bare physiological requirements of keeping them alive and allowing them to produce children. Marx believes that all or most of the surplus value of the working class is expropriated by the landed and capitalist classes. In his exposition of previous labour theories of value he deals first with Steuart, then with the Physiocrats, before turning to Smith, whom he treats at the greatest length:

> [T]his vacillation and this jumbling up of completely heterogeneous determinations of value do not affect Smith's investigations into the nature and origin of surplus-value, because in fact, without even being aware of it, whenever he examines this question, he keeps firmly to the correct determination of the exchange-value of commodities – that is, its determination by the quantity of labour or the labour-time expended on them. (*Theories of Surplus Value*, Chapter 3, cited from www.marxists.org/archive/marx/works/1863/theories-surplus-value/ch03.htm)

By Marx's standards, that is high praise for Adam Smith, although it leaves the transformation problem open.

I have already expressed my view that the labour theory of value, in any form, is an intellectual dead end. It sets up a conflict between the real and the nominal price of goods that seems to breed confusion, not clarity. Certainly in the crude 'labour embodied in production' version, and even in Smith's more sophisticated 'labour value embodied in the price of acquisition' version, the labour theory of value seems to focus entirely on supply and not on demand. If it takes the same amount of labour to produce a given unit volume of gold and of coal, it seems strange to say that the 'value' of the gold and the coal is the same. The classical notion that price is determined by supply and demand, also in Smith, seems a much clearer idea. Nevertheless, Marxists have an undeniably legitimate claim on him.

THE CONSERVATIVE SMITH

The website of the Adam Smith Institute (ASI) contains an interview with its hero, conducted in 1994 by a noted conservative Smithian, the late Edwin West. Here are some of the things that Professor West has Smith say:

> Your question presents my central hypothesis as being that 'unencumbered' markets work best. In *The Wealth of Nations* my understanding of freedom from 'encumbrance' is summarized in my call for 'natural liberty'. This condition presumes a well-designed constitution, respect for the rule of law and the absence of any preferential treatment of special interests.
>
> In a 1991 article,[4] Scully and Slottje selected a total of 15 attributes of economic freedom. These included freedoms of property, international financial transactions, movement, information, peaceful assembly and communication through the print media. A special feature of the analysis was the weighting of the attributes in their construction of an index of economic liberty. After constructing a number of summary indexes, the authors found each of them to be robust. All the rankings indicated that economic growth and real domestic product per capita are positively correlated with economic liberty. So I do indeed feel vindicated!

> One Asian country, in fact, comes much closer to my ideal market economy than does modern America. Hong Kong has had considerably more economic freedom than the United States since the 1950s. There have been no tariffs and no import or export quotas except those such as textile export quotas forced upon Hong Kong by US protectionists. Americans, therefore, do not always favour the level playing field . . . Taxes in Hong Kong have ranged between 10 percent and 20 percent of the national income, which is very much lower than in the United States where government spending is now about 44 percent of the national income. Besides this there is an absence of price controls, and Hong Kong does not have America's minimum wage laws. As well there has been little evidence of the suppression of human freedoms such as freedom of speech and the press. It is true that there has been little in the way of political representation but I was never impressed, anyway, by the ability of democracy to foster economic prosperity. As it is, the level of per capita income in Hong Kong has quadrupled since the 1950s despite a tenfold increase of population; and all this happened without anything in the way of foreign aid.

> To be minimally consistent with the recommended political economy in *The Wealth of Nations*, President Reagan would have had to abolish all of the

> following: minimum wages, tariffs, export subsidies, agricultural marketing boards, taxes on capital, 'free' education at government schools and the whole US system of central banking.
> (Source: www.adamsmith.org/index.php/smith/more_about/an_interview_with_adam_smith/)

The Institute's own selections of quotations from Smith include the 'invisible hand' passages from both *TMS* and *WN* and three passages to illustrate Smith's view on 'human nature and economic growth'. Of the three, one is Dugald Stewart's 'easy taxes' passage from Smith's now lost manuscript of 1755 (see Chapter 6). Here are the others:

> Consumption is the sole end and purpose of all production; and the interest of the producer ought to be attended to, only so far as it may be necessary for promoting that of the consumer (*WN* IV.viii.49).
>
> The uniform, constant and uninterrupted effort of every man to better his condition, the principle from which publick and national, as well as private opulence is originally derived, is frequently powerful enough to maintain the natural progress of things toward improvement, in spite both of the extravagance of government, and of the greatest errors of administration. Like the unknown principle of animal life, it frequently restores health and vigour to the constitution, in spite, not only of the disease, but of the absurd prescriptions of the doctor. (*WN* II.iii.31, with Glasgow edition spelling restored)

What do these extracts tell us about the conservative interpretation of Adam Smith? Conservatives have ample opportunity to quote Smith on the extravagance of government and the errors of administration. They are also right to point out that governments which call themselves conservative, such as the Reagan and now the Bush Administrations in the USA, do not always follow Smith's strictures against rent-seeking lobbies and the policies that they recommend, such as tariffs, export subsidies and agricultural marketing boards.

On the other hand, it is a stretch to believe that Smith was opposed to minimum wage legislation, in the light of the pro-labour comments that I have quoted. As to 'free' education at government schools, that is not exactly what Smith recommends:

> The expence of the institutions for education and religious instruction, is likewise, no doubt, beneficial to the whole society, and may, therefore, without injustice, be defrayed by the general contribution of the whole society. This expence, however, might perhaps with equal propriety, and even with some advantage, be defrayed altogether by those who receive the immediate benefit of such education and instruction, or by the voluntary contribution of those who think they have occasion for either the one or the other. (*WN* V.i.i.5)

Education is partly a private and partly a public good. Recognising this, Smith does not advocate that all the cost should fall on the public purse. In contemporary terms, the Labour government's proposal in 2003 that students in English universities should pay a realistic fee was closer to the spirit of Adam Smith than the Conservative Opposition's principled stand for 'free' education at government universities. The ASI is entitled to retort that it did not write the 2005 Conservative manifesto.

As to central banking, it seems that the ASI, or at least Edwin West, would go much further than Smith. Having lived through the collapse of the Ayr Bank, Smith did not recommend an unregulated banking sector.

> The success of this operation [the lending and borrowing practices of the Ayr Bank], therefore, without increasing in the smallest degree the capital of the country, would only have transferred a great part of it from prudent and profitable, to imprudent and unprofitable undertakings. (*WN* II.ii.77)

Nevertheless, as with the Marxist Smith, there is undeniably a legitimate interpretation of Smith that favours a libertarian conservative policy. If I were the director of the ASI, I would have showcased the following. It comes from a paragraph at the end of Book IV of *WN*, designed to link his preceding discussion of mercantile (and Physiocrat) errors with his succeeding discussion, in Book V, of the role of the state:

> All systems either of preference or of restraint, therefore, being thus completely taken away, the obvious and simple system of natural liberty establishes itself of its own accord. Every man, as long as he does not violate the laws of justice, is left perfectly free to pursue his own interest his own way, and to bring both his industry and capital into competition with those of any other man, or order of men. The sovereign is completely discharged from a duty, in the attempting to perform which he must always be exposed to innumerable delusions, and for the proper performance of which no human wisdom or knowledge could ever be sufficient; the duty of superintending the industry of private people, and of directing it towards the employments most suitable to the interests of the society. According to the system of natural liberty, the sovereign has only three duties to attend to; three duties of great importance, indeed, but plain and intelligible to common understandings: first, the duty of protecting the society from the violence and invasion of other independent societies; secondly, the duty of protecting, as far as possible, every member of the society from the injustice or oppression of every other member of it, or the duty of establishing an exact administration of justice; and, thirdly, the duty of erecting and maintaining certain publick works and certain publick institutions, which it can never be for the interest of any individual, or small number of individuals, to erect and maintain; because the

> profit could never repay the expence to any individual or small number of individuals, though it may frequently do much more than repay it to a great society. (*WN* IV.ix.51)

It is perhaps unlucky for the ASI that there are few real libertarian conservatives in mainstream politics, although organisations like the ASI take more comfort from the politics of conservative libertarians in excommunist countries in central and eastern Europe than in (what they would doubtless regard as) the pseudo-conservatism of the British or American right.

THE SOCIAL-DEMOCRATIC SMITH

The (John) Smith Institute, unlike the Adam Smith Institute, does not fill up its website with quotations from Adam Smith, since that is not its purpose. But its mission statement begins:

> The Smith Institute was founded in memory of the late John Smith QC MP, and its work is focussed on the interaction of fairness and enterprise – an area of political economy that was of particular interest to John (www.smith-institute.org.uk/john-smith.htm).

Its publications include the transcripts of the Edinburgh Enlightenment Lecture series in which Chancellor Gordon Brown asked the questions that set up the framework for this book, and also a book based on another speech of Chancellor Brown's, given to the Catholic overseas aid charity CAFOD in 2004. The (Adam) Smithian implications of this speech are considered below.

My case for the social-democratic Smith as the truest Adam Smith begins with the negative points made above. Although both Marxists and libertarian conservatives have a legitimate claim on Smith, their claims can be exaggerated. The labour theory of value is not at the heart of Smith's economics. Marxists believe that there will always be downward pressure on the wages of the proletariat. Smith believed that their real wages had been steadily rising under what he did not yet call capitalism. As to the libertarian conservative interpretation, it is true that Smith preferred unencumbered markets. But the great defect, for me, of the libertarian conservative interpretation is that it does not acknowledge the depth of Smith's analysis of market failure, nor of his case for redistributive taxation. At worst, it seems that some libertarian conservatives stop reading *WN* before they reach Book V. I do not for a moment accuse the directors of the ASI of that, but very little of *that* Smith appears in their presentation of him.

So, how do I read Smith as an apostle of 'the interaction of fairness and enterprise', to use the Smith Institute's words? First, as to fairness. To say that Adam Smith was a man of the Left in his own time is anachronistic. The words 'left' and 'right' in their political sense date back only to the French Revolution, where they denote the positions of opponents and supporters of the king in the National Assembly, as viewed from the presiding chair. But we can talk about conservatism and radicalism in eighteenth-century thought, and class Smith without hesitation as a radical. I have already said a great deal about his radicalism in ethics and religion, which I do not need to repeat.

Smith was rather cynical about politics: unworried by the fact that he did not have a vote, but very happy to be a backroom adviser to Wedderburn and Dundas. But I think I detect a tone of political earnestness when he is talking about fairness between social classes, which is not present in other political parts of his work. He wishes to see, in that tired old image, a level playing field among Rent, Wages and Profit: as we would say, among the three main factors of production, namely land, labour and capital. He thinks that Rent is taxed too lightly, while Wages are taxed, albeit indirectly, and regulated too heavily. And for him, the explanation is straightforward. Those who live by Rent and Profit are in a position to make laws; those who live by Wages are not. You won't read that in Dugald Stewart, but you can read it very easily in many passages of *WN*. 'Whenever the legislature attempts to regulate the differences between masters and their workmen, its counsellors are always the masters' (*WN* I.x.c.61). That remained true of the British House of Commons until 1906 – or perhaps until 1945. The Labour Party began life as the Labour Representation Committee, whose mission was to get trade unionists into the Commons in order to reverse the Taff Vale judgement. This they achieved in 1906. But Labour ministers did not enter government until 1915; the first Labour government was formed in January 1924 and lasted less than a year and the first Labour majority government was formed in 1945.

One might say that the Labour Party does not have a unique claim to be the party of Wages, which would be fair comment. The first working-class MPs were elected as Liberals in 1874. Contemporaries believed that the electoral reforms of 1867 or 1885 lowered the franchise threshold sufficiently so that the median voter[5] was now a working man. The leader of the opposition to the 1867 bill, Robert Lowe, bitterly said: 'I believe it will be absolutely necessary that you should prevail on our future masters to learn their letters' (*Hansard* third series, 188, 15 July 1867, col. 1549). But in fact the patchy enfranchisement of working-class men makes it unlikely that the median voter was from the working class until well into the twentieth century – perhaps after the franchise extension of 1918. Universal suffrage in the UK came only in 1928. Even then, the House of Lords, almost exclusively a house of the landed interest, had maintained its veto over all legislation until 1911 (McLean and Nou 2005) and over all non-financial legislation towards the end of a parliament since then. Smith's fairness argument for tilting policy towards Wages remained good for a remarkably long time, although no longer now.

I argued earlier that Smith's maxims of taxation warrant both progressive taxation and redistribution. In both of those senses it is fair to see him as a 'fairness', that is 'equity', as well as an 'enterprise', that is 'efficiency', theorist of public finance. Nowadays, economists are mainly interested in the efficiency aspects of a tax regime, arguing that the equity aspects are about making normative judgements, which is not the task of economics. But, of course, most discussions of tax policy by non-economists are much more about the equity issues than about the efficiency issues.

For Smith, a tax system is fair if it conforms with maxim I:

> The subjects of every state ought to contribute towards the support of the government, as nearly as possible, in proportion to their respective abilities; that is, in proportion to the revenue which they respectively enjoy under the protection of the state.

I have already commented (in Chapter 4) on how radical that is. 'In proportion to their respective abilities' authorises at least proportionate taxation, and probably progressive taxation – that is, a tax regime where the rich pay a higher proportion of their income in tax than the poor. 'In proportion to the revenue which they respectively enjoy under the protection of the state' is yet more radical. Smith is part of the tradition descending through Hobbes and Hume which insists that people enjoy income and wealth *only* because there is a state that guarantees it to them by organising external defence, internal police and a structure of contract law. Therefore the state has a legitimate claim on what it costs to maintain these things.

One part of the Adam Smith Institute website celebrates Tax Freedom Day, which in 2005, it states, fell on 31 May. As it explains, 'the average taxpayer works for the government from New Year's Day until sometime in late May – a date which the Adam Smith Institute calculates each year as TAX FREEDOM DAY' (source: www.adamsmith.org/tax/what-is-tfd.php). To bolster its claim on Smith as the patron of tax freedom, it posts (once again) the Dugald Stewart extract celebrating 'easy taxes' on this part of its site. I think this is a misunderstanding. By 'easy taxes' I do not think that Smith meant 'low taxes'. He meant 'taxes that conform to my maxims of taxation'.

Of course, Smith would entirely agree with the Adam Smith Institute that taxes must promote enterprise – not only in the sense that the state should not tax citizens in order to do things it should not be doing, but in more expansive senses. Taxes should promote enterprise by taxing bads rather than goods: by giving people an incentive to increase their economic activity, or at least not to 'obstruct the industry of the people, and discourage them from applying to certain branches of business which might give maintenance and employment to great multitudes' (*WN* V.ii.b.6). Smith recognises that this can involve a complex balance. He is not averse to taxing luxuries but that risks encouraging smuggling. The higher the duty, the more people are tempted to smuggle. He is utterly opposed to prohibitive duties which 'employ taxation as an instrument, not of revenue, but of monopoly' (*WN* V.ii.k.27).

It is for reasons of both equity and efficiency, therefore, that Smith is drawn to a tax on ground-rents (*WN* V.ii.e.10). It is equitable because the incidence falls on the landowner who can afford to pay, and whose property is protected by the state. It is efficient because it does not distort economic activity. As ground-rents (also known as economic rent or Ricardian rent) do not result from any economic activity, it follows that taxing them cannot reduce economic activity. Smith started the line of reasoning that led through Ricardo and Henry George to Lloyd George's budget of 1909 (McLean and Nou 2005).

As to enterprise itself, that is the main subject of *WN*. Here too, as previously noted, Smith seemed sympathetic to the idea that progress was due to artisans like his acquaintance James Watt. Until recently, supporting both fairness and enterprise, as Smith did, made for a fairly unusual political combination. In the latest manifestation of social democracy it seems to be coming back into fashion after a 200-year gap. Therefore, my answers to Gordon Brown's four questions are:

> Is Smith, the author of the invisible hand, also the Smith of the helping hand? YES.
>
> Would the Adam Smith who has been the inspiration behind the right-of-centre Adam Smith Institute be more likely to feel at home with the left-of-centre John Smith Institute? YES.
>
> Or is the Smith of 'The Theory of Moral Sentiments' the Jekyll to 'The Wealth of Nations'' Hyde? NO.

> Is it possible two centuries and more on from his famous work 'The Wealth of Nations' to find a way of reconciling his apparently contrasting views: that social behaviour is influenced by sympathy and that economic behaviour is motivated by self-interest? YES. THEY ARE NOT 'CONTRASTING VIEWS' BUT TRUE STATEMENTS BOTH.

GORDON BROWN AND ADAM SMITH

Gordon Brown's four questions were rhetorical. It is not hard to guess what answers he wished to hear. In my view, the only one where even a respectable argument can be made against the answer Brown expected to hear, which are the answers I have just given, is Question 2: *Would Adam Smith feel more at home in the (John) Smith Institute than in the Adam Smith Institute?*

John Smith (1938–94), the leader of the Labour Party after whom the Smith Institute is named, was more of a *bon viveur* than Adam Smith. Adam's favourite luxury was sugar lumps stolen from the dining table; John's was whisky. But where John Smith faithfully echoed his namesake was in his attitude to the Scottish village school. In Ardrishaig, Argyll, where he grew up, 'there was no class-consciousness or divisions and there was a sense of unity about the place', he told Sue Lawley in 1991, as recalled in a memorial book coedited by Gordon Brown. John Smith called Dunoon Grammar School, where he boarded for three years, 'a useful reminder that many state schools in Scotland have a prouder history than some more pretentious establishments in the so-called private sector' – an unmistakable dig at Fettes College, Edinburgh, the alma mater of his Shadow Cabinet colleague Tony Blair. 'I want to turn the whole of education in the world into the type of education I got' (Brown and Naughtie 1994, pp. 151, 121, 65 in that order). Smith's view of Scottish education was highly romanticised but emotionally powerful – for him as for many Scots. The same could be said of his eighteenth-century namesake.

Adam Smith probably loved the Church of Scotland less than either John Smith (who was an elder of Cluny Church, Edinburgh) or Gordon Brown (whose father was minister of Kirkcaldy parish church). But I think all three shared a delight in its institutional effects on Scottish life.

This has been a subterranean theme of this book, which needs to be brought into the open. *Once a Presbyterian, always a Presbyterian, even if you reject the doctrines of the Church of Scotland.* I said earlier that Adam Smith's tastes for frugality and egalitarianism are just that – tastes. They are not moral imperatives. But it is uncanny how similar are Gordon Brown's tastes. Both the eminent sons of Kirkcaldy are puritanical about ostentation in clothes or tastes. 'Prudence' is the favourite word of both. As already noted, in the 1790 revisions of *TMS* Smith adds a story about the obstinate Protestant general and finance minister to King Henri IV of France, the duc de Sully, being hastily summoned to meet the new king Louis XIII:

> He observed the favourites and courtiers whispering to one another, and smiling at his unfashionable appearance. 'Whenever your majesty's father,' said the old warrior and statesman, 'did me the honour to consult me, he ordered the buffoons of the court to retire into the antechamber'. (*TMS* I.iii.3.6, p. 64)

I doubt whether Gordon Brown would go so far as to talk about 'buffoons of the court' but his appearance every year at the Lord Mayor's Dinner, blue business suit and red tie surrounded by the dress suits, white ties and tails of the City's finest, does remind me of Adam Smith's anecdote. As does another of Robert Burns's poems (reproduced in full in the Appendix):

> What though on hamely fare we dine,
> Wear hoddin grey, an' a that;
> Gie fools their silks, and knaves their wine;
> A Man's a Man for a' that:
> For a' that, and a' that,
> Their tinsel show, an' a' that;
> The honest man, tho' e'er sae poor,
> Is king o' men for a' that.
>
> Ye see yon birkie, ca'd a lord,
> Wha struts, an' stares, an' a' that;
> Tho' hundreds worship at his word,
> He's but a coof for a' that:
> For a' that, an' a' that,
> His ribband, star, an' a' that:
> The man o' independent mind
> He looks an' laughs at a' that.
>
> (Robert Burns, *A Man's a Man for A' That*, 1795)

Similar themes echo through Brown speeches. The most recent as I write this is his speech to the 2005 Labour Party conference, in which he said:

> Why am I in politics? I will never forget what I was brought up to believe. I learned from my parents not just to do my best and to work hard but to treat everyone equally, to respect others, to tell the truth, to take responsibility. I learned from my mother and father that for every opportunity there was an obligation, for every demand a duty, for every chance given, a contribution to be made.

> And when they said to me that for every right there was a responsibility, for them that was not just words. What they meant was quite simple and straightforward, for me my moral compass. In return for what we received we had a duty to put something back[:] one moral community of fairness to all, responsibilities from all. (G. Brown, speech to Labour Party conference 2005, transcript on Labour Party website at www.labour.org.uk/index.php?id=news2005&ux_news[id] =ac05gb&cHash=30c74d8de6)

Adam Smith runs through that passage like the letters in a stick of rock.

In economic policy, I noted that Brown set out his stall in a speech to the Social Market Foundation that has now been published in *Political Quarterly* (Brown 2003). Here are some extracts, collated with extracts from Adam Smith.

> Indeed, in almost every area of current controversy – the future of the Private Finance Initiative, of health care, of universities, of industrial policy, of the European economic reform agenda, of public services generally – the question is, at root, what is the best relationship between individuals, markets and government to advance the public interest.
>
> *THE third and last duty of the sovereign or commonwealth is that of erecting and maintaining those public institutions and those public works, which, though they may be in the highest degree advantageous to a great society, are, however, of such a nature that the profit could never repay the expense to any individual or small number of individuals, and which it therefore cannot be expected that any individual or small number of individuals should erect or maintain.* (*WN* V.i.c.1)
>
> Take higher education. Our universities operate in an increasingly global market place and at the same time their excellence depends upon drawing upon the widest pool of talent – making change inevitable and necessary. And one of the central questions round the world is the extent to which universities should become, in effect, the seller, setting their own price for their service, and the prospective graduate the buyer of higher education at the going rate, whether through an up front or deferred system of payment, and what are the consequences for equity and efficiency as well as choice of such arrangements.
>
> *The expence of the institutions for education . . . is likewise, no doubt, beneficial to the whole society, and may, therefore, without injustice, be defrayed by the general contribution of the whole society. This expence, however, might perhaps with equal propriety, and even with some advantage, be defrayed altogether by those who receive the immediate benefit of such education and instruction, or by the voluntary contribution of those who think they have occasion for either the one or the other.* (*WN* V.i.i.5)
>
> Take the Private Finance Initiative. The argument is whether, at a time of unprecedented need for investment in our public infrastructure, for example in hospitals and schools, the private sector can provide the benefits of

efficiency and value for money to promote what most agree is the public interest: schooling and health care free for all at the point of need.

In several different parts of Europe the ton or lock-duty upon a canal is the property of private persons, whose private interest obliges them to keep up the canal. If it is not kept in tolerable order, the navigation necessarily ceases altogether, and along with it the whole profit which they can make by the tolls. If those tolls were put under the management of commissioners, who had themselves no interest in them, they might be less attentive to the maintenance of the works which produced them. (*WN* V.i.d.7)

Markets, they [the Archbishop of Canterbury and the Chief Rabbi] would suggest, may be the best way of constructing exchanges, and thus providing many goods and services, but are not good ways of structuring human relationships. They also argue that while, generally, markets are good at creating wealth they are less good at guaranteeing fairness and opportunity for all – and certainly not normally good at dealing with their social consequences.

In the progress of the division of labour, the employment of the far greater part of those who live by labour, that is, of the great body of the people, comes to be confined to a few very simple operations, frequently to one or two. But the understandings of the greater part of men are necessarily formed by their ordinary employments. The man whose whole life is spent in performing a few simple operations, of which the effects are perhaps always the same, or very nearly the same, has no occasion to exert his understanding or to exercise his invention in finding out expedients for removing difficulties which never occur. He naturally loses, therefore, the habit of such exertion, and generally becomes as stupid and ignorant as it is possible for a human creature to become. (*WN* V.i.f.50)

Smith and Brown agree that the central question of political economy is where the boundary between the market and the state should lie, in the face of partial market failure.

There is a particular affinity between Smith's and Brown's views on international trade and poverty. Addressing members of the Catholic aid charity CAFOD in December 2004, Chancellor Brown said:

It is my belief that even if we are strangers in many ways, dispersed by geography, diverse because of race, differentiated by wealth and income, divided by partisan beliefs and ideology, even as we are different diverse and often divided, we are not and we cannot be moral strangers for there is a shared moral sense common to us all:

Call it as Lincoln did – the better angels of our nature;
Call it as Winstanley[6] did – the light in man;
Call it as Adam Smith did – the moral sentiment;
Call it benevolence, as the Victorians did; virtue; the claim of justice; doing one's duty.
Or call it as Pope Paul VI did – 'The good of each and all'. . .

> And as Adam Smith – often wrongly seen as the patron of free market capitalism without a conscience – put it: the philosophy of 'all for ourselves and nothing for other people' was a 'vile maxim'. 'Perfection of human nature was to feel much for others and little for ourselves, to restrain our selfish and indulge benevolent affections'.[7] And in that spirit and as he died Smith, not just the writer about the 'invisible hand' but about the 'helping hand', was writing a new chapter for his 'Theory of Moral Sentiments' entitled 'On the Corruption of our Moral Sentiments' which is occasioned by 'the disposition to admire the rich and great and to despise or neglect persons of poor and mean condition'[8] . . .
>
> Next, to put our duties to each other at the centre of policy, we also insist on a progressive approach to trade. And fair trade is not just about the financial gains, it's also about giving people dignity – enabling people to stand on their own two feet and using trade is a springboard out of poverty. You know the damage that rich countries' protectionism has done to entrench the poverty of the poorest countries. We spend as much subsidising agriculture in the European Union as the whole income of all the 689 million people in Sub Saharan Africa taken together. The money that the US spends just in subsidising 25,000 cotton farmers dwarfs the total income of Burkino Faso where two million people are dependent on cotton for their livelihoods. And for every dollar given to poor countries in aid, two dollars are lost because of unfair trade.
>
> So 2005 is the time to send a signal and to agree a new policy.
>
> First, it is time for the richest countries to agree to end the hypocrisy of developed country protectionism by opening our markets, removing trade-distorting subsidies and in particular, doing more to urgently tackle the scandal and waste of the Common Agricultural Policy shows we believe in fair trade [sic].
>
> Second, it is time to move beyond the old Washington consensus of the 1980s and recognise that while bringing down unjust tariffs and barriers can make a difference, developing countries must also be allowed to carefully design and sequence trade reform into their own Poverty Reduction Strategies. ('Speech by the Chancellor of the Exchequer at CAFOD's Pope Paul VI memorial lecture', 08.12.2004. Quoted from HM Treasury website at www.hm-treasury.gov.uk/newsroom_and_speeches/press/2004/press_ 105_ 2004. cfm. Some punctuation added)

Here Brown makes his debts to Smith explicit – to *TMS* and to *WN*, both of which he quotes. However, the Smith–Brown approach to international trade and poverty relief differs from that of many of the UK aid charities. Brown puts free trade first, as did Smith before him. As Smith wanted to dismantle the East India Company, so does Brown want to dismantle the Common Agricultural Policy, which he sees as one of the great causes, or at least aggravators, of poverty in Africa. In the last paragraph of the extract above, Brown seems to give cautious approval to African countries' infant-industry protection. But it is a very guarded approval. It differs markedly from Christian Aid's characterisation of free trade as 'slavery'.

Therefore, Smithian social democracy fits some, but not all, of the ideas that we tend to call social-democratic. It favours government intervention to counter market failure; redistributive taxation; and trade liberalisation for the benefit of all including the poor of the world. It does not favour producer groups; public ownership of trading enterprises (where there are no market failure issues); or protection, either in rich or in poor countries. The UK Social Democratic Party, founded in 1981 and mostly merged with the Liberals in 1989, contained a Smithian wing but also a more producerist wing. This tension contributed to, although it did not cause, its implosion in 1988–9 (Crewe and King 1995). Similar tensions exist in the present-day Liberal and Labour parties into which the shattered fragments of the SDP have gone – and indeed in the Conservative Party as well.

It would be going too far to claim that Gordon Brown's Adam Smith is 'the only' Adam Smith. For sure, there are some parts of Smith's arguments, especially in *WN*, to which the modern Right can legitimately lay claim. But, taking Smith's work as a whole, I think he can only be classed as an egalitarian and left-wing philosopher.

What are the main arguments associated with Adam Smith's Gordon Brown (and equivalently with Gordon Brown's Adam Smith)? I would argue that six main arguments are common to the two Kirkcaldy economists:

- *An attack on rent-seeking*: in Smith, the merriment and diversion of people of the same trade meeting together; in Brown, mistaking producer interests for the public interest.
- *An attack on (not a defence of) selfishness as the sole motive of life*: in Smith, once the Adam Smith Problem is dismissed as a red herring, it is clear that selfishness is in no way the sole motive of life – not even in the discussions in *WN*; in Brown, discussions of the moral limits of markets.
- *Understanding market failure*: Smith was no doubt influenced by Hume, who first defined what we now call 'public goods' and 'market failure' in 1738; but Smith elaborates Hume's ideas in Book V of *WN*. Brown places understanding market failure at the heart of his discussion.
- *The state has a role to correct market failure . . .* in Smith, by providing Defence, Publick works and Publick institutions such as

education. The same list appears in all modern discussion of public goods, including Brown's.

- *. . . but not necessarily to provide public goods itself*. This is the most distinctive common theme. Smith, one of the first people to understand what a public good is, nevertheless held back from saying that the state should always provide them. He had the example of Louis XIV's France to hand to tell him why that was a bad thing. Likewise, Brown has the example of the earlier history of producerism and corporatism in the UK, and in continental Europe, to hand.
- *The principles of optimal taxation*: Smith's maxims of taxation are the starting-point of all modern discussion. Brown announced that he had them at his side while preparing the 2002 Budget. Even the most sympathetic observer must doubt whether all of the UK taxes over which Brown presides satisfy all of Smith's maxims. Notably, TV licensing, National Insurance contributions and council tax violate maxim I. Section 106 planning agreements are an example of a disguised tax which violates maxim II. Council Tax again violates maxim III and any tax with high enforcement costs, such as (again) TV licences, violates maxim IV (I pursue these arguments in McLean 2005b). But being aware of the maxims is at least a good start to tax reform.

Adam Smith's gravestone in Canongate Churchyard, just up the road from Panmure House, is Stoically plain. The inscription says

> Here
> are deposited
> the remains of
> ADAM SMITH
> Author
> of the
> Theory of Moral Sentiments
> and
> Wealth of Nations:
> He was born, 5th June, 1723.
> And
> he died
> 17th July, 1790

That is all. But it is all that is needed. The plain and unvarnished Adam Smith, without any addition before or behind, is one of the chief architects of the modern world.

NOTES

1. *Langtonian*: citizen of the 'Lang Toun' [long town] of Kirkcaldy. Thanks to Kirkcaldy Tourist Information Centre for this information.
2. See 'Epictetus (c. 55–c. 135 CE)', in *The Internet Encyclopedia of Philosophy* at www.iep.utm.edu/e/epictetu.htm. The Greek name 'Epictetus' simply means 'the acquired one'.
3. Thomas Blacklock (1721–91) was blinded by smallpox as a baby. He published several volumes of poems and sermons, and an article on blindness for the *Encyclopedia Britannica*. His attempt to become minister of Kirkcudbright was frustrated by the local Austere deciding that a blind man could not be their pastor. After hearing Burns's Kilmarnock poems he wrote to Burns dissuading him from emigrating to Jamaica and urging him to come to Edinburgh instead.
4. West's Smith is presciently referring to Scully and Slottje (1991).
5. For median voter theory see Downs (1957) and Black (1958). A student introduction is in McLean (1987), Chapter 3.
6. Gerrard Winstanley (c.1609–76) was one of the radical thinkers of the English Civil War, founder of the 'Diggers' who tried to establish a commune in St George's Hill, Surrey, in 1649–50. His religious doctrines most closely resembled the Quaker belief in the 'light within'.
7. 'All for ourselves, and nothing for other people, seems, in every age of the world, to have been the vile maxim of the masters of mankind' (*WN* III.iv.10). 'And hence it is, that to feel much for others and little for ourselves, that to restrain our selfish, and to indulge our benevolent affections, constitutes the perfection of human nature' (*TMS* I.i.5.5).
8. *TMS* I.iii.3, added for the 1790 edition. See discussion in Chapter 3.

Appendix

Is there for honest Poverty
That hings his head, an' a' that;
The coward slave – we pass him by,
We dare be poor for a' that!
For a' that, an' a' that.
Our toils obscure an' a' that,
The rank is but the guinea's stamp,
The Man's the gowd for a' that.

What though on hamely fare we dine,
Wear hoddin grey, an' a that;
Gie fools their silks, and knaves their wine;
A Man's a Man for a' that:
For a' that, and a' that,
Their tinsel show, an' a' that;
The honest man, tho' e'er sae poor,
Is king o' men for a' that.

Ye see yon birkie, ca'd a lord,
Wha struts, an' stares, an' a' that;
Tho' hundreds worship at his word,
He's but a coof for a' that:
For a' that, an' a' that,
His ribband, star, an' a' that:
The man o' independent mind
He looks an' laughs at a' that.

A prince can mak a belted knight,
A marquis, duke, an' a' that;
But an honest man's abon his might,
Gude faith, he maunna fa' that!
For a' that, an' a' that,
Their dignities an' a' that;
The pith o' sense, an' pride o' worth,
Are higher rank than a' that.

Then let us pray that come it may,
(As come it will for a' that,)
That Sense and Worth, o'er a' the earth,
Shall bear the gree, an' a' that.
For a' that, an' a' that,
It's coming yet for a' that,
That Man to Man, the world o'er,
Shall brothers be for a' that.

Robert Burns, *A Man's a Man for A' That*, first published anonymously in 1795. For the publishing history of this poem, see Noble and Scott Hogg 2001, pp. 512–16.

> [I]t is chiefly from this regard to the sentiments of mankind, that we pursue riches and avoid poverty. For to what purpose is all the toil and bustle of this world? what is the end of avarice and ambition, of the pursuit of wealth, of power, and preheminence? Is it to supply the necessities of nature? The wages of the meanest labourer can supply them . . . The most perfect modesty and plainness, joined to as much negligence as is consistent with the respect due to the company, ought to be the chief characteristics of the behaviour of a private man.

Adam Smith, *The Theory of Moral Sentiments* 1759; sixth edn 1790 (probably the one used by Burns in 1795), I, iii, 2, 1 & 5.

Notes on Further Reading

Two centuries and a half have elapsed since the first criticisms of *TMS* rolled in from Smith's friends. Nobody can read 250 years of scholarly criticism if they are to have a life. In these notes I list the shortcuts that I have found helpful, in the hope that readers wishing to go further may find them helpful too. By inference, those who are inclined to think I am completely wrong may find helpful the shortcuts that I do *not* find helpful.

ADAM SMITH'S WRITINGS

Almost nobody need now go beyond the splendid Glasgow Edition of the Works of Adam Smith, available at a wonderfully low price, thanks to the Liberty Fund of Indianapolis. Searchable copies of *TMS* and *WN* are available on the Adam Smith Institute website, www.adamsmith.org; and a full searchable text of *WN*, all searchable from the home page, is at www.online-literature.com/adam_smith/wealth_nations/. However, I have found all the search engines I have used somewhat unreliable. Some do not give correct book and chapter references when they find a passage. The most reliable way of finding a passage, with 2005 technology, seems to be to search a pdf file of one of the books, using Adobe's internal search engine. The more old-fashioned search engines are more reliable at the moment. In particular, the Index volume of the Glasgow Edition, newly produced for, and funded by, the Liberty Fund, is a boon – and Smith's original index for the third edition of *WN*, which it includes, is a delight ('*Church*, the richer the church, the poorer the state'; '*Hose*, in the time of Edward IV, how made').

For the posthumous history of Smith's writings in various languages, Tribe (2002) is useful.

ADAM SMITH'S LIFE

Only four biographies matter; but all four of them do. Dugald Stewart's *Account* (1793, with later notes) is to be found at the end of the volume of the Glasgow edition containing *EPS*. John Rae's *Life* (1895) was edited with valuable additional notes by Jacob Viner (1965). W. R. Scott's *Adam Smith as Student and Professor* (Scott 1937; unfortunately, unlike the other three, it is now hard to find) is vast and chatty and has a magnificently politically incorrect discussion of gipsies and tinkers; it does, however contain important detail, for example on Smith as university administrator, that is available nowhere else. The current life is Ross (1995). The letters both from and to AS in *The Correspondence of Adam Smith* (Glasgow edition, cited in this book as *Corr.* followed by item number) bring him to life. The letters between AS and David Hume, and those written around the time of Hume's death, are the most memorable.

The astonishing revival of interest in Smith and the Scottish Enlightenment is pushing many scarce contemporary works back into print. They round off our picture of Smith's life and his intellectual environment. One is the autobiography of the appalling name-dropper Alexander ('Jupiter') Carlyle (Carlyle [1860] 1990). Sir Walter Scott says that he was so nicknamed because he was 'the grandest demigod I ever saw'. Others include the first modern editions of the works of Gershom Carmichael, John Millar (Millar 1990) and Thomas Reid.

On Smith's work as a special economic adviser, see Scott (1935) and Winch (1978). The claims I make for this neglected side of Smith are more extensive than either Scott or Winch make, so they should not be held responsible for mine.

As with other eighteenth-century scholars, Smith's library (most complete catalogue Mizuta 2000) is a window into his world, as is Thomas Jefferson's (Gilreath and Wilson 1989).

ADAM SMITH'S ENVIRONMENT

A good rule of thumb to follow in opening a book on Smith is to ask 'Does the author show awareness that Smith was a Scot, and that eighteenth-century Scotland was very different from eighteenth-century England?' If the answer is no, it is very unlikely that the book will be helpful. Following this rule of thumb, I have found the scholars who have worked with (what became) the Glasgow edition (especially A. S. Skinner; D. D. Raphael; A. L. Macfie; and I. S. Ross) to be among the most helpful guides. From an earlier generation, W. R. Scott (1937) still matters, although as noted his book is now not easy to get hold of. The rare book collections of Glasgow University, and the University Archives, contain important primary materials for Smith, as noted in the text.

There is an increasing amount of literature on the relationships among the Scottish, American and French Enlightenments. I am indebted especially to the pioneer work of Douglass Adair (1974, 2000 – note that these books were actually written in the 1940s) and to Richard B. Sher and his collaborators (for example Sher 1985; Sher and Smitten 1990; Hook and Sher 1995; and Sher's entries on Scottish Enlightenment figures in the new *Dictionary of National Biography*). I also found the contextual work of Samuel Fleischacker (2002, 2003) helpful. Some years ago, I started exploring all three sides of the Scots–American–French triangle in work of my own with collaborators (McLean and Hewitt 1994; McLean and Urken 1995). The Adair seam has been mined by Wills (1978), Howe (1989) and Galvin (2002) among others. Although I have not yet laid hands on a copy, the blurb for Himmelfarb (2004) announces that she gives the British Enlightenment priority, both intellectual and temporal, over the French – an Enlightenment that, she argues, 'resonates strongly today, in America perhaps even more so than in Europe' (Publisher's description from www.loc.gov/catdir/description/random052/20030 60576.html).

For the politics and political economy of the 1707 Union, see McLean and McMillan (2005) and the works we cite there. My attitude to the Union is profoundly influenced by not the most recent, but in my view the best history of Scotland: Mitchison (1970) and by a brilliant British Academy Lecture by Neil MacCormick (1998). Two sparkling books on the physical products of the Scottish Enlightenment are Youngson (1966) and Bathurst (1999). Guides to the Scottish Enlightenment are proliferating. My prejudice in favour of guides to the Scots written by Scots biases me in favour of some earlier treatments, such as Daiches (1986) and Davie (1991), however much I disagree with Davie's views on the Scottish educational system. However, recent and more accessible guides include Broadie (2003) and Herman (2003). Herman, whose first sentence announces that he is not a Scot, is entertaining but sometimes unreliable on dates. The best way to get a feel for Adam Smith's Edinburgh is to spend a day walking round it. Most of it is still there.

Robert Burns, like Adam Smith, comes to life through his letters – see Roy (1985) and, for the go-between Mrs Dunlop, Wallace (1898).

ADAM SMITH'S PHILOSOPHY

More (and better) is being written now about Smith's philosophy, and its place in the history of ideas, than at any time since 1759. It is pouring out from academic presses so fast that I am certain to have missed important contributions. However, I have found Griswold (1999), Otteson (2002) and Fleischacker (2004) helpful; my disagreements with them are as noted in the text. An approach from the direction of literary criticism, itself one of Smith's interests, is Brown (1994). The new *Adam Smith Review* (Vol. 1 2004) is keeping the pot on the boil.

A useful starting point for the view (which I reject) that the Adam Smith Problem still matters is Dickey (1986), who interprets the changes in *TMS* between 1759 and 1790 as evidence that the problem is real. Rothschild (2001) is an important treatment that spans Scotland and France; economics, philosophy and intellectual history. I agree with almost all her interpretations.

ADAM SMITH'S ECONOMICS

By contrast, writing about Smith as an economist is rather in eclipse. 'The history of Smith scholarship and the history of economists' views on Smith have frequently lived entirely separate lives' (Winch 1976, p. 71). Economists are very present-oriented. If the latest theorem is not in Smith, they are generally unlikely to cite him. Furthermore, the history of economic thought is regarded as something of a backwater. Old studies (such as Viner 1965 and Schumpeter 1954) are therefore still valuable. The essays in the bicentenary book edited by Wilson and Skinner (1976) are an eminent exception to the neglect of Smith by economists. The same editors' earlier collection (Skinner and Wilson 1975) spreads its net wider but also includes a number of important essays by economists, or essays on Smith's economics (overlapping but not identical sets). I find Fry's (1992) collection of the opinions of ten economics Nobel Laureates on Smith generally less revealing. The problem may be that a Nobel Prize lifts the laureate to such lofty heights that the detail is lost. At the frontier of Smith's (putatively Austrian) economics and his philosophy, I have found Otteson (2002) and Petsoulas (2001) helpful. But I have found that there is no substitute for actually reading *WN*. It is full of delights and surprises. Many of them are well known; many are not, and I am sure I have missed many more. If a non-specialist reader starts feeling bogged down, he or she should skip to IV.vii (the discussion on colonies) or V.i (on taxation, public expenditure and the role of the state). These chapters punch as hard as they did in 1776.

In recent decades, much of the interest even in the economic arguments in *WN* has come from non-economists. For instance, Gertrude Himmelfarb, who probably would not sympathise with the main arguments of this book, nevertheless draws extensive attention to Smith's pro-labour arguments in favour of equality and making policy fair to the poor. See her *The Idea of Poverty* (1984), pp. 42–63 and 531.

I guess that the most controversial point in my discussion of Smith's economics is my dismissal of the value of any labour theory of value. For an opposite view see Dobb (1973).

ADAM SMITH TODAY

This book was triggered by a challenge from Gordon Brown, and I have been substantially influenced by some of his recent speeches and writings, both when they accord a prominent place to Adam Smith (for example Brown 2004) and when they do not (for example Brown 2003). Other work in political economy that colours my view of Smithian social democracy includes the whole *opus* of Mancur Olson (Olson 1965, 1982, 2000), although I concede that it contains contradictions, especially between the 1982 and 2000 books (McLean 2000). The new macroeconomics owes most to the seminal (and now Nobel prizewinning) work of Kydland and Prescott (1977). They and other writers have shown how the old belief that a government could fine-tune the economy by fiscal and monetary manipulation was, literally, incredible. When policy-makers realised that this was so, they were liberated from trying to run the economy in a way that Adam Smith would have told them was impossible, and could return to Smithian political economy. In a book that is in a sense a companion to this one, I have explored this with my co-editor Colin Jennings, and contributions from Peter Jay, Sir Alan Budd, Ed Balls and Christopher Allsopp among others (McLean and Jennings 2006). Readers who find Chapter 7 of this book disappointingly trite or overly compressed should look there before attacking me for triteness or over-compression.

As to a modern Smithian social policy, I recommend a close reading of *TMS*. In spite of the proliferation of high-quality commentary on it since 1976 (as previously noted), there is, as with *WN*, no substitute for actually reading it. Smith's egalitarianism comes out (to me at least) as fresh and radical as in 1790. A recent Smithian work in social policy, by an academic who is also a UK government adviser, is Le Grand (2003). Le Grand's motivating quotation from George Eliot ('Fancy what a game of chess would be if all the chessmen had passions and intellects . . .') must come straight from the 'man of system' passage of *TMS*. At least, if Eliot did not know this passage, her image is a quite extraordinary coincidence.

Quite possibly the part of my modern social democratic Smith whom readers will find least comfortable is the robust advocate of global free trade and sceptic about charity. For a robust Smithian defence of global free trade against such well-meaning enemies as Christian Aid, see Wolf (2004).

References

Adair, D. (1974), *Fame and the Founding Fathers*, ed. T. Colburn, New York. Published for the Institute of Early American History and Culture at Williamsburg, VA, by Norton.

Adair, D. (2000), *The Intellectual Origins of Jeffersonian Democracy: republicanism, the class struggle, and the virtuous farmer*, Lanham, MD: Lexington Books.

Addison, W. I. (1901), *The Snell Exhibitions from the University of Glasgow to Balliol College, Oxford*, Glasgow: James MacLehose & Sons.

Appleby, Joyce, and Ball, Terence (eds) (1999), *Thomas Jefferson: Political Writings*, Cambridge: Cambridge University Press.

Armitage, D. (1995), 'The Scottish Vision of Empire: Intellectual Origins of the Darien Venture', in J. Robertson (ed.), *A Union for Empire: Political Thought and the British Union of 1707*, Cambridge: Cambridge University Press, pp. 97–118.

Artemieva, Tatania V. (2002), 'Adam Smith in Russian Translation', in Tribe 2002, pp. 153–67.

Axelrod, Robert, and Hamilton, W. D. (1981), 'The evolution of cooperation', *Science* 211, pp. 1390–6.

Axelrod, Robert (1984), *The Evolution of Cooperation*, New York: Basic Books.

Bain, David Haward (2000), *Empire Express: building the first transcontinental railroad*, New York: Penguin.

Baker, Keith (1975), *Condorcet: from natural philosophy to social mathematics*, Chicago: University of Chicago Press.

Bathurst, Bella (1999), *The Lighthouse Stevensons: the extraordinary story of the building of the Scottish lighthouses by the ancestors of Robert Louis Stevenson*, London: HarperCollins.

Black, Duncan (1958), *The Theory of Committees and Elections*, Cambridge: Cambridge University Press.

Broadie, Alexander (ed.) (2003), *The Cambridge Companion to the Scottish Enlightenment*, Cambridge: Cambridge University Press.

Brown, Gordon (2003), 'State and Market: Towards a Public Interest Test', *Political Quarterly* 74 (3), pp. 266–84.

Brown, Gordon (2004), 'Speech by the Chancellor of the Exchequer at CAFOD's Pope Paul VI memorial lecture', 8 December, on HM Treasury website at www.hm-treasury.gov.uk/newsroom_and_speeches/press/2004/press_105_2004.cfm.

Brown, Gordon, and Naughtie, James (eds) (1994), *John Smith: life and soul of the party*, Edinburgh: Mainstream Publishing.

Brown, Tom (2005), 'Students drop "bad role model" Adam Smith', *Sunday Times*, Scottish edition, 2 October.

Brown, Vivienne (1994), *Adam Smith's discourse: canonicity, commerce and conscience*, London: Routledge.

Burke, Edmund ([1790] 1993), *Reflections on the Revolution in France*, edited with an introduction by L. G. Mitchell, Oxford: Oxford University Press (World's Classics edition).

Carlyle, Alexander ([1860] 1990), *The Autobiography of Dr Alexander Carlyle of Inveresk 1722–1805*, ed. J. Hill Burton and R. B. Sher, Bristol: Thoemmes.

Chomsky, Noam (1965), *Aspects of the Theory of Syntax*, Cambridge, MA: MIT Press.

Condorcet, Sophie, marquise de ([1793] 1994), *Lettres sur la sympathie*, ed. J. P. de Lagrave, Montreal: L'Etincelle. Originally written 1793 and published 1798 as an appendix to her translation of *TMS*.

Crewe, Ivor, and King, Anthony (1995), *SDP: the birth, life and death of the Social Democratic Party*, Oxford: Oxford University Press.

Daiches, David (1986), *The Scottish Enlightenment: an introduction*, Edinburgh: Saltire Society.

Davie, G. E. (1991), *The Scottish Enlightenment: and other essays*, Edinburgh: Polygon.

Dawkins, Richard (1976), *The Selfish Gene*, Oxford: Oxford University Press.

Dawkins, Richard (1986), *The Blind Watchmaker*, Harlow: Longman.

Defoe, Daniel (1724–7), *A tour thro' the whole island of Great Britain*, 3 vols, vol. III in two parts, London: printed and sold by G. Strahan [and others].

Devine, T. M. (1999), *The Scottish Nation 1700–2000*, London: Penguin.

Devine, T. M. (2003), *Scotland's Empire, 1600–1815*, London: Allen Lane.

Dickey, Laurence (1986), 'Historicizing the "Adam Smith Problem": conceptual, historiographical, and textual issues', *Journal of Modern History* 58 (3), pp. 579–609.

Dobb, Maurice (1973), *Theories of value and distribution since Adam Smith: ideology and economic theory*, Cambridge: Cambridge University Press.

Downs, Anthony (1957), *An Economic theory of democracy*, New York: Harper & Row.

Ellis, Joseph J. (1998), *American Sphinx: the character of Thomas Jefferson*, New York: Vintage Books.

Ellis, Joseph J. (2001), *Founding Brothers: the revolutionary generation*, New York: Alfred A. Knopf.

Faccarello, Gilbert, and Steiner, Philippe (2002), 'The Diffusion of the work of Adam Smith in the French Language: an outline history', in Tribe (2002), pp. 61–119.

Farrand, Max (ed.), *The Records of the Federal Convention of 1787*, 4 vols, New Haven, CT: Yale University Press.

Fay, C. R. (1956), *Adam Smith and the Scotland of his Day*, Cambridge: Cambridge University Press.

Ferguson, Adam ([1767] 1995), *An Essay on the History of Civil Society*, ed. F. Oz-Salzberger, Cambridge: Cambridge University Press.

Fleischacker, Samuel (2002), 'Adam Smith's Reception among the American Founders', *William & Mary Quarterly* 3rd series 59, pp. 897–924.

Fleischacker, Samuel (2003), 'The impact on America: Scottish philosophy and the American founding', in Broadie (2003), pp. 316–37.

Fleischacker, Samuel (2004), *On Adam Smith's* Wealth of Nations*: a philosophical critique*, Princeton, NJ: Princeton University Press.

Fletcher, Andrew (of Saltoun) ([1697] 1997), *A Discourse of Government with relation to Militia's*, in *Political Works*, ed. J. Robertson, Cambridge: Cambridge University Press, 1997, pp. 1–35.

Fry, Michael (ed.) (1992), *Adam Smith's Legacy: his place in the development of modern economics*, London: Institute of Economic Affairs.

Galvin, R. W. (2002), *America's Founding Secret: what the Scottish Enlightenment taught our founding fathers*, Lanham, MD: Rowman & Littlefield.

Gamble, Andrew (1996), *Hayek: the iron cage of liberty*, Cambridge: Polity Press.

Gilreath, James, and Wilson, Douglas L. (1989), *Thomas Jefferson's Library: a catalog with the entries in his own order*, Washington, DC: Library of Congress.

Green, Ian (2004), 'Warner, John (bap. 1581, d. 1666)', in *Oxford Dictionary of National Biography* on-line edition at www.oxforddnb.com.

Griswold, C. L. Jr (1999), *Adam Smith and the Virtues of Enlightenment*, Cambridge: Cambridge University Press.

Haakonssen, K. (2002), 'Introduction' to A. Smith, *The Theory of Moral Sentiments*, Cambridge: Cambridge University Press, pp. vii–xxx.

Haddon, Mark (2003), *The Curious Incident of the Dog in the Night-time*, London: Cape.

Hague, William (2004), *William Pitt the Younger*, London: HarperCollins.

Hansard: Parliamentary Debates (House of Commons), six series, each in multiple volumes, cited by series, vol. and column.

Hartwell, R. M. (1995), *A History of the Mont Pelerin Society*, Indianapolis: Liberty Fund.

Hayek, F. A. von (1988), *The fatal conceit: the errors of socialism*, London: Routledge.

Herman, A. (2003), *The Scottish Enlightenment: the Scots' invention of the modern world*, London: Fourth Estate.

Hertz, Noreena (2001), *The silent takeover: global capitalism and the death of democracy*, London: Heinemann.

Himmelfarb, Gertrude (1984), *The Idea of Poverty*, London: Faber & Faber.

Himmelfarb, Gertrude (2004), *The roads to modernity: the British, French, and American enlightenments*, New York: Knopf; distributed by Random House.

Hogg, James ([1824] 1969), *The private memoirs and confessions of a justified sinner: written by himself, with a detail of curious traditionary facts and other evidence by the editor*; edited with an introduction by John Carey, Oxford: Oxford University Press.

Hook, A., and Sher, R. B. (eds) (1995), *The Glasgow Enlightenment*, East Linton: Tuckwell Press.

Howe, D. W. (1989), 'Why the Scottish Enlightenment was useful to the Framers of the American Constitution', *Comparative Studies in Society and History* 31 (3), pp. 572–87.

Hume, David ([1738] 1911), *A Treatise on Human Nature*, London: Dent (Everyman), 2 vols.

Insh, G. P. (1932), *The Company of Scotland Trading to Africa and the Indes*, London: Charles Scribner's Sons.

Jefferson, Thomas (1984), *Writings*, ed. Merrill D. Peterson, New York: The Library of America.

Jones, John (1988), *Balliol College: a history 1263–1939*, Oxford: Oxford University Press.

Jones, John (1999), *John Snell's Exhibitions 1699–1999*, Exhibition catalogue, Balliol College, Oxford.

Jones, John (2004), 'Snell, John (1628/9–79)', in *Oxford Dictionary of National Biography* on-line edition at www.oxforddnb.com.

Kennedy, Gavin (2005), *Adam Smith's Lost Legacy*, Basingstoke: Palgrave.

Kernell, Samuel (2003), 'The True Principles of Republican Government: Reassessing James Madison's Political Science', in S. Kernell (ed.), *James Madison: the Theory and Practice of Republican Government*, Stanford, CA: Stanford University Press, pp. 92–125.

Klein, Naomi (2000), *No logo: no space, no choice, no jobs*, London: Flamingo.

Krueger, Anne O. (1974), 'The political economy of the rent-seeking society', *American Economic Review* 64 (3), pp. 291–303.

Kydland, F., and Prescott, E. (1977), 'Rules rather than discretion: The inconsistency of optimal plans', *Journal of Political Economy* 85, pp. 473–90.

Lane, Joan (2004), 'Small, William (1734–75)', in *Oxford Dictionary of National Biography* on-line edition at www.oxforddnb.com.

Le Grand, Julian (2003), *Motivation, Agency, and Public Policy: of knights and knaves, pawns and queens*, Oxford: Oxford University Press.

Locke, John ([1690] 1988), *Two Treatises of Government*, ed. P. Laslett, Cambridge: Cambridge University Press.

McCall Smith, Alexander (2004), *The Sunday Philosophy Club*, London: Little, Brown.

McCall Smith, Alexander (2005), *Espresso Tales*, Edinburgh: Polygon.

MacCormick, Neil (1998), 'The English Constitution, the British State, and the Scottish Anomaly', *Proceedings of the British Academy* 101, pp. 289–306.

McLean, Iain (1987), *Public Choice*, Oxford: Blackwell.

McLean, Iain (2000), 'The divided legacy of Mancur Olson', *British Journal of Political Science* 30, pp. 651–68.

McLean, Iain (2003), 'Before and after Publius: the sources and influence of Madison's political thought', in S. Kernell (ed.), *James Madison: the Theory and Practice of Republican Government*, Stanford, CA: Stanford University Press, pp. 14–41.

McLean, Iain (2004), 'Thomas Jefferson, John Adams, and the *Déclaration des droits de l'homme et du citoyen*', in Robert Fatton Jr and R. K. Ramazani (eds), *The Future of Liberal Democracy: Thomas Jefferson and the Contemporary World*, New York: Palgrave Macmillan, pp. 13–30.

McLean, Iain (2005a), *The Fiscal Crisis of the United Kingdom*, Basingstoke: Palgrave.

McLean, Iain (2005b), 'Can local taxation be progressive?', *Public Policy Research* 12 (2), pp. 111–17.

McLean, Iain (2005c), 'Scotland after Barnett: towards fiscal autonomy', in G. Hassan, E. Gibb and L. Howland (eds), *Scotland 2020: hopeful stories for a northern nation*, London: Demos, pp. 134–48.

McLean, Iain, and Hewitt, Fiona (1994), *Condorcet: foundations of social choice and political theory*, Cheltenham: Edward Elgar.

McLean, Iain, and Urken, Arnold B. (ed. and transl.) (1995), *Classics of Social Choice*, Ann Arbor, MI: Michigan University Press.

McLean, Iain, and Linsley, Benjamin (2004), *The Church of England and the State: reforming establishment for a multi-faith Britain*, London: New Politics Network.

McLean, Iain, and McMillan, Alistair (2005), *State of the Union*, Oxford: Oxford University Press.

McLean, Iain, and Nou, Jennifer (2005), 'Why Should We Be Beggars with the Ballot in Our Hand? Veto Players and the Failure of Land Value Taxation in the UK 1909–1914', Nuffield College, Working Papers in Politics, no. 2005-W11, at www.nuff.ox.ac.uk/Politics/papers/.

McLean, Iain, and Jennings, Colin (eds) (2006) *Applying the Dismal Science: when economists give advice to governments*, Basingstoke: Palgrave.

Madison, James, Hamilton, Alexander, and Jay, John ([1788] 1987), *The Federalist Papers*, ed. I. Kramnick, Harmondsworth: Penguin.

Madison, James (1999), *Writings*, ed. Jack N. Rakove, New York: The Library of America.

Mandeville, Bernard ([1732] 1924), *The Fable of the Bees: or, Private vices, publick benefits*, with a commentary critical, historical, and explanatory by F. B. Kaye, 2 vols, Oxford: Clarendon Press. Facsimile reprint of 1924 edition published by Liberty Fund, Indianapolis, 1988.

Mandeville, Bernard ([1732] 1997), *The Fable of the Bees and other writings*, ed. and abridged E. J. Hundert, Indianapolis, IN: Hackett Publishing.

Marwell, Gerald, and Ames, Ruth (1981), 'Economists Free Ride, Does Anyone Else? Experiments on the Provision of Public Goods, IV', *Journal of Public Economics* 15, pp. 295–310.

Millar, John ([1779] 1990), *The Origin and the Distinction of Ranks*, ed.

J. V. Price, Bristol: Thoemmes.

Minowitz, Peter (1993), *Profits, priests, and princes: Adam Smith's emancipation of economics from politics and religion*, Stanford, CA: Stanford University Press.

Mitchison, Rosalind (1970), *A History of Scotland*, London: Methuen.

Mizuta, H. (2000), *Adam Smith's Library: a Catalogue*, Oxford: Clarendon Press.

Mueller, Dennis C. (2003), *Public Choice III*, Cambridge: Cambridge University Press.

Noble, Andrew, and Scott Hogg, Patrick (eds) (2001), *The Canongate Burns: the complete poems and songs of Robert Burns*, Edinburgh: Canongate.

Olson, Mancur (1965), *The Logic of Collective Action: public goods and the theory of groups*, Cambridge, MA: Harvard University Press.

Olson, Mancur (1976), 'Comments by Mancur Olson', in Wilson and Skinner 1976, pp. 105–12.

Olson, Mancur (1982), *The Rise and Decline of Nations: economic growth, stagflation, and social rigidities*, New Haven, CT: Yale University Press.

Olson, Mancur (2000), *Power and Prosperity: outgrowing communist and capitalist dictatorships*, New York: Basic Books.

Oncken, August (1897), 'The consistency of Adam Smith', *Economic Journal* 7, pp. 443–50.

Otteson, James R. (2002), *Adam Smith's Marketplace of Life*, Cambridge: Cambridge University Press.

Paley, William (1802), *Natural theology: or, Evidence of the existence and attributes of the Deity*, London: R. Faulder.

Petsoulas, C. (2001), *Hayek's Liberalism and its Origins: the idea of spontaneous order in the Scottish Enlightenment*, London: Routledge.

Pitcairn, R. (ed.) (1842), *The Autobiography and Diary of James Melvill . . .*, Edinburgh: Wodrow Society.

Price, Richard (1991), *Political Writings*, ed. D. O. Thomas, Cambridge: Cambridge University Press.

Rae, John ([1895] 1965), *Life of Adam Smith*, originally published London: Macmillan 1895. New edition incorporating Viner (1965), Fairfield, NJ: Augustus Kelley.

Raphael, D. D. (1985), *Adam Smith*, Oxford: Oxford University Press.

Raphael, D. D. and Macfie, A. L. (1976), 'Introduction' to Glasgow edition of *TMS*. See Smith, Adam for bibliographic details.

Rasmussen, Dennis C. (2005), 'Rousseau's "Philosophical Chemistry" and the foundations of Adam Smith's thought', Paper prepared for American Political Science association annual meeting, Washington, DC, September.

Ricardo, David (1817), *On the principles of political economy, and taxation*, London: John Murray.

Ross, I. S. (1995), *The Life of Adam Smith*, Oxford: Clarendon Press.

Rothschild, Emma (2001), *Economic sentiments: Adam Smith, Condorcet, and the Enlightenment*, Cambridge, MA: Harvard University Press.

Roy, G. Ross (ed.) (1985), *The Letters of Robert Burns* 2nd edn, 2 vols, Oxford: Clarendon Press.

Schama, Simon (1989), *Citizens: a chronicle of the French Revolution*, Harmondsworth: Penguin.

Schofield, Norman (2002a), 'Evolution of the Constitution', *British Journal of Political Science* 32 (2), pp. 1–20.

Schofield, Norman (2002b), 'Quandaries of War and of Union in North America: 1763 to 1861', *Politics & Society* 30 (1), pp. 5–49.

Schumpeter, Joseph (1942), *Capitalism, Socialism, and Democracy*, London: Allen & Unwin.

Schumpeter, Joseph (1954), *History of Economic Analysis*, ed. E. B. Schumpeter, New York: Oxford University Press.

Scott, W. R. (1935), 'Adam Smith at Downing Street, 1766–7', *Economic History Review* 6, pp. 79–89.

Scott, W. R. (1937), *Adam Smith as Student and Professor*, Glasgow: Jackson & Son.

Scully, G., and Slottje, D. (1991), 'Ranking economic liberty across countries', *Public Choice* 69 (2), pp. 121–52.

Sharp, Andrew (ed.) (1998), *The English Levellers*, Cambridge: Cambridge University Press.

Sher, Richard B. (1985), *Church and university in the Scottish Enlightenment: the moderate literati of Edinburgh*, Princeton, NJ: Princeton University Press.

Sher, Richard B., and Smitten, Jeffrey R. (eds) (1990), *Scotland and America in the Age of the Enlightenment*, Edinburgh: Edinburgh University Press.

Sher, Richard B. (2004a), 'The Poker Club, *act.* 1762–84', in *Oxford Dictionary of National Biography* on-line edition at www. oxforddnb.com.

Sher, Richard B. (2004b), 'Blair, Hugh, 1718–1800', in *Oxford Dictionary of National Biography* on-line edition at www.oxforddnb.com.

Sher, Richard B. (2004c), 'New light on the publication and reception of the *Wealth of Nations*', *Adam Smith Review* 1, pp. 3–29.

Sinclair, J. (1837), *Memoirs of the Life and Works of Sir John Sinclair, Bart*, Edinburgh: Blackwood.

Skinner, Andrew S. (2004), 'Steuart, Sir James, of Coltness and Westshield, third baronet (1713–80)', in *Oxford Dictionary of National Biography* on-line edition at www.oxforddnb.com.

Skinner, Andrew S., and Wilson, Thomas (eds) (1975), *Essays on Adam Smith*, Oxford: Clarendon Press.

Sloan, Herbert (1995), *Principle and Interest: Thomas Jefferson and the problem of debt*, New York: Oxford University Press.

Smith, Adam (1982–2002), *The Glasgow Edition of the Works and Correspondence of Adam Smith*, 8 vols, Indianapolis: Liberty Fund. (Facsimile reprints of the edition published by Oxford University Press between 1976 and 2001.)

Steuart, Sir James ([1767] 1998), *An Inquiry into the Principles of Political Oeconomy*, ed. A. S. Skinner, N. Kobayashi and H. Mizuta, 4 vols, London: Pickering & Chatto.

Thomas, Peter D. G. (2004), 'Townshend, Charles (1725–67)', in *Oxford Dictionary of National Biography* on-line edition at www.oxforddnb.com.

Tribe, Keith (ed.) (2002), *A Critical Bibliography of Adam Smith*, London: Pickering & Chatto.

Tullock, Gordon (1967), 'The welfare costs of tariffs, monopolies, and theft', *Western Economic Journal* 5 (3), pp. 224–32.

Tytler, A. F. (1807), *Memoirs of the life and writings of the Honourable Henry Home of Kames*, 2 vols, Edinburgh: William Creech; London: T. Cadell and W. Davies.

Vindication (1738), *A Vindication of Mr Hutcheson from the Calumnious Aspersions in a late pamphlet. By Several of his Scholars.* Glasgow.

Viner, Jacob (1965), *Guide to John Rae's* Life of Adam Smith, in Rae ([1895] 1965), pp. 5–145.

Wallace, W. (1898), *Robert Burns and Mrs Dunlop*, London: Hodder & Stoughton.

Watson, J. Steven (1960), *The Reign of George III* (*The Oxford History of England*, vol. XII), Oxford: Clarendon Press.

Wilberforce, R. and S. (eds) (1840), *The Correspondence of William Wilberforce*, 2 vols, London: John Murray.

Wills, Garry (1978), *Inventing America: Jefferson's Declaration of Independence*, New York: Random House (Vintage Books).

Wilson, T., and Skinner, A. S. (eds) (1976), *The Market and the State: Essays in Honour of Adam Smith*, Oxford: Clarendon Press.

Winch, Donald (1976), 'Comment by Donald Winch', in Wilson and Skinner 1976, pp. 67–72.

Winch, Donald (1978), *Adam Smith's Politics: an essay in historiographic revision*, Cambridge: Cambridge University Press.

Wolf, Martin (2004), *Why Globalization Works*, New Haven, CT: Yale University Press.

Yergin, Daniel, and Stanislaw, Joseph (2002), *The Commanding Heights: the battle for the world economy*, revised edition New York: Simon & Schuster.

Young, Hugo (1990), *One of Us: a biography of Margaret Thatcher*, 2nd edn, London: Pan.

Youngson, A. J. (1966), *The Making of Classical Edinburgh, 1750–1840*, Edinburgh: Edinburgh University Press. Latest edition, with pagination of main text unchanged, 2002.

Index